How to Open & Operate

a Financially Successful

Private
Investigation
Business

By Micheal J. Cavallaro

HOW TO OPEN & OPERATE A FINANCIALLY SUCCESSFUL PRIVATE INVESTIGA-TION BUSINESS: WITH COMPANION CD-ROM

Copyright © 2011 Atlantic Publishing Group, Inc.
1405 SW 6th Avenue • Ocala, Florida 34471 • Phone 800-814-1132 • Fax 352-622-1875
Web site: www.atlantic-pub.com • E-mail: sales@atlantic-pub.com
SAN Number: 268-1250

Library of Congress Cataloging-in-Publication Data

Cavallaro, Michael J.
 How to open & operate a financially successful private investigation business : with companion CD-ROM / by Michael J. Cavallaro.
     p. cm.
 Includes bibliographical references and index.
 ISBN-13: 978-1-60138-331-0 (alk. paper)
 ISBN-10: 1-60138-331-2 (alk. paper)
 1. Private investigators. 2. Small business--Management. I. Title. II. Title: How to open and operate a financially successful private investigation business.
 HV8081.C38 2010
 363.28'90681--dc22
                              2010022530

PROJECT MANAGER: Melissa Peterson
PEER REVIEWER: Marilee Griffin
INTERIOR LAYOUT: Rhana Gittens
FRONT COVER DESIGN: Meg Buchner • megadesn@yahoo.com
BACK COVER DESIGN: Jackie Miller • millerjackiej@gmail.com

Printed on Recycled Paper

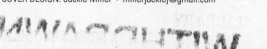

We recently lost our beloved pet "Bear," who was not only our best and dearest friend but also the "Vice President of Sunshine" here at Atlantic Publishing. He did not receive a salary but worked tirelessly 24 hours a day to please his parents. Bear was a rescue dog that turned around and showered myself, my wife, Sherri, his grandparents Jean, Bob, and Nancy, and every person and animal he met (maybe not rabbits) with friendship and love. He made a lot of people smile every day.

We wanted you to know that a portion of the profits of this book will be donated to The Humane Society of the United States. *–Douglas & Sherri Brown*

The human-animal bond is as old as human history. We cherish our animal companions for their unconditional affection and acceptance. We feel a thrill when we glimpse wild creatures in their natural habitat or in our own backyard.

Unfortunately, the human-animal bond has at times been weakened. Humans have exploited some animal species to the point of extinction.

The Humane Society of the United States makes a difference in the lives of animals here at home and worldwide. The HSUS is dedicated to creating a world where our relationship with animals is guided by compassion. We seek a truly humane society in which animals are respected for their intrinsic value, and where the human-animal bond is strong.

Want to help animals? We have plenty of suggestions. Adopt a pet from a local shelter, join The Humane Society and be a part of our work to help companion animals and wildlife. You will be funding our educational, legislative, investigative and outreach projects in the U.S. and across the globe.

Or perhaps you'd like to make a memorial donation in honor of a pet, friend or relative? You can through our Kindred Spirits program. And if you'd like to contribute in a more structured way, our Planned Giving Office has suggestions about estate planning, annuities, and even gifts of stock that avoid capital gains taxes.

Maybe you have land that you would like to preserve as a lasting habitat for wildlife. Our Wildlife Land Trust can help you. Perhaps the land you want to share is a backyard—that's enough. Our Urban Wildlife Sanctuary Program will show you how to create a habitat for your wild neighbors.

So you see, it's easy to help animals. And The HSUS is here to help.

THE HUMANE SOCIETY
OF THE UNITED STATES.

2100 L Street NW • Washington, DC 20037 • 202-452-1100
www.hsus.org

DEDICATION

This book is dedicated with love,
to Erin Johns

TABLE OF CONTENTS

Chapter 1: Determining Your Prospects in the Private Investigation Profession   17

Chapter 2: What it Takes to Become a Private Investigator   49

Chapter 3: What You Will Need to Open Your Business   69

Chapter 4: Finding Clients & Getting Paid 145

Chapter 5: How to Investigate Different Cases   175

Chapter 6: Working a Case   205

Chapter 7: Maintaining Your Business, Avoiding Pitfalls, and Reaping Benefits 221

Chapter 8: Working with Law Firms & Enforcement Agencies 247

Chapter 9: Ethical & Legal Issues   263

Chapter 10: Long-term Financial Goals for Your Business   285

Conclusion   299

Appendix A: Checklists and Forms   301

INTRODUCTION

Think back to a time when you discovered something that was meant to be hidden from public view. Was it an open diary with your name written somewhere in it? Perhaps your mother was having a muted phone conversation in the next room. Maybe someone in your neighborhood turned out to be different from who he or she seemed to be.

We investigate things because our basic makeup as human beings compels us to bring organization and arrangement to the chaos of things beyond our understanding and control. If you are reading this book, you may be looking to do more than just a little investigating. You may be someone who believes your skills, interests, and desire for self-employment are reasons for seriously considering this as your profession.

Private investigation is an information business. Someone needs to know something, and he or she has contacted you, the private investigator, because your skills and training can deliver, record, and process the information he or she is looking for. Information is often used in many ways, and not always for the purpose of impartiality. Advertising and marketing agencies may use information in ways that conveniently skew results to the benefit of their clients' products. Broadcast news organizations look for breaking news to disseminate to as many viewers as possible. They editorialize, fray the boundaries of neutrality, and maybe even lie.

Conversely, your responsibility as a private investigator is to gather information that may never be divulged to anyone but your client. That means you will have to gather information discretely, without crossing legal boundaries or arousing the suspicion of others. Should your client want information for the purposes of making it public record, the information must be unbiased, untainted, and most importantly, it must be factual.

You may be asking yourself a few questions right now. Am I interested in pursuing a career in private investigation? Do my skills and background match up? How long will it take to achieve my goals? These are all important questions, so our first order of business in Chapter 1 will be to evaluate your skills and career choices to help you determine if this is the career for you. Try not to worry about what stage in life you are entering or leaving. If you are a college graduate, recent or otherwise, this book is for you. If you are an analytical thinker, this book is for you. If you are a current or retired law enforcement official looking for an entrepreneurial opportunity, this book is for you.

While many resourceful books have been written on the procedures you must know to operate successfully as a private investigator, this book has been written with the intention of taking you through a step-by-step process of becoming an investigator and, ultimately, starting and operating your own agency with a high degree of success. For this reason, our discussion has been organized in sequential order to cover career choices, entrepreneurial planning, career training, legal protocols, investigative techniques, job-related industries, business management practices, and long-term goals. How you approach your business concept is paramount to putting you in business and keeping you there once you have established yourself as a viable private entity. Over the course of this book, you should come to understand both the training and management protocols that others before you have followed toward success.

Additionally, the information contained in this book will also include case studies at the end of each chapter. A case study is an interview with a professional in the field of private investigation. These professionals have been through the process you are just beginning. Their insight will help you see how the topics in each chapter have been applied in real life. Be sure to make note of the charts and resources listed throughout the book and in the appendices. For example, when preparing for your first surveillance operation, consult the itemization checklist that appears in the book's Appendix beforehand. Or, to find training, networking, or small business financing, refer to the table of contents to locate the organizations and Web sites listed in the specific chapters covering these related topics. A companion CD-ROM has also been included with this book to make the resources more readily available as you apply the concepts to your career. The CD-ROM includes a sample business plan, retainer agreements, and other reference points designed to help you mold an original document or plan.

I hope you are excited about the possibilities of becoming a private investigator. It is a lot of hard work and not as glamorous as television or movies would have you believe, but the rewards are both broad and substantial. That is, after all, what the life of a private investigator is all about.

CHAPTER 1

Determining Your Prospects in the Private Investigation Profession

Detective work requires a number of different skill sets, and contrary to popular belief, it is far different from what you may have seen on television. Since Hollywood first glamorized the profession in the early 1930s, faithful adaptations to the actual efforts of trained professionals have been few and far between. Most private investigators have an abundance of interesting stories to tell, but with rare exceptions, they are never involved in high-speed car chases, shootouts, or flagrant acts above the law. In the 1941 classic *The Maltese Falcon*, Humphrey Bogart plays a private investigator whose client wants her sister to leave an abusive husband. After hearing the case, Bogart says, "It's simply a matter of having a man at the hotel this evening to shadow him when he leaves. If she still doesn't want to leave him after we've found her…well, we have ways of managing it." Bogart's brash promise makes his character look cool, but investigators are bound by strict laws when it comes to investigating someone. An investigator's job is methodical, often solitary. They may spend three uneventful hours parked in front of a hotel, and 30 seconds recording an incident crucial to their client's case.

The job can have its share of exciting moments, but the level of danger or risk involved depends on the nature of the case. Some areas of investigation, such as investigating cyber crime, collecting evidence for civil cases, or searching public records contain little or no danger at all. Other areas, such as criminal investigation, fraud, serving subpoenas, surveillance, and executive protection assume a level of expected or unexpected risk. If the risk is expected, an investigator has a level of control over the danger involved. He or she is able to plan in advance and use his or her skills in ways that minimize the possibility of being harmed. *See Chapter 6 for more information on surveillance techniques.* Conversely, unexpected risks leave investigators unprepared for a potentially dangerous situation that may bring harm to themselves or the client's case. One's ability to control a given situation will go a long way in determining one's success as a private investigator. In other words, the better your training as a private investigator, the more success you will have in working a case legally and giving your clients what they want.

Professional conduct is never more crucial than in the initial stages of an investigator's career. If intuition tells you certain activities are pushing the limits of the law, the activity should be halted until verified or an alternate method has been found. Being mindful of state and federal laws is especially important in the early part of an investigator's career. It will pay off later because he or she will have established a reputation for being a trustworthy professional. Why is reputation important? For starters, a good portion of business may come from lawyers who need information for their clients. Lawyers have large networks, and you do not want to run the risk of being blacklisted by lawyers and their networks or having clients find out you are a liability rather than an asset. Networking is the lifeblood of any one- or two-man agency. Investigators who destroy their networking prospects are forced to rely on advertising, which can be an extremely unaffordable and ineffective way to find clients, particularly for start-up businesses operating on a limited budget. It is entirely possible to gain traction in this business simply by word of mouth due to the need in related industries for investigators who are professional, trustworthy, cautious, and dependable. Therefore, a good reputation will earn a lot of future business. For these reasons, it is not advisable to take your cue from the cavalier attitudes and cowboy tactics demonstrated by characters in movies or television shows.

Investigators are often amused by the technical errors committed in Hollywood films. In the 1997 comedy *Liar Liar*, Jim Carrey plays a California lawyer who is magically unable to lie for a day. When Carey attempts to seek a settlement in the wake of his client's marital infidelity, the opposing counsel brings into evidence an audio recording of his client's philandering activities with another man. Just before the opposing counsel plays the tape, the private investigator who conducted the surveillance effort is asked to testify the details of his assignment, including what he witnessed and when he witnessed it. The scene itself makes for great comedy, except for one problem. The state of California, under California Penal Code 631 to 632, states that any audio recording between two uninformed parties is illegal. California is just one of 12 states that employ the two-party consent law. Because both parties were unaware they were being recorded, the evidence proving marital infidelity would never have been admissible in court.

In addition to technical errors, the Hollywood stereotype of private investigation is frequently gender-biased. When was the last time anyone saw a female private detective in the movies? While it is true that many investigators are male, the number of females entering the profession is increasing. According to *PI Magazine*, roughly 15 percent of the 60,000 detectives in the United States are women. In fact, women may have an advantage in this area because fewer subjects under surveillance may actually suspect them. Physically, a woman may be less equipped to handle bodily danger, but her training to handle these situations is largely the same as her male counterparts, and a number of self-defense classes can be taken to avoid personal harm. Male or female, those willing to carry a gun must always have a permit and must always know the responsibilities of carrying one.

Private Investigation: A Brief History

Who was the first ever private investigator? Ironically enough, some say it was a French criminal by the name of Eugene Francois Vidocq. His agency, Les Bureau des Reseignments (Office of Intelligence), was established in 1833. Much to the distaste of law enforcement officials who tried to shut the business down, Vidocq was believed to have frequently hired ex-convicts. In 1842, Vidocq was arrested for suspicion of unlawful imprisonment, as well as taking money on false pretenses after solving a major embezzlement case. He was sentenced to five years in prison, but won his case in the court of appeals. Despite his criminal background, Vidocq has been described as a sympathizer to the poor and someone who never reported anyone who stole money to survive. He is also credited for having introduced record keeping, criminology, and ballistics to criminal investigation.

The more popular figure credited as being the first private investigator is Allan Pinkerton. Pinkerton was Scottish and sought refuge in the United States in 1842 after becoming involved in Chartism and being threatened with arrest for his actions. Pinkerton established himself in America by serving as a deputy sheriff. In 1850, he partnered with a Chicago attorney by the name of Edward Rucker and formed the North-Western Police Agency. The agency, which later became known as the Pinkerton National Detective Agency, served as a private militia for businessmen looking to weaken labor strikes. The man who came to America in search of justice had ironically founded an agency that would become one of the most antagonizing forces against the youth labor movement in America. His militia, which had more guards than the entire U.S. standing army, kept strikers out of factories during the Homestead Strike of 1892, the Pullman Strike of 1884, and several others.

As America's railway system became a main driver in the countries economic growth, Pinkerton's agency was appointed to solve numerous train robberies hurting the country's development. They went after such historical figures as Jesse James, the Reno Brothers, and Butch Cassidy and the Sundance Kid. History credits Pinkerton with inventing the concept of "going undercover" and the use of surveillance in undercover situations. Because of their success, Pinkerton's agency was also handed responsibilities pertaining to matters of national security. Their efforts included obtaining military intelligence through agents posing as confederate soldiers and thwarting an assassination plot of Abraham Lincoln in Baltimore, Maryland during his 1862 inauguration.

By the 1920s, America's "protected" economic strength eventually created a middle class that could afford the services of private investigators everywhere. As the American economy became more robust, commercialization of the service expanded into newly created industries.

Today, new types of work exist for private investigators, including insurance fraud claims, infidelity cases, and some of the more recent areas of specialization, such as computer forensic investigation.

Private Investigation Today

According to the Bureau of Labor Statistics (BLS), 37 percent of all current private investigators have the education level equivalent to a bachelor's degree. The second highest education level reported showed only some college education or no degree at all. Individuals without a degree have a reasonable chance of earning a private investigation license or working as an unlicensed investigator, as 21 percent of private investigators are currently doing so. According to the BLS' *Occupational Handbook* for 2010-2011, these numbers are projected to increase as the demand for private investigators increases in a time of heightened security, employee background checks, cyber crime, and increasing litigation. The BLS projects 22 percent growth in the field over the next decade, a rate faster than the average number of non-related occupations, which the Bureau expects to grow only 7 to 13 percent.

This growth projection also forecasts increased competition in the field, as the business attracts more qualified professionals. According to these statistics, your chances of becoming an investigator are very good if you have limited education or no prior experience. However, the level of competition will make increasing your training and service offerings imperative after you become a licensed or unlicensed private investigator. This is especially important given that a number of applicants entering the field may already have experience in law enforcement, insurance, or the military. Lack of experience should not be a deterrent because their previous training will not license them any quicker. A law enforcer's experience in another area will not set them apart from you because training will be different in terms of requirements, knowledge of laws, and the degree of field work dissimilarity between law enforcement and private investigation.

Of the total number of private investigators working, 34 percent of jobs are in security services for corporations or individuals, while 9 percent work in department stores, and 30 percent are self-employed, according to the BLS. The remaining percentage of investigators work for law firms, employment services, insurance agencies, credit agencies, and the state and local government. So, if you plan to open and operate your own financially successful private investigation business, your direct competition may be roughly $2/3$ of all investigators who are self-employed, and even less if you choose a niche and a skill set of service offerings wisely.

The numbers break down favorably for employment opportunities, but what about wages? The answer to that question depends on several factors because wages can vary according to your area of specialty, your employer, and where your business is located. Agencies bill their clients in range between $40 and $150 per hour. The average national rate is approximately $52 an hour and slightly less in lower income areas. Individuals with a specialty area or advanced degree normally bill their client in the $65-$100 per hour range. The average salaried private investigator makes $47,130, according to the Bureau of Labor Statistics.

Investigators who seek to own an agency have the potential to make over six figures. However, they must weigh the positive and negative aspects of owning a business. If the business is structured wisely, the capacity to earn more will increase, and tax liability will decrease. Conversely, one must be prepared to accept the fact that statistics will not play in the owner's favor. It is reported by the Small Business Administration that half of new businesses typically fail within five years, but if a business makes it past five years, it is in good company. Small firms account for roughly 44 percent of the private U.S. payroll, hiring half the number of employees in the private sector. Also, half of all businesses usually fail for a reason. They can, and have, failed as a result of poor planning, poor management, poor location, and surprisingly, unexpected growth. If you manage to avoid these pitfalls, your business will likely succeed.

Assessing Your Skills & Background

What type of person are you? Are you observant and usually attuned to what is happening around you? Can you react quickly and make quick judgments? Do you possess a meticulous attention to detail? Concentration and focus in this field is paramount because your ability to collect evidence depends on it. If you are someone who forgets things, lacks organization, reacts slowly, gets bored easily, or has an attention deficit, this may not be the job for you. If you have what it takes to become an investigator but struggle with these qualities, you can train your mind with memory exercises, and create mental games to keep your mind alert and occupied. Puzzles and riddles are a good way to improve your logical reasoning, pattern recognition, and non-linear thinking. You will be surprised by how the smallest techniques will keep you actively alert on the job. For example, if you get tired in the middle of a particularly long and uneventful surveillance, bring chewing gum or energy drinks. Some investigators make a common practice out of talking to themselves; others listen to the radio to take the edge off when tailing a potentially dangerous subject in traffic.

According to brain training and fitness research group Vivity Labs, Inc., "Memory can be affected by many factors, including level of stress, rest, nutrition, medical status, medications, alcohol, exercise, sensory function, hormones, and information processing ability." During free time, Vivity Labs suggests engaging in stress relieving activities, such as jogging or yoga, as well as eating foods that contribute to the wellness of the brain and memory, such as fish, fruits, nuts, and vegetables. "Information that you need to encode will be recalled better if you repeat the information to yourself several times. If you have problems remembering names of people you meet, continue to use their names in every sentence when speaking to them. This is a type of normal repetition that is polite and helpful to your processing."

Communication skills are just as important as the power of observation. As a private investigator, many clients will become aware of your business through networking. How investigators sell themselves determines who is willing to hire them. It does not matter how well you have been trained. If you stutter, potential clients may assume a nervous twitch could interfere with getting information or conducting surveillance operations. Lawyers will dread putting you on the stand as a witness to their case. Subjects will know you are following them if you act skittish. In short, you must be calm, composed, and in control of every situation because it will make you appear professional.

Communication skills are valuable to private detectives because they are in the business of obtaining information. Without these skills, people will be more hesitant to give you the information you need. Information can come from a variety of sources: a potential witness, relative, neighbor, coworker, or court clerk. Detectives who do not know how to finesse people, stroke their egos, and make them feel at ease will get nowhere. To understand what motivates people, you must also be a good listener and hear what they are saying as fact and by implication.

Because law enforcement officials are trained to communicate and deal with people, a retired captain looking to become a private investigator may have more experience than the average person. Having a law enforcement background can be an asset, but it will not earn a license or advanced degree faster than anyone else. Inexperienced people usually enter the field with a bachelor's degree in criminal justice. Some people with accounting degrees find the prospects of working fraud cases interesting, and now with the rise of DNA matching and cyber crime, forensic science degrees are being pursued. The states that will allow unlicensed investigators are:

- Alabama
- Alaska
- Colorado
- Idaho
- Mississippi
- Missouri
- South Dakota
- Wyoming

Some of these states, however, do require a private investigation license within their major cities. To verify the rules, find your state's government Web site by visiting **www.globalcomputing.com/states.html** and clicking the state where you reside or plan to operate. Also, find each state's licensing office by going to the CrimeTime.com Web site (**www.crimetime.com/licensing. htm**). These links are valuable for checking out-of-state requirements if an investigation leads elsewhere. One caveat on unlicensed investigators: They often find themselves on the lower end of the pay scale. Licensed investigators do contract unlicensed investigators for routine and legal purposes, like public record retrieval, but the unscrupulous practices of some unlicensed investigators has deterred this practice lately.

In 2008, two unlicensed investigators from BNT Investigations plead guilty in a federal court to obtaining confidential information on their subjects. This is a serious breach of law that could leave the licensed investigator responsible for invasion of privacy. The best way to avoid these headaches is to obtain a license. For the individual whose time and money falls short of this goal, earning a living as a process server depends on the ability to serve quickly and in high volume. Process servers are people who physically deliver and serve official documents, such as subpoenas, to certain parties involved in legal matters. The National Association of Process Servers (**www.napps.org**) can provide tips on how to make a living as one.

Retired police or military officers looking to become private investigators may have certain expectations about the job. One thing to understand is that police work is a public service, whereas private investigation is a private sector business. One major difference between police work and private investigation is that police officers conduct public investigations. Private investigators are contracted to work cases privately and under supreme confidentiality. What detectives discover is not for public record. Sometimes, the only people who may ever know the details of a case are the detective, the client, and the client's lawyer. Police officers work their cases in such a way as to produce evidence for a trial and public conviction. In these cases, many police officers could be working multiple leads and sharing information with one another. Unless the private investigator is farming out contract work to another investigator, the detective does not share information with anyone but his client. The following is a comparison between the work of a police officer and a private investigator:

Characteristics of Police Work Versus Private Investigation

Police Work	Private Investigation
Community Service	Business
Must Investigate all cases	Chooses to decline or accept cases
Can interrogate	Can be called in to perform an interrogation and record depositions
Case not confidential	Case confidential
Can make arrests	Can only make citizen's arrests and must immediately deliver the person to law enforcement
Has authorized use of force	Use of force not authorized unless self-defense

May be authorized to wiretap with court order	Wiretapping unauthorized without one- or two- party consent
Authorized to conduct surveillance	Should notify police before conducting surveillance in public
Authorized to carry a weapon	Must always carry permit with weapon
Uses state labs to process evidence	Must pay private labs to process evidence
Broader access to public records	Limited access to some public records, such as driver's license or credit information
Can process crime scenes	Should immediately call in crime scene if first to arrive and can process a crime scene after police have processed it.

Due to the nature of his or her work in public service, a police officer's schedule may be more unpredictable than a private investigator's. Because police officers are the first responders to crime, they may suddenly be called to investigate a crime scene or a domestic disturbance. They are often called in to patrol certain areas. A private investigator's day revolves more around preplanning and flexibility of schedule. A typical day or night on the job might include doing any number of things. The following is an example of what a typical day might look like as a private investigator.

 Private Investigator Daily Ledger

8:30 a.m.: Check pay database for information pertaining to missing persons case

9:00 a.m.: Meet with potential client to determine whether to accept or decline a case

9:30 a.m.: Write reports. Transfer evidence from ongoing investigation to computer or an external hard drive (videos and surveillance logs)

10:30 a.m.: Arrive at county jail to take deposition from witness in civil case with lawyers present.

> 12:00 p.m.: Lunch with a lawyer
>
> 1:30 p.m.: Arrive at courthouse for testimony and cross-examination with copy of evidence relevant to case hearing
>
> 3:00 p.m.: Arrive at surveillance site, establish position, and set up recording equipment to observe a subject
>
> 5:00 p.m.: Observe and record subject leaving surveillance site
>
> 5:30 p.m.: Follow subject in mobile surveillance to public place and record subject's activities

Mock schedule aside, most detectives do not have many days that follow a rigorous 9-to-5 schedule. Be prepared to work irregular hours. A detective may have three hours in the afternoon with nothing going on, and a stakeout at 3 a.m. to observe and report on a subject's suspicious activities. The beauty of the job is having a certain amount of control over one's schedule, yet it is anything but typical.

Learning About the Industry

At this point, you should have some general idea of what private investigation involves and whether this is a profession that aligns with your skills, background, and interests. Process serving will be the quickest way into the profession, but if the ultimate goal is to open a private investigation business, getting a license is paramount. Before seeking any type of training, it is a good idea to know everything about the industry, what aspect of the industry to train for, and what that training will require. It is also recommended you first begin your career with an agency instead of opening a business immediately after obtaining an investigator's license. As we will discuss in Chapter 3, working for an agency is a safe and sensible way to build the necessary cash requirements for your future business and gain the experience necessary to successfully start your own business. The first step is to research the industry and answer several important questions:

- What type of training do I need to become a licensed investigator?
- Where can I find the best training and what should I expect to learn?

- How long will training take?
- What area of specialty should I seek?

A great way to begin research is to locate online databases. EInvestigator.com (**www.einvestigator.com**) contains a resource library of resource books or topics of interest listed alphabetically. This comprehensive list contains information on different fields within the industry and provides links to professional businesses that specialize in each field. Online magazines are also a good resource for learning about the industry. One of the most popular online magazines is *PI Magazine*, run by editor-in chief Jimmie Mesis. His Web site has each state's licensing requirements and offers a frequently asked questions sheet on private investigation, a directory of upcoming seminars and conferences, and an e-mail address linked to private investigators who field specific questions related to areas of specialization.

A third resource for researching the private investigation business is national organizations. The National Association of Investigative Specialists (NAIS) focuses on marketing services, developing new investigative techniques, and providing training programs. The association's Web site, **www.pimall.com/ nais/dir.menu.html**, provides numerous links to resources related to private investigation, including a state-by-state directory, allowing the reader to find and contact a local detective agency enrolled in membership to NAIS. The United States Association of Professional Investigators (USAPI) is another national organization offering an accredited training program. The association's Web site can be found at **www.usapi.org**.

Databases listing academic universities specializing in criminal justice can also be used for research. According to US News and World Report, the three most reputable criminal justice programs are at Syracuse University, Drury University, and University of Louisville. Criminal justice programs by state can be found on the Austin Peay State University's Web site at **www.apsu. edu/oconnort/jusgrad.htm**. Once you have identified a program you are interested in, you must research it to determine whether the program's course studies match the kind of training desired. The key to getting a proper degree in criminal justice is to select the right school. If you have trouble selecting a criminal justice program with a university, try contacting The Accrediting Counsel for Continuing Education and Training. They have been officially recognized by the U.S. Department of Education since 1978, and their mission is to "identify, evaluate, and enhance" education through peer review of accredited institutions. Their commissioners are readily available and can suggest the right program. *For these and additional resource sites, see the Appendix located in the back of this book.*

Lastly, the most important determining factor in training selection should include what you want to do as a private investigator. To make this determination, you need to first understand the different cases private investigators handle. The most common types of cases are:

- Divorce, infidelity, and child custody cases
- Background searches
- Missing persons cases
- Fraud cases
- Workers' compensation cases
- Bounty hunting
- Collection and repossession

All private investigation cases involve two people: the client and the subject. The client is the person you will be working for. The subject is the person you will be collecting information on. At this stage, use research to become familiar with what these cases typically involve. When handling a divorce case, an investigator will most likely be asked to produce evidence documenting the behavior or actions taken by a client's spouse. The purpose of producing such evidence is so it can be used in court to render a decision in the client's favor. If the client suspects infidelity and is seeking a financial settlement, evidence needs to be collected on the spouse's philandering activities. If the case is a child custody suit, the investigator will be called on to produce evidence that proves the spouse is unfit for guardianship. When working these cases, the objective is to obtain video footage that objectively reflects the client's claims. Therefore, when thinking about which training program you would like to attend, find one that offers training in basic and advanced surveillance techniques.

Investigators handling a background search will be asked to produce documentation of a subject's past. Every person leaves a paper trail that forms a detailed picture of their past. Credit card purchases, loans, social security numbers, liens, reported residencies, arrest records, employee and marital records, business licenses, cell phone records, and Internet searches are some of the resources at the private investigator's disposal. The purpose of obtaining this documentation in background search cases will be to provide the client with a better understanding of whom they are associating with. A background search is the process of gathering information through public record retrieval. The process must be legal and in consideration of privacy laws. Clients in background search cases will often be employers looking to verify the credentials of a prospective employee or someone looking to verify the trustworthiness of someone they recently started dating. For example, private investigators are sometimes contacted by women who suspect something odd about the person they have recently met. Their partner's wandering eye or bad temper has tipped them to relationship trouble they would rather avoid.

In a missing persons case, the investigator is asked to locate someone who has gone intentionally or unintentionally missing. Handling a missing persons case can sometimes overlap with certain aspects of divorce, custody, or background searches. In a divorce or custody case, for example, a spouse may have disappeared with a child illegally in his or her custody. In these cases, the investigator begins with a background search to gain information on the subject's most recent whereabouts. Investigators typically treat these cases as a missing persons case rather than a divorce case because evidence of infidelity or unfit guardianship may have already been proven. The goal is to find the subject and inform the client so appropriate legal action may be taken. Other missing persons cases involve runaway teens, estranged relatives, or people who have skipped out on a legal obligation, such as rent, car insurance, or alimony payments. The technique employed in these types of cases is called *skip tracing*. Skip tracing is the methodical process of locating a subject who has intentionally or unintentionally "skipped town." In this process, the investigator is able to determine the persons's new location by utilizing the minimal clues they have left behind.

Skip tracing is often the method used in bounty hunting, collection and repossession cases, and fraud investigation. The first step is to begin a skip search using the person's minimal clues and to ultimately locate him or her to serve a subpoena stating the intention to take legal action. If the subject has skipped town after having already been served with a subpoena, the case becomes a bounty hunt. In bounty hunting, investigators locate and physically return the skip for a monetary reward.

Workers' compensation cases are fraud cases, but not all fraud cases are about workers' compensation. In workers' compensation cases, your client will be an employer or insurance company looking to verify a claim made by an employee collecting insurance on an injury sustained at work. If the claim is believed fraudulent, documented evidence must be collected to support the charge or proves the claimant was injured outside the workplace. If fraud — in either case — is proved, the client becomes exempt from making payments, and the employee is subject to prosecution.

In fraud cases not pertaining to workers' compensation, the objective may change slightly because evidence may not come from video surveillance. Fraud constitutes false representation, usually for monetary purposes, and results in damage to another individual. Fraud can include identity theft, bankruptcy fraud, false billing, tax fraud, embezzlement, investment fraud, marital fraud, securities fraud, forgery, or professional quackery.

Before You Open Your Business

Roughly 21 percent of all private investigators are self-employed. Most planned their business down to the very last detail. It is recommended to start planning years in advance, even before training begins.

Why is early planning so important? For starters, the resources necessary to open and sustain a business may take years to actually acquire, so start planning and building right now. Start-up money, for example, is the key resource that floats a business through the first six months of operation. How you plan to finance your start-up costs will go a long way in determining whether you join the 50 percent of businesses that stay in business after the first five years or the 50 percent of businesses that end up failing. A business plan can help facilitate this process.

A business plan is a comprehensive document that may run between 30 and 50 pages long. You should have detailed analysis on your industry's market segmentation, cash flow requirements, and operations plan. The importance of writing a business plan is twofold. First, you want to have a realistic plan that concretely and systematically sets reachable goals that deter operational pitfalls. The second reason is financing. If you do not have the proper start-up cash requirements, you will have to find a lender who has seen your business model and believes in it. Lenders will refuse to lend money out of blind faith. They want to know the money they are lending has a high probability of being paid back over time. The more detailed the business plan, the greater the chance of convincing them the principle amount will be paid back at the interest rate you agreed to pay. If you plan to open and operate a private investigation business, it makes sense to start a business plan only after professional training is completed. *See Chapter 3 for step-by-step instructions on how to create a business plan.*

Before creating a plan, the first order of business is to determine your cumulative cash requirements. A cumulative cash requirement is the amount of money you will spend on starting a business plus the money needed to cover your net losses until the company reaches profitability.

After you receive a private investigation license and have begun working for an agency, it is advisable to start saving enough money to live off of for at least six months in the event that your new business does not profit enough money to cover your basic living expenses. Six months is roughly the amount of time a business is considered a start-up and accrues start-up expenses. Some believe a business owner should hold off on starting a business until 12 months of personal support money is acquired. However, some start-up expenses should begin diminishing after six months.

To know how much money is needed, estimate the cost of your living expenses to the nearest dollar. Basic cost of living expenses include:

- Rent or mortgage payment
- Car (lease or loan payments and occasional repairs)
- Gas
- Car insurance
- Phone bill
- Food bill
- Utility bill
- Entertainment
- Credit card payments

The lower your monthly expenses, the less support money you will need to sustain yourself through six months without a substantial income. To determine your cost of lifestyle, account for every cent that regularly goes out of your pocket and into someone else's. Multiply that number by six to see the amount of reserve money necessary to cover your expenses for the first six months of being a business owner.

After you determine the cost of living, it is also necessary to determine start-up costs. You should aim to determine the expenses required to sustain the business for the first six months of operation. Saving now for these expenses can help make the first few months run smoothly should your new business not be as profitable as you previously planned.

Calculating your future cost of living expenses as well as operating costs and weighing it against a current salary will determine the amount of time it will take save for these expenses. Monthly expenses may include:

- Renewals for licenses, fees, and permits
- Surveillance costs
- Administrative wages
- Car expenses
- Advertising
- Database subscriptions
- Utility bill
- Telephone/cell service
- Rental equipment
- Lease payments
- Accounting fees
- Contract labor
- Repairs & maintenance (computer, cameras, vehicle, etc.)
- Office supplies
- Medicare
- Taxes
- Travel expenses
- Meals
- Fines and penalties

Essential Factors to Success

There are six factors essential to the long-term success of any business:

1. Passion is the prime ingredient. A successful business is "more than a business" to its owner.

2.   A solid business foundation is built on a strong strategic plan.

3.   Excellent customer relations are the hallmark of success.

4.   Quality, reliability, and service are emphasized.

5.   Procedures, products, pricing, and all the strategic necessities of the business are regularly evaluated and monitored by the owner.

6.   A flexible business remains successful as it adapts readily to changes in the industry, technology, and market.

Almost everyone has dreamed of owning a business. Often, these dreams are the result of dealing with difficult bosses, low pay, long hours, swing shifts, and other frustrations that come from working for someone else. In the safe confines of the imagination, the vision of owning a business is immensely satisfying: You are your own boss, you make your own decisions, and you do not have to answer to anyone else. What could be better?

While there are elements of truth in this vision of business ownership, it is also true that in reality, business owners have problems too. The problems are different from the frustrations faced by employees, but they are serious and stomach wrenching just the same. You will want to know your personal capacity to deal with the problems of business ownership before you jump out of the workforce and take over the boss's chair.

National Research

Wherever you decide to do business as a private investigator, you will need to research local demographics and market conditions. To collect national research specific to the private investigation industry, contact the United States Association of Professional Investigators, or go to the association's Web site at **www.usapi.org.** The home page displays a national directory list of members in each state. You can listen to podcasts on the Web site, contact members in other states, read about industry news, or get information on attending regional seminars and conferences.

A 2009 issue of *Forbes* magazine noted the transient impulses caused by the historic recession of 2008 and 2009 and listed the 10 best metro and small metro areas to start a business in. Criteria for the ratings included local cost of doing business, crime rate, education attainment, living costs, projected income, and job growth. Also research local per-capital income levels, housing prices, family sizes, and other factors likely to impact business.

Small-Metro Best Cities to Work —
Best Places for Business and Careers:

- Sioux Falls, South Dakota (#3 in cost of doing business)
- Greenville, North Carolina (#4 in cost of doing business)
- Morgantown, West Virginia
- Bloomington, Indiana
- Columbia, Missouri (#6 in educational attainment)
- Bismark, North Dakota (#10 in projected job growth)
- Fargo, North Dakota
- Lafayette, Indiana
- Iowa City, Iowa (#5 in educational attainment)
- Auburn, Alabama (#1 in projected job growth)

Metro Best Cities to Work —
Best Places for Business and Careers:

- Raleigh, North Carolina (#4 in projected job growth)
- Fort Collins, Colorado (#6 in educational attainment)
- Durham, North Carolina (#8 in educational attainment)
- Fayetteville, Arkansas
- Lincoln, Nebraska
- Asheville, North Carolina (#2 in cost of doing business)
- Des Moines, Iowa
- Austin, Texas (#8 in projected job growth)
- Boise, Idaho
- Colorado Springs, Colorado

Market Area Research

"Market" is one way of referring to a city or a metropolitan statistical area (MSA). MSA is a term used in census research. Decide on a target city for your business. Focus on the parts that would be good for your business. Targeting locations will give you some idea about which areas have more demand for your services and which have less. After you narrow down your choices, visit the sites. Take pictures, make notes, and evaluate the various sites to determine which is best for your agency.

Evaluate these specifics about any location you are considering:

- How many similar private investigation businesses are located in the area?
- What were competitors' volumes of sales the previous year?
- What is the population of the immediate area?
- Is the population increasing, stationary, or declining?
- Are the residents of all ages or old, middle-aged, or young?
- What is the average sales price and rental rates for area homes?
- What is the per capita income?
- What is the average family size?
- Is the location suitable for a private investigation business?

Population and demographics

Population and demographics are factors to consider when choosing your location. The U.S. Census Bureau (**www.census.gov**) can supply important information and statistics about the private investigation industry.

Trends and activities in a demographic breakdown should be narrowed to your service offerings. For example, a private investigator looking to specialize in divorce, infidelity, and child custody cases might look for a demographic area that favors:

- Family income
- Divorce rates
- Number of divorce lawyers in the area
- High number of child custody suits in official court records
- Few private investigators specializing in divorce/infidelity

A private investigator looking to specialize in workers' compensation cases might look for areas heavily populated with:

- Construction companies
- Geographical booms in real estate construction
- Industrialized areas (petroleum plants, automotive manufacturing facilities)

A good source for information is your local chamber of commerce. To contact a chamber in another area, visit the Chamber of Commerce.com Web site (**www.chamberofcommerce.com**). You can get in touch with the association related to the private investigation industry, and peers will assist you with economic and lifestyle patterns for your business research. Your library and online sources can also provide valuable information. There are research librarians who can help you find the information you need. You can find market statistics for different areas of the United States by visiting the DemographicsNow Web site (**www.demographicsnow.com**).

For additional data and statistics, visit the following sites online:

- QuickFacts: **http://quickfacts.census.gov/qfd/index.html**
- SearchBug: **www.searchbug.com/sitemap.aspx**
- MelissaDATA: **www.melissadata.com/lookups/index.htm**

Also, the American Community Survey (**www.census.gov/acs**) provides additional information from the supplemental census survey. This information includes demographics by county and metropolitan statistical areas (MSAs). An MSA is an area with at least one major city and includes the county or counties located within the MSA. This survey is replacing the Census Bureau's long survey. It provides full demographic information for communities each year, not every ten years. The CenStats Databases (**http://censtats.census. gov**) provide economic and demographic information that you can compare by county. The information is updated every two years. On the County Business Patterns (**www.census.gov/econ/cbp**) Web site, economic information is reported by industry. Statistics, updated every year, include the number of establishments, employment, and payroll for more than 40,000 ZIP codes across the country. Metro Business Patterns provides the same data for MSAs. American FactFinder (**http://factfinder.census.gov**) allows you to evaluate all sorts of U.S. census data.

Scouting the competition

Never underestimate the value of knowing your competition. Make a list of the other agencies in your market. Which ones target the same population that you will? Find out what they are selling and their prices. Sources for finding out who your competitors are include:

- **Telephone book:** The phone book will give you the number and location of your competitors.
- **Chambers of commerce:** These organizations have lists of local businesses. Verify whether it is a complete list and not just a list of chamber members.
- **Local newspapers:** Study the local advertisements and help wanted ads. There could also be a weekly entertainment section with information about local private investigation businesses.

Take a detailed look at your competition once you narrow down your choices. The best way to find information about your competition may be by visiting them. Be creative. For example, you could visit every law firm in the area and ask which local investigation agencies they work with. Contact businesses that would be in line for investigative services. When visiting a potential competitor, ask yourself the following questions afterward:

- What did and did not seem to work for that particular private investigation agency?
- Have there been any social or business trends in the area the competitor is operating in that changed the market outlook?
- How many potential clients and industry-related businesses are in the area in which the competitor is operating?
- Did you like the surroundings inside and outside of the agency?
- How busy was the agency during a peak time?
- What makes the area have a demand for investigative services?
- What is the business likely to pay in office rent in that area?
- Do they offer any unique services?
- How much manpower does the competitor have?
- What was the atmosphere?

Starting from Scratch versus Buying a Franchise

If you plan to start your business from scratch, your costs will be lower and you will not have to follow the plans and policies of a franchise or deal with the reputation of a previous business owner. You will be in complete control and have the prospect of success or of failure on your shoulders. It will be up to you to find customers, market your services, research your vendors and potential partners, hire any employees, and set up your office. This is a huge challenge, but if you have a vision in mind, you may be eager to take it on. Remember — planning is key. The following quiz can help you determine whether business ownership is right for you and whether you should buy a franchise or strike out on your own.

Personality Quiz

1. I am happiest when I am completely in charge of a project and using my own ideas.
    (Yes___ Sometimes___ No___)

2. I prefer to have a group of people brainstorm alternatives and then come to a group consensus to set priorities and make decisions.
    (Yes___ Sometimes___ No___)

3. I like to have someone else with more experience set my targets and goals, so I can meet or exceed them. **(Yes___ Sometimes___ No___)**

4. I am excited about starting from scratch.
    (Yes___ Sometimes___ No___)

5. I enjoy building teams as long as I am the leader. **(Yes___ Sometimes___ No___)**

6. I feel uptight if someone asks me a question and I do not immediately know the answer.
    (Yes___ Sometimes___ No___)

7. I enjoy pleasing the people I work for.
    (Yes___ Sometimes___ No___)

8. I want to help my employees feel successful, and I know how to encourage others.
    (Yes___ Sometimes___ No___)

9. My primary goal is to make a lot of money fast and have lots of leisure time.
    (Yes___ Sometimes___ No___)

10. I like the idea of coming to work later in the morning and seeing my employees already working.
    (Yes___ Sometimes___ No___)

11. I know I do not know how to do everything, but I am willing to ask for advice and even pay for it.
    (Yes___ Sometimes___ No___)

12. I would rather learn on the job by trial and error than pay for help.
    (Yes___ Sometimes___ No___)

13. I would rather sit in my office making phone calls and setting appointments than working outside, getting sweaty.
    (Yes___ Sometimes___ No___)

14. I do not care if I have to follow someone else's rules if I benefit from their expertise and make more money faster.
    (Yes___ Sometimes___ No___)

15. I work outdoors, and I play outdoors. It is my favorite place to be.
    (Yes___ Sometimes___ No___)

16. I hate being cooped up in an office.
    (Yes___ Sometimes___ No___)

17. I have excellent mechanical skills.
    (Yes___ No___)

18. I know I am good at what I do, but I know my limits. **(Yes___ Sometimes___ No___)**

19. I am orderly by nature. I live by the motto: "a place for everything and everything in its place."
    (Yes___ Sometimes___ No___)

20. Even if my work area seems messy, it is organized to suit my needs.
    (Yes___ Sometimes___ No___)

21. I like the challenge of getting along with difficult people.
    (Yes___ Sometimes___ No___)

22. One of my goals is to inspire others to succeed. I want to be a role model in my community.
    (Yes___ Sometimes___ No___)

23. I would like a job where I can get my hands dirty.
    (Yes___ Sometimes___ No___)

24. I prefer the wilderness to a manicured golf course.

(**Yes**___ **Sometimes**___ **No**___)

25. I keep my checkbook balanced and promptly reconcile bank statements.

(**Yes**___ **Sometimes**___ **No**___)

26. I pay my taxes on time.

(**Yes**___ **Sometimes**___ **No**___)

27. I know the local regulations for the business I want to open.

(**Yes**___ **No**___)

28. I feel comfortable negotiating prices with customers and vendors.

(**Yes**___ **Sometimes**___ **No**___)

29. I like to associate with people from different backgrounds.

(**Yes**___ **Sometimes**___ **No**___)

30. I will tell an employee the result I want and let him or her figure out how to achieve it.

(**Yes**___ **Sometimes**___ **No**___)

31. I am rarely satisfied, and I always strive for improvement.

(**Yes**___ **Sometimes**___ **No**___)

32. I have always enjoyed working with numbers.

(**Yes**___ **No**___)

33. I am willing to change any business practice or product at a moment's notice if I hear of something that might work better.

(**Yes**___ **Sometimes**___ **No**___)

34. I hate having someone else tell me what to do or how to do it.

(**Yes**___ **Sometimes**___ **No**___)

35. I am done with formal education forever.

(**Yes**___ **No**___ **Maybe**___)

36. I will ask customers for feedback regularly. If I do not hear complaints, I will not change anything in the business.

(**Yes**___ **Sometimes**___ **No**___)

37. I like to shop for bargains.

(**Yes**___ **Sometimes**___ **No**___)

38. I do not take chances; I plan for all possibilities.
(Yes____ Sometimes____ No____)

39. I can be fine without a regular paycheck for a while.
(Yes____ Sometimes____ No____)

40. I am eager to open this business. It is like a parachute jump — a leap into the unknown.
(Yes____ Sometimes____ No____)

41. I have enough of my own money and resources to start this business immediately.
(Yes____ Sometimes____ No____)

42. I know where to get more money if I need it.
(Yes____ Sometimes____ No____)

43. I am living from paycheck to paycheck now, and I am tired of it.
(Yes____ Sometimes____ No____)

44. I want customers ready and waiting the day I open my doors.
(Yes____ Sometimes____ No____)

45. I have many ideas about marketing my business and I know how to get it done.
Yes____ Sometimes____ No____)

46. I already have a company name picked out.
(Yes____ No____)

47. I already know what kind of customers I want to serve.
(Yes____ No____)

48. I dream about this business at night.
(Yes____ Sometimes____ No____)

49. I have a picture in my head of me running my own business.
(Yes____ Sometimes____ No____)

50. My family and friends are supportive of my business ideas.
(Yes____ Sometimes____ No____)

Scoring:

Business ownership may be appropriate for you if you answered "yes" on questions 1, 4, 5, 8, 12, 33, 34, 39, 41, 42, 48, 49, and 50. This response shows that you have an independent spirit and are willing to take full responsibility for the job you are undertaking. A "yes" response on question 2 suggests that you might want to form a partnership or at least consider bringing employees, family, or other advisers to help you make business decisions.

A person well suited to franchise ownership might answer "yes" to questions 3, 14, and 50. Someone who answers "yes" to 41, 42, and 44 may find purchasing an existing business more appropriate than starting from scratch. Delegating skills are highlighted by "yes" answers to questions 18 and 30.

A good attitude that will be helpful in business is demonstrated by "yes" answers to questions 11, 21, 22, 38, and 40. Skills and affinities useful to business operation are shown in "yes" answers to 15, 16, 17, 19, 20, 23, 25, 26, 27, 28, 29, 31, 32, 37, 45, 46, and 47.

Finally, those who answer "yes" to questions 9, 10, 13, 24, 35, 36, and 43 may find the reality of business ownership difficult. This does not mean you cannot run a successful business, just as a "no" to certain questions in the skills and affinities group does not mean you cannot succeed. However, it does mean that you may need to select partners, advisers, or get some specific training to make the path of your business growth possible and realistic. It is always helpful to consider delegating work that is in an area where your skills are not supreme. Also, remember that showing your employees that you are dedicated to doing the job will inspire them to make their best effort, too.

CASE STUDY: MATCHING YOUR SKILLS TO A PRIVATE INVESTIGATION

Pierre McLean, president
Peace of Mind Private Investigators
P.O. Box 1004, Forked River, NJ 08731
macself@aol.com
www.peaceofmind-pi.net
Phone: (609) 971-0356
Fax: (609) 971-3999

Becoming a private investigator was something that happened by circumstance. After being a New Jersey law enforcement officer for 11 years, I had resigned from the department to own a full service car wash. My new business might have worked out, except I wound up being defrauded by the previous owner. I used my prior law enforcement experience to conduct a fraud investigation on the seller and provided critical evidence to my attorney, who used it to structure an effective and successful case representation on my behalf. I enjoyed the experience so much that I decided to apply for a private investigator's license and open an agency instead of a car wash.

One thing I learned about private investigation is that you can come from just about any background. It is possible to become a private investigator whether you have a degree in criminal justice, previous experience in the military or law enforcement, or no experience or degree at all. I came to private investigation as a law enforcement officer and Marine Corps veteran. My previous qualifications made getting a private detective license an easier transition, but I had no experience or private investigative knowledge. I purchased multiple books on being a private investigator and conducting private investigations, learning everything I could about the business and being licensed. I completed applications to several established agencies to work as an employee and/or subcontractor. I worked for four agencies over the course of two years, both as an employee and subcontractor.

Eventually, I was able to offer my services to the public. I sought certifications in areas of interest and specialization to establish competency and define my niche. Early research will help you decide if the profession is for you. My research also helped me identify the cost upfront. The collective amount for training was about $3,000. This pertained to getting three industry specific certifications in surveillance, insurance claims investigations, and fraud investigations, which allowed me to find a niche and receive higher compensation in my practice. I sought certifications through the National Association of Investigative Specialists (NAIS) and currently hold designations as Certified Surveillance Investigator (CSI) and Certified Insurance Claims Investigator (CICI).

CHAPTER 2
What it Takes to Become a Private Investigator

Forty states require private investigators to be licensed, 22 of them require a licensing examination, and ten allow you to operate with just a business license. To know the exact requirements, contact your state's licensing office. In some states, such as Ohio, private investigators are licensed by the Department of Homeland Security. Arizona licenses are granted by the Department of Public Safety. California licenses come from the Bureau of Security and Investigative Services. State-by state links to licensing offices can be found at the *PI Magazine* Web site (**www.pimagazine.com/private_investigator_license_requirements.html**) and the *Pursuit Magazine* Web site (**http://pursuitmag.com/investigator-licensing**).

There are no academic requirements to qualify for training as a private investigator, but some states require less training for applicants with an academic background. Whether you have a business license and want to open an agency, a bachelor's degree in criminal justice, no academic background, or previous investigative experience in law enforcement, the quickest way to acquire a license is to seek full-time internship at a licensed private investigation agency. Proof of internship must be legally granted and experience must be documented before submitting a license application. Private investigation internships normally take two years to complete. Those with a bachelor's degree in criminal justice, criminology or law enforcement administration in the state of Florida will only need to intern for one year at an agency. After completing an internship, you will be eligible to submit an application package to the licensing office in your state. If all the requirements have been met, the state will formally issue a private investigator's license to operate within that state. Keep in mind that internships require long hours due to surveillance operations that may require working at night. Agencies recognize this and will pay interns for their services. Starting pay can range from $10 to $16 per hour plus mileage reimbursement for travel expenses incurred during fieldwork.

It is not uncommon for a private investigation firm to require their interns to sign a non-compete or confidentiality agreement before starting an internship. This agreement prohibits the intern from sharing sensitive information regarding case files, practices, or activities with anyone outside the agency. Interns who refuse to sign it will not be employed by the agency. Those who break the agreement could be subject to prosecution.

Some firms start their interns on a part-time probationary period of six months and gradually increase the hours by caseload. Agencies are extremely cautious about who they hire. Often, they will require permission to conduct an extensive background check, so it is important to make sure you do not have a criminal record before contacting an agency for internship. In fact, any record with your name on it should be clear. If you own a car, make sure the car is insured, especially because you will be expected to have a vehicle for the purposes of training. If your driver's license is expired, it should be renewed before you begin the internship. If you do have a criminal record, contact your state's licensing office and ask if the criminal conviction disqualifies you from being licensed by the state. If it does not, write to the agency explaining the nature of the incident, state you have contacted the licensing office, and provide reasons why you believe your skills and personality would be a valuable addition to the agency.

Developing Your Skills for Internship

Stressing your skills to a training program or agency is an important part of the interview process because competition for internship positions can be high. If you have skills that align with the needs of the prospective agency, it will increase your chances of being awarded an internship with the agency of choice. When researching an agency in your area, take into account the agency's areas of specialty. For example, if you previously worked for an insurance agency, consider interning with an agency that specializes in insurance fraud. This might make you a more attractive prospect over another applicant. If you have an accounting degree or license, consider an agency that handles asset investigations.

Photography skills are not a prerequisite for securing an internship, but interns are likely to perform stationary and mobile surveillances during training. Interns who seek training from a firm specializing in marital infidelity will be working with a number of different cameras, and knowledge of how to operate f-stops, light filters, and optical zoom lenses are required. Taking a photography workshop before the internship will help you to become familiar with these features. To learn how to use a digital single reflex camera from professionals, The Nikon School (**www.nikonusa.com/Learn-And-Explore/Nikon-School/index.page**) offers classes at hotels and convention centers around the country for about $119. Interns need to learn how to use an optical zoom lens on a digital camera. Optical zoom capability involves physically moving the lens to achieve a greater focal length and increase the size of the image. The image is what the lens actually sees. These images prevent the picture from having to be altered by a digital process. Digital zoom uses software that blows up the pixels, resulting in loss of clarity, which is the most important aspect of obtaining visual evidence on a subject. If you buy a digital camera to use while in your internship and for your own business, look for the optical zoom capability. The most common camera used by private investigators has an optical zoom lens with a 100-300 mm range.

Having prior experience working with optical zoom lenses will improve your standing with an agency if the agency requires working with that type of equipment. For example, investigators who specialize in workers' compensation cases require the use of video because most hard evidence lies in the subject's continual range of motion.

Communication skills are also an important aspect of private investigation. Private investigation can be solitary work, involving many hours alone on surveillance, but it is surprising how much of the job actually involves dealing with people, whether through conducting witness interviews, interrogation of suspects, talking to neighbors about someone, or being called for cross-examination. It is common for interns to be assigned tasks such as creating marketing campaigns, writing reports, and dealing with clients. Part of your work as a private investigator will involve questioning witnesses and interrogating suspects. Television often gives a skewed impression of what suspect interrogation is really like. A good communicator is not just someone who articulates himself or herself well; he or she is also someone who reads non-verbal cues, such as body language, and uses communication techniques to get information from people who may be unwilling to give it. During an interview with an agency, those with a degree in communications should stress what they learned from the coursework.

Most communication between people is non-verbal and psychologically manifested by body language. Reading body language is like reading a book. Each gesture is like a word that cannot have readable meaning until formed in a "sentence" of at least three or four gestures. Body language experts are trained to read body language and use techniques that can redirect a person's behavior toward a desired end. For example, a suspect with her arms folded and legs crossed indicates a closed off, defensive posture. To the trained eye, this is a sign that the suspect may not be open to talking, or he or she may just be folding her arms because he or she is cold. If the suspect touches his nose after being asked a question directly related to your case, it is your first sign the suspect may be lying. Psychological and biological research shows that when people consciously lie, the blood vessels in their nose constrict, causing a compulsion to itch. As an expert communicator, your goal in this kind of interrogation is to set subjects at ease rather than harangue and accuse them in ways that have been made popular by crime dramas on television.

Intern Progress Reports

When interviewing with a private investigation agency, your prospective employer will be closely observing how well you communicate answers, especially in the form of nonverbal cues. How well you represent yourself will tell them a lot about how you would represent the agency if asked to meet with clients or attend trade conventions to network with potential clients and other professionals.

Whichever agency you choose, make sure the employer has an adequate basic training program. Some red flags are easy to detect. For example, if they dodge some of the interview questions or do not allow communication with former interns, it may be signs of a suspicious agency. To assess the quality of training, ask the following questions when contacting a prospective agency:

- What specific training programs does your company offer?
- Do you start interns off at part-time or full-time hours?
- Do you have a probationary period? If so, is there a pay increase after the probationary period?
- How do you document intern training?
- Do you process intern progress reports to the Division of Licensing (DOL), or do you leave processing responsibilities to the interns?
- How will this training complete the necessary number of hours required by the state?
- What type of private investigator license do your investigators have?
- May I speak with someone who recently interned at your agency?

A good agency will supply you with most of the equipment you will need for your assignments. Spending more than $1,000 on a camera may cast a poor reflection on the agency and could indicate their inability to provide adequate training and equipment. If you do not already own them or your internship does not provide them, the items you may be asked to buy for basic training program will include:

- Binoculars
- 8mm camera
- 35mm camera
- Camera tripod
- Cell phone
- Tape recorder
- Laptop
- Black tape
- Backpack
- Camouflage
- Wristwatch
- Maps
- Identification cards to prove your credentials

To qualify for state licensing at the end of an internship, you must have documented proof of training. These documents should be submitted in the form of semi-annual progress reports to the state licensing division. They should also be notarized and backed up with a copy in the event they become lost in processing. If internship training is not reported or the documents become lost, all the hours of training are essentially lost unless you have a back-up copy. Should this happen, the state might deny licensure.

Keep in mind that most agencies are small and have little room for advancement. Most do not have higher and lower ranking positions. If you are hired to work as a licensed investigator by the company after your internship, advancement in the agency will materialize in the form of increased salary and assignment status. The most important thing to verify when deciding on an internship is the licensure class of the investigators you will be working with. As requirements vary from state to state, so do the types of licenses. In Ohio, a Class C license only certifies trainees for security guard work, while a Class B license certifies private investigators. In Florida, an internship gives the trainee a CC Class license. After processing, the application package qualifies interns as private investigators with a C license. If an agency turns out to be unlicensed yet willing to train, look for another agency immediately, as this type of behavior is illegal in states that require licensure. For example, any unlicensed party offering to provide a regulated service in the state of Texas is guilty of a Class A misdemeanor under the Private Security Act in Chapter 1702 of the Occupations Code. The likelihood of encountering this problem is not great because most agencies will not risk the stiff penalties involved with this activity. However, it is good to be aware of unscrupulous practices. Internship duties include:

- Completion of company training programs and initiatives
- Assist investigations with lead investigator
- Prepare investigative reports
- Handle customer service
- Prepare advertising and marketing campaigns
- Give presentations
- Attend social business functions
- Meet prospective clients
- Administrative tasks

After completing the required number of hours for internship, interns must package the application to the appropriate licensing office. The first step is to complete any exams the state may require. The state exam for Washington investigators covers state law and licensing regulation (45 percent of the exam), federal law (30 percent of the exam), court systems (7.5 percent of the exam), legal procedures (10 percent of the exam), and public information resources (7.5 percent of the exam). In California, the Bureau of Security and Investigative Services requires applicants who have completed their training to take an examination to "determine proficiency of the applicant to engage in the business for which the license is required."

The next step is to make sure semi-annual reports have been processed to show the completed number of hours required for internship. Afterward, contact the licensing office and ask them to send an application form. Read the application form very carefully when it arrives. Most forms will list their application requirements at the top. There should be no surprises at this stage because you will have heeded these requirements before applying for internship. Some states require private investigators to be at least 25 years of age; others require them to be at least 18 years of age. The state of Florida will deny an application to those who were dishonorably discharged from the military or convicted of a crime and served a sentence longer than one year. An application can be accepted if a period of ten years has passed since they were convicted. Along with the paper application, several items will also need to be submitted. In the state of Michigan, for example, you are required to submit:

- Fingerprints
- Two recent photos, no larger than 1 ¼"x1 ¼"
- Employee verification forms
- Official transcript (if qualifying by degree)
- Bond or liability insurance
- Five notarized personal references from individuals who have known applicant for a period of at least five years

Most applicants required to pass an examination must also provide documentation confirming their passing grade. Some states allow a grace period to those who have not completed the examination upon submitting their application. In Florida, applicants are allowed to complete a mandatory 40-hour course in additional to the internship within 180 days of their application date.

Applicants must also submit the registration form. This form will ask you to fill out personal information, the federal identification number of the agency where the internship was provided, and their professional license number.

Depending on the license you are applying for, the processing fee may cost several hundred dollars. This is usually paid in the form of a check or money order.

Niches for Investigators without a License

Unless you reside in a state that does not require a license, investigating without a license severely limits the activities of an investigator. Those who decide to become unlicensed investigators in states that require licensure may not be contracted by licensed investigators. Unlicensed investigators are legally restricted in what they are allowed to do as investigators, which limits their usefulness to licensed investigators. It also increases the licensed investigator's liability if the unlicensed investigator does something he or she is not licensed to do. Unlicensed investigators will, however, be able to get work as a processing agent, serving subpoenas and routinely performing public record retrieval.

If it seems encouraging to know that prior experience is not a necessity to be an investigator, the news is about to get even better. Many people who do not have the time or resources to obtain a license as a private investigator can perform unlicensed investigation in public record retrieval. These investigators can earn up to several thousand dollars per month just from pulling records for clients and lawyers involved in civil or criminal cases.

Unlicensed private investigators are very much involved in the court process because many of them make a living as process servers. When the court orders someone to appear in court, they must be notified in person. Process servers are given the responsibility of serving a *subpoena*, or official document notifying a person they have been ordered to appear in court. Some states have certain requirements that you must follow before this task can be performed, so check with a local sheriff's office or an official state Web site to see if any requirements exist. Keep in mind that local police departments do not like competition from process servers. Process servers typically charge less than police departments because of their ability to serve subpoenas in much higher volumes. The National Association of Process Servers (NAPPS) is an international organization dedicated to helping process servers by protecting their rights and providing industry information. The association's Web site, **www. napps.org**, is a good resource for anyone interested in working as an unlicensed private investigator. It provides state-by-state networking links, state charter support associations, consultation on opening a process server business, and information regarding conferences.

You may also work for a corporation or conduct business as a *registered agent*, who deals directly with a process server in receiving all legal documents pertaining to lawsuits, subpoenas, and tax forms. If you have been working as an unlicensed investigator, the chances of becoming a registered agent are good because most public corporations are required to carry one for tax and legal purposes. Businesses that fail to maintain a registered agent can potentially lose their business license. This is a particularly good niche for unlicensed investigators with a degree in accounting. In fact, some individuals are strictly in the business of being a registered agent because they can represent thousands of businesses for a fee. The function of a registered agent is to track and report to the company about their filing status for any documents that need to be officially filed, track legislative changes, and report due dates for filing official documents. Businesses can appoint corporate officers within the company as registered agents, but an outside registered agent avails a company the embarrassment of being served a subpoena in front of its employees. If you become a process server, this is a job option to consider at some point in the future.

Additional Training & Niches for Licensed Investigators

Your opportunities in the field of private investigating will increase with advanced degrees and training after becoming officially licensed. While the top licensed investigators make over $60,000 a year, several niche areas pay six-figure salaries. Training in niche areas is a good way to build the savings needed to open a business at some future date.

Certified Fraud Examiner

Training to become a Certified Fraud Examiner (CFE) provides expertise in the area of fraud prevention, detection, and deterrence. According to the Association of Certified Fraud Examiners (ACFE), CFEs earn 22 percent more than investigators who work in the anti-fraud industry. To meet the requirements for training, applicants must have a bachelor's degree and at least two years experience in:

- Accounting or auditing
- Criminology and sociology
- Fraud investigation
- Loss prevention
- Law

As an accountant or auditor, one's experience in anti-fraud measures should include system evaluation, risk analysis, designing protection schemes, and the ability to detect financial inconsistencies in business ledgers. If you have experience in criminology, it must be specifically related to white-collar crime. Those who already have a background in fraud investigation must have experience related to civil or criminal cases. Insurance fraud investigators, for example, are the most likely to seek training as a CFE. If you have worked as a security director and have experience with loss prevention, you also qualify for CFE training. An investigator license in security guard training will not suffice as qualification. However, experience in fraud litigation does qualify an applicant for training.

Investigators who meet these background requirements should submit an application for CFE certification to the Board of Regents. The Board of Regents sets admission standards and is responsible for admissions. It also enforces a code of ethics to ensure ACFE standards. Eligibility for certification is based on a point system. Previous experience as an investigator will award an applicant significant points. If your prior experience equals at least 40 points, you may apply for the CFE exam given by the Board of Regents. Investigators looking to become certified will need to accumulate 50 points. In other words, a bachelor's degree automatically earns 40 points and qualifies the applicant to take the exam before accumulating the necessary two years of experience required in a related field. Passing the CFE exam before meeting the two year's experience requirement is a good way to increase the prospects of getting a job in one of the five previously mentioned fields in fraud detection. After meeting the two-year requirement, the applicant will earn the last tem points necessary for certification. The requirements can also be met in other ways, such as having other types of degrees or professional certifications. To determine your score and whether you qualify, go to the ACFE's Web site (**www.acfe.com**). By clicking the "qualifications" menu, calculate your current point score based on experience or level of certification. The AFCE holds annual conferences in the United States, Europe, and Canada. Attendance fees are extremely high for both members and non-members, but these conferences are excellent places to network with some of the field's top practitioners.

To facilitate the process, go to the ACFE's Web site and become a member of the association. This can easily be done by filling out an information field for name, e-mail, and physical address. It is not possible to apply for the test by circumventing membership. When membership is applied for, calculate the point score, and print out the online application form. Registrants should fill out and submit the application, along with an application prep course and exam fee of $250, proof of education, and the association's three download-able CFE recommendation forms to:

Association of Certified Fraud Examiners
Attn: Certification Department
716 West Avenue
Austin, TX 78701 USA
Phone: (800) 245-3321 / +1 (512) 478-9000
Fax: (512) 478-9297

After studying the prep course, the exam will test knowledge in:

- Fraudulent financial transactions
- Legal elements of fraud
- Investigation methods
- Criminology
- Ethics

When you pass the exam and receive CFE certification from the Board of Regents, you will be obligated to pay an annual membership fee of $150. If the membership expires, you will have to be reinstated as a CFE by submitting a reactivation fee of $150 and application. If the membership has expired for longer than three years, you will be required to retake the certification exam.

Your job functions as a CFE will intercede the functions of a private investigator in several ways. A CFE typically investigates and identifies fraud and hidden assets and specializes in data recovery and computer forensics. He or she calculates damages as a result of fraud, examines financial transactions in business ledgers, interviews suspects, writes reports, and testifies in court. However, CFEs are typically paid more for their services than a regular investigator who investigates fraud cases. More importantly, they are needed in a variety of industries. Industries with the highest percentage of CFEs include public accounting, bookkeeping, banking, and organizations at the state and federal level.

Certified Forensic Accountants

Some CFEs go on to become Certified Forensic Accountants (Cr.FA). Your casework in this field will often involve issues of money laundering, embezzlement, insurance fraud, securities fraud, credit card fraud, financial statement fraud, and bankruptcy fraud. Cr.FAs are typically employed by public accounting firms that specialize in consultation. A public accounting firm may outsource you for any number of services, including financial information analysis, evidence integrity analysis, and computer design application. For employment as a Cr.FA, you can find a list of the top public accounting firms at the AcountingMajors.com Web site (**www.accountingmajors.com/ accountingmajors/articles/top100.html**). Working as a Cr.FA will test your knowledge of accounting procedures, regression analysis, and knowledge of computer forensics. This type of training requires a bachelor's degree in accounting, coursework in criminal justice, and designation as both a Certified Public Accountant (CPA) and CFE. The American College of Forensic Examiners (ACFEI) offers advancement in this type of forensic science and education. To enroll, go to visit the ACFEI Web site (**www.acfei.com/ forensic_certifications/crfa/**).

Executive protection services

Another niche in the private investigation field is in bodyguard or executive protection services to top-level company executives. Licensing in this area varies from state to state. If you are unlicensed and have decided to pursue training for executive protection services, contact the licensing office in your state to find out which license is required. If you already have a private investigator license, you may only need additional training. Training is offered by most executive protection services. These agencies offer classes in unarmed combat, martial arts, environment simulation, tactical driving, first aid, and more advanced training classes. To pursue training in this area, trainees are required to obtain a license to carry a weapon. To obtain this license, you must be trained in the use of firearms. This may include taking courses offered by the National Rifle Association (NRA) or other training facilities for certification, or it may involve obtaining a gun permit from the state. As a bodyguard, you may have to carry weapons other than guns that are considered deadly weapons, such as batons or certain types of knives. These weapons are not covered in the certification by the NRA, yet the state may require a class or certification fee to carry one.

Bodyguard services require skills similar to private investigation, yet the goals are somewhat opposite. The goal in conducting stationary surveillance in private investigation is remaining undercover. For bodyguard and executive protection services, you are openly conducting surveillance and making threat assessments in public, called "crowd screening" and "crowd control." During mobile surveillance, private investigators must tail but never get ahead of their subjects, whereas bodyguards are trained to assess the situation and escape if necessary. A bodyguard conducts a number of routine investigative searches, such as examining an area for explosives or debugging a room.

Bodyguards also work with local police departments to assess potential threats and security weaknesses prior to their client's arrival. For example, if a client happens to be a high-profile executive who faces threats from a radical group, you may be sent a day before his or her arrival to coordinate security logistics in a hotel he or she is traveling to. Responsibilities could include determining the location of entrances and exits and meeting with service staff members who have access to the rooms. One of the highest levels of executive protection services is the United States Secret Service. This agency is assigned with protecting the life of the President of the United States, his family, and other federal officials. Keep in mind that security guard services may require a different license or training than executive protection services. If you pursue a career in security guard services, you will be assigned with maintaining security at an event or one specific location, rather than protecting one individual.

Communication forensics investigators

If specializing in security services seems too dangerous, training in communication or computer forensics also is a great way to earn a living. Communication forensics involves the process of analyzing evidence found within computers and various forms of digital storage. An increasing number of lawyers are introducing computer forensics into evidence for their civil and criminal cases thanks to information that can be gleaned from a *digital artifact*, such as a hard drive, electronic document, or packet. For example, if a lawyer is attempting to prosecute someone accused of pedophilia, the lawyer may issue a warrant to have the defendant's hard drive seized for digital forensic examination. If evidence in digital storage uncovers lewd e-mails to underage persons, the evidence contained in the digital artifact may be used to strengthen the prosecution's case.

In 2005, communication forensics investigators played a vital role in catching Dennis Lynn Rader, now infamously known as the "BTK Killer." From 1974 to 1991, Rader had committed a string of brutal murders near Wichita, Kansas. One of Rader's trademarks was to send detailed letters about the slayings to local police. The BTK Killer had eluded punishment for years until data on a floppy disk sent by Rader led examiners to determine the identity of the killer. During his interrogation by investigators, Rader admitted to having already planned his next murder. If not for the investigators who uncovered the vital trace evidence on the disk, Rader would have managed to kill his 11th victim.

Communication forensics investigators perform routine interrogations and interviews with subjects in the same vein as private investigators, only a forensic examiner looks to obtain digital information rather than physical evidence. One of the ways investigators ensure evidence cannot be erased or changed when entering digital storage into evidence is to calculate a *cryptographic hash*, which is a computer function that allows a computer forensic specialist to know when stored electronic data has been accidentally or intentionally altered in some way. Other practices include *writeblocking*, which prevents data from being added to a device admitted as evidence; *live analysis*, which attempts to identify computer hackers who leave no trace; and *imaging*, which duplicates an entire hard drive.

This field has become so sophisticated that job seekers can find a niche within a niche. Many branches fall under the communication forensics umbrella, including network forensics, mobile device forensics, firewall forensics, and database forensics. The use of digital forensics is not simply limited to introducing evidence against defendants in a criminal case. Suppose you have a client who is looking for a reason to fire a particularly ineffective employee. The employer is within his or her right, but feels the employee may try to sue for unfair termination. Now, suppose the client has reason to believe the employee has been using work hours to visit Internet sites expressly banned by the employee manual. As a communication forensics investigator, your job would be to collect, examine, analyze, and report the trace evidence left behind on the employee's computer.

In a different scenario, suppose the client suspects an employee is breaking the confidentiality agreement by communicating trade secrets via cell phone with a direct competitor. Expert investigators in the field of mobile device forensics would use their training to collect, examine, analyze, and report trace evidence from the employee's mobile device. Private investigators need a valid reason to search through private information on devices belonging to the subject. Likewise, communication forensics investigators may need legal authority or a warrant to search through an employee's digital media files, even if the property belongs to the employer.

If you have an interest in this field, the Information Assurance Certification Review Board offers an exam that will ask you to analyze mock evidence files. Exam fees are $499 and just over 1,000 people have this certification as of July 2009. To seek certification in communications forensics, e-mail or contact the organization at:

Information Assurance Certification Review Board
1515 N. Harlem
Suite #307
Oak Park, IL, 60302
exams@iacertification.org

Surveillance equipment installation

Communications forensics is a common career avenue for private investigators who cannot handle the long and abnormal hours they normally keep. If you enjoy working with equipment and eventually grow tired of tailing suspects and operating late-night stakeouts, you might also look into offering your technical services. Installing surveillance equipment is a profitable niche because it pools three types of clients: homeowners looking to set up a do-it-yourself system, publicly funded institutions such as school districts that monitor their students, and corporations with multiple locations trying to coordinate their entire system. In the corporate sector, installation experts serve many popular restaurants that have been franchised.

In recent years, violent outbreaks in schools have forced legislators to make school safety a priority by installing Internet-capable digital video recorders (DVR). Surveillance equipment is commonly installed to utilize an existing local area network on campus to allow a remote station to consolidate its cameras. If you install surveillance equipment, your success will depend on your familiarity with the latest equipment and how well you integrate cameras, video servers, and multiplexers to record, store, and playback surveillance footage.

Whether you are a private investigator or someone who specializes in surveillance installation, you will need to know how specific laws impact your career. Laws will decide who can install cameras and where they can be installed. Cameras in public places cannot be placed in areas where the subject under surveillance expects a reasonable amount of privacy, such as bathrooms or teacher's lounges. Clients may also be individuals looking to document a husband's or wife's activities while they are away from home. In most of these cases, these clients will want to install the multiple security camera DVRs that can be set for playback. Recording a person on video without permission is legal in some states as long as you do not record the audio. Some states allow audio recording if one party is privy to the recording, while others require both parties to be knowledgeable of the recording and give their consent.

If you are thinking about a career in surveillance installation, find out if your internship training will cover surveillance installation. Agencies that do not specialize in surveillance installation will only do this for their clients if the privacy laws in their state allow it. If your state does not allow surveillance installation without permission of the party under surveillance, it is likely you will not receive training on how to install surveillance equipment inside a home or office. In this case, try seeking additional training by contacting a technical school.

Technical surveillance countermeasures survey

Investigators with government security clearance may be hired to uninstall equipment by clients who believe they are being recorded by a device installed without their permission. In this instance, the investigator will be hired to conduct a technical surveillance countermeasures survey (TSCM) and will need to know how to "debug" a room. Spectrum analysis checks for transmitters, including devices that transmit audio and video devices connected to power lines. TSCM specialists should also know how to conduct a telecommunications system analysis, which tests telephone lines for modifications designed to intercept and record.

Conducting physical inspections requires knowledge of where devices are typically hidden inside a room. This niche can be extremely lucrative because many investigators are not qualified in this area. Those who are qualified charge between $3,500 and $5,000 for a day's worth of inspection, as well as approximately a $250 consultation fee. An investigator will typically charge $1,000 to $2,500 for a limited bug sweep.

Technical training in debugging or security installation may be necessary for investigators who have not set up surveillance equipment for clients before. Many of the best TSCM specialists have degrees in engineering or experience in government security. Only Nevada and North Carolina require a license for this specialization. Government training, however, can take up to several years. The most popular government training TSCM course is North America Interagency Training Center (ITC). For commercial training, the REI Center for Technical Security offers courses that take less time to complete. A private investigator without security clearance can seek commercial TSCM training to increase his or her service offering. However, these investigators should think about charging less for their services than a government-trained specialist.

CASE STUDY: WHY TRAINING IS KEY TO SUCCESS

Kelly E. Riddle, president
Kelmar & Associates, Inc.
2553 Jackson Keller, Ste. 200, San
Antonio, TX 78230
kelmar@kelmarpi.com * www.kelmarpi.com
Phone: (210) 342-0509
Fax: (210) 342-0731

I have 31 years experience in the private investigation industry and have owned my own business since 1989. I am the author of ten books about private investigation and am the president-elect of the Texas Association of Licensed Investigators. I began my career in law enforcement, but left and took a job as an investigator for an insurance company. I was hired by an international private investigation company that ended up selling out to Pinkerton, which is one of the largest national firms in the country. I needed a job, which is why is started my own firm.

Because I had experience in insurance investigations and knew many adjusters, I had a ready-made market. I started with four investigators on staff and $28,000 in billing my first month. However, over the years, I have had to retool and find the latest niche. The largest hurdle for any private investigator is getting your name known and getting business. You can be the best investigator, but it will not matter if you are not good at marketing and getting business.

I have a degree in criminal justice and had seven years in law enforcement and six years as a private investigator before opening my business, so I had a good background and had many contacts. My minor was in business administration, so I also had a grasp of the business side of things.

You should get training early in your career is because it widens the scope of what you are able to do as a private investigator. By increasing your service offering, you increase your client base, but I advise people not to stop their training once they have become licensed investigators. Showing you are up-to-date with industry standards keeps you in the mainstream of the industry and can be a good marketing tool. Even the most experienced investigator can learn from others who have developed specialty services.

CHAPTER 3
What You Will Need to Open Your Business

At the end of the training period, most private investigators who are looking to start a business will seek employment with an agency to build their cumulative cash requirements. Using the initial preparations you made regarding your business plan, you should begin to expand your plan while you work. Having a polished plan by the time cash requirements are reached allows the entrepreneur to get started with fewer problems. A detailed business plan will be your navigational guide through the critical start-up period and proof to lenders or strategic partners that you are capable of starting a business.

Business plans are your road map to success. The only way you can reach your goal of succeeding with your business is by having a plan. It is difficult at best to establish and operate a business when you do not quite know how to go about it — let alone trying to accomplish it without a thorough assessment of what you want to accomplish, how you plan to go about it, and what financial support you have to accomplish it. As you prepare to undertake the enormous task of starting a new business, evaluate your situation as it stands today and visualize where you want to be three to five years from now. To work your way up to owning and operating a successful business, you must set goals to reach along the way that will serve as benchmarks on your road to success. A sample business plan for the private investigation industry will be included in the accompanying CD-ROM.

The most important and basic information to include in a business plan:

- Your business goals
- The approach you will take to accomplish those goals
- Potential problems you may encounter along the way, and how you plan to address those problems
- An outline of the organizational structure of the business, as it is today and how you plan it to be in the future
- The capital you will need to get started and keep it in operation

There are various formats and models available for developing business plans. There are even entire books devoted to guiding you through the development of a business plan. However, before you constrain yourself to any one business plan format, take into consideration that business plans should be as unique as the business for which it is being written. No two businesses are the same, and even though there may be some basic similarities, each business is as individual and unique as the owner. Therefore, even though it is recommended that you follow the basic structure of commonly used templates, you should customize your business plan to fit your needs. There are a number of Web sites that provide you with a variety of samples and templates that can also be used as reference, such as Bplans.com (**www.bplans.com**) and PlanMagic (**www.planmagic.com**).

When writing your business plan, stay focused on its ultimate purpose, and take into consideration the many reasons why the plan is being developed and its possible applications. For instance, if you do not have a loan proposal — essentially a condensed version of the business plan used by businesses to request financing — when trying to secure financing, business plans are great supporting documentation to attach to a loan application. Plans are also used as a means of introducing your business to a new market or presenting your business to a prospective business partner or investor.

Parts of a business plan

Cover page

The cover page should be evenly laid out with all the information centered on the page. Always write the name of your company in all capital letters in the upper half of the page. Several line spaces down write the title "Business Plan." Last, write your company's address, the contact person's name (your name), Web site if available, and the current date. The cover sheet is the only thing that will immediately be visible in a professional business plan. Most detective agencies have a registered trademark, which is a company symbol designed to promote recognition and branding. Having a company trademark printed on the cover sheet will make the company seem more viable as a business entity, and thus make the plan appear more professional looking. *You will learn more about trademarks later in this chapter.*

NAME OF COMPANY

Business Plan

Address
Contact Name
Date

Table of contents

Target Market

Product Description

Market Approach Strategy

Marketing

Operations

Strengths and Weaknesses

Financial Projections

Conclusion

Supporting Documents

Body of the business plan

MISSION STATEMENT

It is very important that you present your business and what it is all about at the very beginning of your business plan. A mission statement is only as significant as you intend for it be. It can be written somewhere and then disregarded as unimportant. However, it should be written and placed in important documents such as your business plan and ultimately used as a beacon to always guide your business in the right direction. When writing your mission statement, three key elements that must be taken into consideration and discussed are: the purpose of your business, the services that you provide, and a statement as to your company's attitude toward your employees and customers. A well-written mission statement could be as short as one paragraph but should not be longer than two. For example, a private investigator may want to emphasize his or her oath to serve the client to the best of his or her ability and promise that all information obtained through investigation is strictly confidential and intended for the private use of the client.

EXECUTIVE SUMMARY

The executive summary should be about one to two pages in length, and it should actually be written last, as it is a summary of all the information included in the plan. It should address what your market is, the purpose of the business, where it will be located, and how it will be managed. Write the executive summary in such a way that it will prompt the reader to look deeper into the business plan. It is a good idea to discuss the various elements of your business plan in the order you address them in the rest of the document. The end of the executive summary should include your cumulative cash flow requirement for start-up costs, the estimated short-term return on investment, and competitive advantages. A weak executive summary is an indication of a weak business plan. It is not uncommon for investors to turn down individuals after being unimpressed by the executive summary, so make it a good one.

DESCRIPTION OF PROPOSED BUSINESS

Describe in detail the purpose for which the business plan is being written. State what it is that you intend to accomplish. Describe your goods, services, and the role your business will play in the overall global market. Explain what makes your business different from all competitors. Clearly identify the goals and objectives of your business. The average length for the proposed business description section should be one to two pages.

REGULATORY CONSIDERATIONS

This section should cover regulatory considerations and insurance coverage and allows the investor to perform due diligence on your certifications. Here, the private investigator can provide information on state requirements, his or her professional background, and proof of licensure by supplying a business and investigator's license identification number. All investigators are required by law to carry a certain amount of insurance. Providing your insurance information will show lenders you have protected your business, and if lenders decide to fund it, this assures the money will not be lost as a result of the investigator losing his or her license or being permanently put out of business.

MANAGEMENT AND STAFFING

Clearly identifying the management team and any other staff that may be part of the everyday operations of the business will strengthen your business viability by demonstrating that the business will be well managed. Keep in mind that a company's greatest asset is its employees. State who the owners of the business are, as well as other key employees with backgrounds in the international trade industry. Identify the management talent you have on board (this may even include yourself) as well as any others you may need in the future to expand your business. For instance, you may be the only employee when first opening your business; however, in your plans for expansion, you might think about incorporating someone well versed in a specialized field, such as TSCM debugging, computer forensics, or executive protection services. The management and staffing section of the plan could be as short as one paragraph, if you are the only employee, or it could be as long as a page or two, depending on how many people you have and anticipate having as part of your staff.

MARKET ANALYSIS

The market analysis section should identify your potential customers so you may establish how you plan to market your services later in the business plan. This is where the fruits of your research will really pay off. It might be wise to start this section by providing area demographics.

If you are new to the industry, do your research and include information that you have acquired through research and data collection. There are numerous sources of information available, both online and through printed media, which can provide you with a wealth of knowledge about area demographics. Area demographics will profile who is likely to hire a private investigator for his or her services. It will allow you to break down an area's market segmentation by age, race, average income levels, real estate trends, marital status, or any other category you choose.

There are several ways to access demographics in your area. The U.S. Census Bureau offers demographic information at **www.factfinder.census.gov**. Simply enter your state and ZIP code into the field. Results from a local map will provide information clusters on demographic attributes. These information clusters will form a picture of the trends and activities in the area, which ultimately indicate your likelihood of success in market penetration. If you do not find enough information in FactFinder, try CensusScope (**www.census-scope.org**). This Web site examines demographic trends by color graphs and charts. If you need more information, try a local or college library for reference books or contact a marketing firm about purchasing its surveys.

Trends in demographic breakdown should be narrowed to your service offerings. A private investigator looking to specialize in divorce, infidelity, and child custody cases might look for a demographic area where income level and divorce rates are high and open his or her business near that area. A private investigator looking to specialize in workers' compensation cases might look for areas heavily populated with construction companies or geographical booms in real estate construction. This process will add validity to your presentation, and you will be better prepared to answer any questions that may be presented to you. Essential elements to include in this section include details of the private investigation industry's total market, market segmentation, market penetration, and possible needs; a description of your services; and identification of your competition and your planned strategy and approach to the market. This element of your business plan should be one of the most comprehensive sections of the plan and can be several pages long, depending on the number of products involved and the market you intend to cover. In particular, the *Target Market* portion of this section alone can easily be two to three pages in length.

Industry Background

The international trade industry is vast, so providing a comprehensive description of trading business in the global market would be overwhelming. Instead, focus on the segment of the market that you will be a part of. Include trends and statistics that reflect the direction the market is going and how you will fit into that movement. Discuss major changes that have taken place in the industry in the recent past, which will affect how you will conduct business. Provide a general overview of your projected customer base, such as wholesalers or domestic consumers. Great sources to research online are The U.S. Customs and Border Protection (**www.cbp.gov**), the World Trade Organization (**www.wto.org**), United States International Trade Commission (**www.usitc.gov**), and the International Trade Administration (**www.trade.gov**).

Target Market

This is one of the largest sections of the business plan because you will be addressing key issues that will determine the volume of sales and ultimately, the revenue that you will be able to generate for your business. The target market is who your customer, or groups of customers, will be. By this point, you should have already decided on your role, so it is a good idea to narrow down your proposed customer base to a reasonable volume. If you spread your possibilities too thin, you may be wasting time on efforts that will not pay off and end up missing out on some real possibilities. Identify the characteristics of the principal market you intend to target, such as demographics, market trends, and geographic location of the market.

Discuss what resources you used to find the information you needed on your target market. For example, state whether you used the World Trade Organization's Web site or U.S. Customs' statistical data. Elaborate on the size of your primary target market — your potential customers — by indicating the possible number of prospective customers, what their purchasing tendencies are in relation to the product or services your anticipate providing, their geographical location, and the forecasted market growth for that particular market segment. Discuss the avenues you will use to reach your market. Include whether you plan to use the Internet, printed media, or trade shows. Explain the reasons why you feel confident that your company will be able to effectively compete in such a vast industry. Discuss your pricing strategies to be able to compete in the global market, such as discount structures in the form of bulk discounts or prompt payment discounts. Finally, you must address potential changes in trends that may favorably or negatively impact your target market.

Product Description

Do not just describe your product or service — describe it as it will benefit or fill the needs of potential customers, and center your attention on where you have a clear advantage. This section should elaborate on the services your investigation business offers.

Market Approach Strategy

How do you anticipate entering such a vast market? Do you anticipate carving out a niche? Determining how to enter the market and what strategy to use will be critical for breaking into the market.

MARKETING STRATEGY

In order to operate a financially successful business, you must not only maintain a constant flow of income, but also boost your profits by increased sales. The best way to accomplish this is through an effective marketing program, such as promoting your products and services by advertising, attending trade shows, and establishing a presence on the Internet. The marketing strategy element of the business plan identifies your current and potential customers, as well as the means you will use to advertise your business directly to them. The marketing strategy portion of your business plan is likely to be several pages long — at least three to four pages — depending on how much detail you include in the plan. For a large, well-established business it would probably be more appropriate to prepare a separate marketing strategy plan; however, for the start up company, it would be appropriate to include the marketing strategy plan as part of the business plan. Even as part of the business plan, the marketing strategy section should include the following elements: products and services, pricing strategy, sales/distribution plan, and advertising and promotions plan.

In this section, the business planner explains how the agency will develop its image and message to the public and plan for increasing sales to maintain a competitive advantage. The body of this plan should include:

- Network and advertising strategies
- Media kit
- List of media outlets
- Demographic charts/client purchasing characteristics
- Rationale for marketing approach and service pricing
- Similarities and differences to direct competitors
- Marketing budget

A private investigator's marketing budget will include the service offering fees and reflect the economic health of the total market. For example, many process servers rely on their vehicle to serve subpoenas and other legal documents. In an economic slowdown, their expenses increase with rising fuel costs. A common solution for most businesses in this type of climate is to make up for rising costs by charging more. However, process servers depend on serving in volume. Serving in volume will decrease if the attorneys they are contracted by cannot afford price hikes. Instead of cutting a marketing budget, the process server might consider expanding it. The process server will need to increase his or her volume to circumvent an economic slowdown affecting his or her current list of clients.

Products and Services

This section will focus on the uniqueness of your services and how your potential customers will benefit from them. Describe in detail the services your business provides, how the services are provided, and what makes the services that you provide unique and different from other businesses in the industry that provide the same service. Address the benefits of using your services instead of those of the competitors.

Pricing Strategy

The pricing strategy segment is about determining how to price your services in a way that will allow you to remain competitive, while still allowing you to make a reasonable profit. You are better off making a reasonable profit rather than pricing yourself out of the market and losing money by pricing your services too high. Therefore, you must take extreme care when pricing your services. The most effective method of doing this is by gauging your costs, estimating the tangible benefits to your customers, and making a comparison of your services and prices to similar ones on the market.

A good rule of thumb is to set your price by taking into consideration how much the services cost you, and then adding what you think would be a fair price for the benefits the services will provide to the end customer. Keep in mind, that when you are determining your cost of the services, you must take into consideration all the costs, such as the cost of labor and materials and administrative work.

You should also address why you feel the pricing of your services is competitive in comparison to others. If your price is slightly higher than that of the competition, then you need to explain why your services are worth the price. In addition, it is noteworthy to point out the kind of return on investment (ROI) you anticipate generating with that particular pricing strategy and within what time frame. ROI is a return ratio that compares the net benefits — in this case, of your services — versus their total cost.

Advertising and Promotion

Discuss how you plan to advertise your services through market-specific channels, such as private investigation industry newsletters, Internet phone books, and private investigation networking associations. Promote your business to a specific market. One of your goals in this section is to break down what percentage of your advertising budget will be spent in which media. For instance, the costs of advertising through trade magazines, trade shows, and via an Internet site differ significantly, and the return on your investment on each one may not be worth what you spent. Therefore, it is wise to carefully evaluate your advertising and promotion plans before putting them into effect.

OPERATIONS

This section will not require much detail because private investigation is a service and overhead does not require the purchase of large and expensive machines. The operations plan might be even shorter if the agency starts as a one-person operation. Private investigators who partner to form an agency will want to emphasize their credentials in the management team section of the business plan.

Under the operations section, all aspects of management and manufacturing operations and logistics services provided will be discussed. Concentrate your discussion on how to improve resources in operations and production, which will facilitate the success of the company. Remember that all of the information outlined in this section needs to be backed by realistic numbers, such as the cost of any equipment and salaries.

Discuss the business's current and proposed location, describing in detail any existing facilities. If you have employees, or anticipate having them, give a brief description of the tasks the employees will perform or other duties to be performed by the administration team.

STRENGTHS AND WEAKNESSES

As it is the case in most industries, the competition in private investigation is tough, with numerous business owners in the market competing for the same prospects. Those who take advantage of their strengths and work to overcome weaknesses will get ahead. In this section of the plan, elaborate on the particulars of your business that have enabled you, and will continue to enable you, to be successful. Discuss those things that set you apart and give you an advantage over your competitors.

There are no strengths without weaknesses, and as hard as it may be to face and deal with the weaknesses that could be holding you back, addressing them will help you to either overcome them or deal with them better. Remember that your competitors have weaknesses to deal with as well. Some weaknesses you may be dealing with at the time you are writing the business plan may be due to inexperience and limited exposure to the market, both of which can be overcome. However, some weaknesses cannot be overcome and must be dealt with head-on, such as legislative changes in privacy laws that may limit an investigator's ability to obtain information. Each of the weaknesses must be discussed in detail as to how you plan to overcome the particular weakness or how you foresee ultimately eliminating it. Although important, discussing strengths and weaknesses should not take away from other focal points of the business plan. Therefore, keep this section relatively short — no more than one page in length.

FINANCIAL PROJECTIONS

Financial projections are normally derived from already existing historical financial information. Therefore, even though your goal in this section is to address financial projections for your business, you should include some historical financial data that will help support your projections. If you are preparing a business plan as part of your start-up process, then historical financial data will obviously not be available, and working with estimates based on similar business' performance will be acceptable. If you are using the business plan as part of the application process for a loan, then be sure to match your financial projections to the loan amount being requested.

When developing your financial projections, you must take into consideration every possible expense, expected and unexpected, yet be conservative in your revenues. It is not critical that your actual revenues exceed the estimated amount; however, it is not a good situation when expenses are more than expected. Your projections should be addressed for the next three to five years breaking down each year with the following information: forecasted income statements, cash flow statements, balance sheets, and capital expenditure budgets. Due to the nature of this section, you can anticipate it taking up several pages of your business plan, as you might want to include some graphs, in addition to the budget forms, to depict the information more clearly.

CONCLUSION

The conclusion is the last written element of the business plan. Use this last opportunity to state your case wisely, highlighting key issues discussed in the plan. Then, wrap it up and close with a summary of your future plans for the expansion and progress of your business. Use language that will help the reader visualize what you will be able to accomplish and how successful your business will be should you receive the support you are requesting.

SUPPORTING DOCUMENTS

Attaching supporting documentation to your business plan will certainly strengthen it and make it more valuable; however, do not over-burden it with too many attachments — finding a balance is important. Before you start attaching documents, ask yourself if that particular piece of information will make a difference. If the answer is no, then leave it out. Documents that you should attach include:

- Copies of the business principals' résumé
- Tax returns and personal financial statements of the principals for the last three years
- A copy of licenses, certifications, and other relevant legal documents
- A copy of the lease or purchase agreement, if you are leasing or buying space

Determine the Legal Structure of Your Business

Deciding which legal structure to build your business under is the backbone of your operation. The legal structure sets the platform for your everyday operations, as it will influence the way you proceed with financial, tax, and legal issues. It will even play a part in how you name your company, as you will be adding Inc., Co., LLC, and such at the end of the name to specify what type of company you are. It will dictate what type of documents need to be filed with the different governmental agencies and how much and what type of documentation you will need to make accessible for public scrutiny, as well as how you will actually operate your business. To assist you in determining how you want to operate your business, a description of the different legal structures is provided as follows, along with sample documents that you may need to file with state and federal agencies, depending on where you live.

Business Entity Chart

Legal Entity	Costs Involved	# of Owners	Paperwork	Tax Implications	Liability Issues
Sole Proprietorship	Local fees assessed for registering business; generally between $25 and $100	One	Local licenses and registrations; assumed name registration	Owner is responsible for all personal and business taxes	Owner is personally liable for all financial and legal transactions
Partnership	Local fees assessed for registering business; between $25 and $100	Two or more	Partnership agreement	Business income passes through to partners and is taxed at the individual level only	Partners are personally liable for all financial and legal transactions, including those of the other partners
LLC	Filing fees for articles of incorporation; generally between $100 and $800, depending on the state	One or more	Articles of organization; operating agreement	Business income passes through to owners and is taxed at the individual level only	Owners are protected from liability; company carries all liability regarding financial and legal transactions
Corporation	Varies with each state, can range from $100 to $500	One or more; must designate directors and officers	Articles of incorporation to be filed with state; quarterly and annual report requirements; annual meeting reports	Corporation is taxed as a legal entity; income earned from business is taxed at individual level	Owners are protected from liability; company carries all liability regarding financial and legal transactions

Becoming a Small Business

A small business is a company with fewer than 500 employees. You will be joining more than 26 million other small businesses in the United States, according to the Small Business Administration. Small companies represent 99.7 percent of all employer firms in the country and contribute more than

45 percent of the total U.S. private payroll. More than half are home-based. Franchises make up 2 percent.

Of those 26 million small U.S. businesses, the SBA states that 649,700 new companies first opened for business in 2006. During the same period, 564,900 of the 26 million closed shop. However, $2/_3$ of newly opened companies remain in business after two years and 44 percent after four years. The odds are with start-ups. Just keep in mind that virtually every company that survives does so because the owners are working hard and care about their company.

Sole proprietorship

Sole proprietorship is the most prevalent type of legal structure adopted by start-up or small businesses, and it is the easiest to put into operation. These businesses are owned and operated by one owner and are not set up as a corporation. Therefore, you will have absolute control of all operations. Under a sole proprietorship, you own 100 percent of the business, its assets, and its liabilities. Some of the disadvantages are that you are wholly responsible for securing all monetary backing, and you are ultimately responsible for any legal actions against your business. However, it has some great advantages, such as being relatively inexpensive to start, and with the exception of a couple of extra tax forms, there is no requirement to file complicated tax returns in addition to your own. Also, as a sole proprietor, you can operate under your own name or you can choose to conduct business under a fictitious name. Most business owners who start small begin their operations as sole proprietors.

If you mishandle a surveillance operation and your subject sues for invasion of privacy, under a sole proprietorship, you personally could be sued and your personal assets could be threatened by litigation. Sole proprietors can deduct business expenses during tax season, but personal income is also taxed. The benefit of a sole proprietorship is you do not need a great deal of resources to create one, and you do not have to worry about legal issues involved with moving profits from a business account to a personal account. If you work as a private investigator in a field that assumes a high level of legal risk, a sole proprietorship might not be the safest business structure to erect. If you work in an area that assumes a low level of risk, operate as a one-person outfit, and do not have a lot of overhead or resources available, a sole proprietorship is a sensible structure to create. Process servers, for example, deal with less risk because they are simply acting on the orders of an attorney to serve a legal document. Most states require private investigators to carry insurance, so the insurance could mitigate any risk involved in opening a sole proprietorship. To create a sole proprietorship, a business owner must apply for an employer identification number with the IRS and file taxes on a Schedule C of a 1040 tax return. Sole proprietors also file a Schedule SE and pay a 15.3 percent self-employment tax on their business income.

General partnership

A partnership is almost as easy to establish as a sole proprietorship, with a few exceptions. In a partnership, all profits and losses are shared among the partners. In a partnership, not all partners necessarily have equal ownership of the business. Normally, the extent of financial contributions toward the business will determine the percentage of each partner's ownership. This percentage relates to sharing the organization's revenues as well as its financial and legal liabilities. One key difference between a partnership and a sole proprietorship is that the business does not cease to exist with the death of a partner. Under such circumstances, the deceased partner's share can either be taken over by a new partner or the partnership can be reorganized to accommodate the change. In either case, the business is able to continue without much disruption.

Although not all entrepreneurs benefit from turning their sole proprietorship businesses into partnerships, some thrive when incorporating partners into the business. In such instances, the business benefits significantly from the knowledge and expertise each partner contributes toward the overall operation of the business. As your business grows, it may be advantageous for you to come together in a partnership with someone who is knowledgeable about international trade and will be able to contribute to the expansion of the operation. Sometimes, as a sole proprietorship grows, the needs of the company outgrow the knowledge and capabilities of the single owner, requiring the input of someone who has the knowledge and experience necessary to take the company to its next level.

When establishing a partnership, it is in the best interest of all partners involved to have an attorney develop a partnership agreement. Partnership agreements are simple legal documents that normally include information such as the name and purpose of the partnership, its legal address, how long the partnership is intended to last, and the names of the partners. It also addresses each partner's contribution both professionally and financially and how profits and losses will be distributed. A partnership agreement also needs to disclose how changes in the organization will be addressed, such as death of a partner, the addition of a new partner, or the selling of one partner's interest to another individual. The agreement must ultimately address how the assets and liabilities will be distributed, should the partnership dissolve.

If two investigators form a business, they must create a partnership and file the same 15.3 percent employment tax as a sole proprietorship. With the benefit of splitting business expenses, their combined efforts can generate more cash flow to keep the business running until it reaches profitability. Agreements between partners are usually cemented in writing, and disputes among partners are covered under the Uniform Partnership Act (UPA), which governs the rules that partners in a business must follow. The UPA covers rules involving partnership assets, fiduciary duties, disputes, and termination of partnership.

Limited liability company

A limited liability company (LLC), often wrongly referred to as limited liability corporation, is not quite a corporation, yet is much more than a partnership. An LLC encompasses features found in the legal structure of corporations and partnerships, which allows the owners — called members in the case of an LLC — to enjoy the same liability protection of a corporation and the record-keeping flexibility of a partnership, like not having to keep meeting minutes or records. In an LLC, the members are not personally liable for the debts incurred for and by the company, and profits can be distributed as deemed appropriate by its members. In addition, all expenses, losses, and profits of the company flow through the business to each member, who would ultimately pay either business taxes or personal taxes — and not both on the same income.

An LLC would be most appropriate for a business that is not quite large enough to warrant assuming the expenses incurred in becoming a corporation or being responsible for the record keeping involved in operating as such. Yet, the extent of its operations requires a better legal and financial shelter for its members.

Regulations and procedures affecting the formation of LLCs differ from state to state, and they can be found on the Internet in your state's "corporations" section of the Secretary of State office Web site. A list of the states and the corresponding section of the Secretary of State's office that handles LLCs, corporations, and such is included in the Corporations section of this book. There are two main documents that are normally filed when establishing an LLC. One is an operating agreement, which addresses issues, such as the management and structure of the business, the distribution of profit and loss, the method of how members will vote, and how changes in the organizational structure will be handled. The operating agreement is not required by every state.

Articles of organization, however, are required by every state, and the required form is generally available for download from your state's Web site. The purpose of the articles of organization is to legally establish your business by registering with your state. It must contain, at a minimum, the following information:

- The LLC's name and the address of the principal place of business
- The purpose of the LLC
- The name and address of the LLC's registered agent (the person who is authorized to physically accept delivery of legal documents for the company)

- The name of the manager or managing members of the company
- An effective date for the company and signature

For instance, articles of organization for an LLC filed in the state of Florida will look something like this:

ARTICLE I - Name
The name and purpose of the Limited Liability Company is:

Fictitious Name International Trading Company, LLC
Purpose: To conduct...

ARTICLE II - Address
The mailing address and street address of the principal office of the Limited Liability Company is:

Street Address: 1234 International Trade Drive
                    Beautiful City, FL 33003

Mailing Address: P.O. Box 1235
                     Beautiful City, FL 33003

ARTICLE III – Registered Agent, Registered Office, and Registered Agent's Signature
The name and the Florida street address of the registered agent are:
                    John Doe
                    5678 New Company Lane
                    Beautiful City, FL 33003

Having been named as registered agent and to accept service of process for the above stated Limited Liability Company at the place designated in this certificate, I hereby accept the appointment as registered agent and agree to act in this capacity. I further agree to comply with the provisions of all statues relating to the proper and complete performance of my duties, and I am familiar with and accept the obligations of my position as a registered agent as provided for in Chapter 608, Florida Statutes.

_____
Registered Agent's Signature

ARTICLE IV – Manager(s) or Managing Member(s)

Title   Name & Address
"MGR" = Manager
"MGRM" = Managing Member

MGR   Jane Doe
                                234 Manager Street
                                Beautiful City, FL 33003

MGRM   Jim Unknown
                                789 Managing Member Drive
                                Beautiful City, FL 33003

ARTICLE V – Effective Date

The effective date of this Florida Limited Liability Company shall be January 1, 2009.

REQUIRED SIGNATURE:

_____

Signature of a member or an authorized representative of a member

Corporation

Corporations are the most formal type of all the legal business structures discussed so far. A corporation can be established as a public or a private corporation. A public corporation, with which most of us are familiar, is owned by its shareholders (also known as stockholders) and is public because anyone can buy stocks in the company through public stock exchanges. Shareholders are owners of the corporation through the ownership of shares or stocks, which represent a financial interest in the company. Not all corporations start as corporations, selling shares in the open market. They may actually start as individually owned businesses that grow to the point where selling its stocks in the open market is the most financially feasible business move for the organization. However, openly trading your company's shares diminishes your control over it by spreading the decision-making to stockholders or shareholders and a board of directors. Some of the most familiar household names, like the Tupperware Corporation and The Sports Authority, Inc., are public corporations. A private investigation agency might become a publicly traded business as a way of obtaining financing. Issuing shares to shareholders allows the company to obtain capital like any other business.

A private corporation is owned and managed by a few individuals who are normally involved in the day-to-day decision-making and operations of the company. If you own a relatively small business, but still wish to run it as a corporation, a private corporation legal structure would be the most beneficial form for you as a business owner because it allows you to stay closely involved in the operation and management. Even as your business grows, you can continue to operate as a private corporation. Corporations also protect personal assets, so if you are sued, the company is sued, not the owner. Private investigators could be sued if they break a privacy law. There are no rules for having to change over to a public corporation once your business reaches a certain size. The key is in the retention of your ability to closely manage and operate the corporation. For instance, some of the large companies that we are familiar with, and tend to assume are public corporations, happen to be private corporations — companies such as Domino's Pizza, L.L. Bean, and Mary Kay Cosmetics.

Whether private or public, a corporation is its own legal entity capable of entering into binding contracts and being held directly liable in any legal issues. Its finances are not directly tied to anyone's personal finances, and taxes are addressed separately from its owners. These are only some of the many advantages to operating your business in the form of a corporation. However, forming a corporation is no easy task and not all business operations lend themselves to this type of setup. The process can be lengthy and put a strain on your budget due to all the legwork and legal paperwork involved. In addition to the start-up costs, there are additional on-going maintenance costs, as well as legal and financial reporting requirements not found in partnerships or sole proprietorships. If you are a one- or two-person private investigation agency, it makes more sense to open a sole proprietorship or a partnership. However, these business structures may not protect your personal assets, so some investigators may prefer a corporation, especially if they employ others.

To legally establish your corporation, it must be registered with the state in which the business is created by filing articles of incorporation. Filing fees, information to be included, and its actual format vary from state to state.

However, some of the information most commonly required by states is listed as follows:

- Name of the corporation
- Address of the registered office
- Purpose of the corporation
- Duration of the corporation
- Number of shares the corporation will issue
- Duties of the board of directors
- Status of the shareholders, such as quantity of shares and responsibilities
- Stipulation for the dissolution of the corporation
- Names of the incorporator(s) of the organization
- Statement attesting to the accuracy of the information contained therein
- Signature line and date

For instance, Alabama's format for filing the articles of incorporation can be accessed through the state's Secretary of State Corporate Division Web site. The Web site contains instructions for filling out and submitting the document along with corresponding filing fees.

STATE OF ALABAMA
DOMESTIC FOR-PROFIT CORPORATION
ARTICLES OF INCORPORATION GUIDELINES

INSTRUCTIONS:

STEP 1: CONTACT THE OFFICE OF THE SECRETARY OF STATE AT (334) 242-5324 TO RESERVE A CORPORATE NAME.

STEP 2: TO INCORPORATE, FILE THE ORIGINAL, TWO COPIES OF THE ARTICLES OF INCORPORATION, AND THE CERTIFICATE OF NAME.

RESERVATION IN THE COUNTY WHERE THE CORPORATION'S REGISTERED OFFICE IS LOCATED. THE SECRETARY OF STATE'S.

FILING FEE IS $40. PLEASE CONTACT THE JUDGE OF PROBATE TO VERIFY FILING FEES.

PURSUANT TO THE PROVISIONS OF THE ALABAMA BUSINESS CORPORATION ACT, THE UNDERSIGNED HEREBY ADOPTS THE FOLLOWING ARTICLES OF INCORPORATION.

Article I The name of the corporation.

Article II The duration of the corporation is "perpetual" unless otherwise stated.

Article III The corporation has been organized for the following purpose(s).

Article IV The number of shares, which the corporation shall have the authority to issue, is____ _____.

Article V The street address (NO P.O. BOX) of the registered office: _____
_____, and the name of the registered agent at that office: _____.

Article VI The name(s) and address(es) of the Director(s).

Article VI The name(s) and address(es) of the Director(s).:

Article VII The name(s) and address(es) of the Incorporator(s).

Type or Print Name of Incorporator
Signature of Incorporator

Rev. 7/03

Any provision that is not inconsistent with the law for the regulation of the internal affairs of the corporation or for the restriction of the transfer of shares may be added.

IN WITNESS THEREOF, the undersigned incorporator executed these Articles of Incorporation on this the _____ day of _____, 20_____.

Printed Name and Business Address of Person Preparing this Document:

Sometimes, finding the correct office within the state government's structure that best applies to your needs can be a challenge. The same office may have a different name in different states. In this case, the name of the office that provides services to businesses and corporations may be called Division of Corporations in one state, Business Services in another, or Business Formation and Registration in another. Therefore, to save you time and frustration while trying to establish a business, here is a shortcut so you can reach the appropriate office for filing articles of incorporation without having to search though the maze of governmental agencies in your state:

State	Secretary of State's Office (specific division within)
Alabama	Corporations Division
Alaska	Corporations, Businesses, and Professional Licensing
Arizona	Corporation Commission
Arkansas	Business/Commercial Services
California	Business Portal
Colorado	Business Center
Connecticut	Commercial Recording Division
Delaware	Division of Corporations

State	Secretary of State's Office (specific division within)
Florida	Division of Corporations
Georgia	Corporations Division
Hawaii	Business Registration Division
Idaho	Business Entities Division
Illinois	Business Services Department
Indiana	Corporations Division
Iowa	Business Services Division
Kansas	Business Entities
Kentucky	Corporations
Louisiana	Corporations Section
Maine	Division of Corporations
Maryland	Secretary of State
Massachusetts	Corporations Division
Michigan	Business Portal
Minnesota	Business Services
Mississippi	Business Services
Missouri	Business Portal
Montana	Business Services
Nebraska	Business Services
Nevada	Commercial Recordings Division
New Hampshire	Corporation Division
New Jersey	Business Formation and Registration
New Mexico	Corporations Bureau
New York	Division of Corporations
North Carolina	Corporate Filings
North Dakota	Business Registrations
Ohio	Business Services
Oklahoma	Business Filing Department
Oregon	Corporation Division
Pennsylvania	Corporation Bureau
Rhode Island	Corporations Division

State	Secretary of State's Office (specific division within)
South Carolina	Business Filings
South Dakota	Corporations
Tennessee	Division of Business Services
Texas	Corporations Section
Utah	Division of Corporations and Commercial Code
Vermont	Corporations
Virginia	Business Information Center
West Virginia	Business Organizations
Washington	Corporations
Washington, DC	Corporations Division
Wisconsin	Corporations
Wyoming	Corporations Division

S Corporation

An S corporation is a form of legal structure under IRS regulations and is designed for the small businesses — "S corporation" means small business corporation. Until the inception of the limited liability company form of business structure, forming an S corporation was the only choice available to small business owners that offered some form of limited liability protection from creditors, yet afforded them with the many benefits that a partnership provides. Operating under S corporation status results in the company being taxed close to how a partnership or sole proprietor would be taxed, rather than being taxed like a corporation.

Operating under the S corporation legal structure, the shareholders' taxes are directly impacted by the business's profit or loss. Any profits or losses the company may experience in any one year are passed through to the shareholders who in turn must report them as part of their own income tax returns. According to the IRS, shareholders must pay taxes on the profits the business realized for that year in proportion to the stock they own.

In order to organize as an S corporation and qualify as such under the IRS regulations, the following requirements must be met:

- It cannot have more than 100 shareholders
- Shareholders must be U.S. citizens or residents
- All shareholders must approve operating under the S corporation legal structure
- It must be able to meet the requirements for an S corporation the entire year

Additionally, Form 253, "Election of Small Business Corporation," must be filed with the IRS within the first 75 days of the corporation's fiscal year.

Electing to operate under S corporation status is not effective for every business; however, it has proven to be beneficial for a number of companies through many years of operation. Private investigators who fall under a lower personal income tax bracket may want to consider an S corporation because it decreases the taxes due as a result of running a corporation. Because of the significant role S corporations play in the U.S. economy, the S Corporation Association of America was established in 1996 serving as a lobbying force in Washington protecting the small and family-owned businesses from too much taxation and government mandates. Membership in the association is comprised of S corporations, both big and small, from throughout the nation. This includes companies such as the Barker Company, a family-owned business that manufactures custom refrigerated and hot display cases for supermarkets and convenience stores based in Keosauqua, Iowa. Another example is the Sumner Group, headquartered in St. Louis, Missouri. The Sumner Group is one of the largest independently owned office equipment dealerships in the nation.

The S corporation structure avoids having to pay taxes on corporate and personal income taxes. If you are a one-person private investigation agency and your personal income is in a lower tax bracket than the corporation, it makes sense to move the profits into the bracket requiring you to pay less tax. However, you are required to transfer the leftover profits from the corporate account into your personal bank account. There is also a risk. If your profits unexpectedly skyrocket, you will be bumped into an income tax bracket in which the tax percentages are much higher than they might have been if you left the money in the corporate account. If you want to avoid double taxation, enjoy corporate tax benefits, and do not expect growth that will bump your income into a much higher bracket, an S corporation may be the best business structure for your agency.

Obtaining Financing for a Profitable Business

It is important that you become familiar with the various sources of financing that are available to you and will provide you with the capital to successfully operate your business. Figures in a business's first operating budget are hardly ever concrete because you are only using numbers that are estimated to come close to what the actual expenses or revenue may end up being. However, it gets easier as you move forward from year to year. Each year that passes gives you a better financial history to work with, and you can actually get close to accurately budgeting your revenues and expenses. The goal of this book is to not only provide all the tools and knowledge you need to open a business, but to operate a *financially successful* one. You would not be a typical entrepreneur if your vision were not larger than the depth of your pocket. It is easy to get caught up in the excitement and go beyond your financial means. This is where establishing a sound budget and adhering to it comes in to play. A budget is only as good as your ability to operate within it.

Funding is the lifeblood of any business. If an investigation agency is to survive, it will need enough funding to cover licensing and incorporation fees, bond or liability insurance, office rent, furniture, equipment, employees, additional operational expenses, and advertising. This is typically considered the first round of financing. At this stage, the agency has become a registered business entity. In an agency's life cycle, three other rounds of financing may be needed. Second-stage financing occurs when the agency has pushed past breakeven and is drawing larger revenues. At this stage, more employees and subcontractors are working for the agency. If the agency has good operating margins, it may be able to fund the costs and risks associated with sudden growth. It is much easier to obtain financing from banks, and there are lending firms that specifically deal with second round financing for businesses. Third-stage financing occurs when the agency is running smoothly and the operation is being overhauled to work out any deficiencies that existed from the start of its operation. The fourth stage may involve the sale of the agency to another company or a group of investors through public shares.

There are several types of investors that a business owner can approach. Investors can be family members, especially in the case of an S corporation that issues limited shares. State and federal agencies offer loan programs, and the Small Business Administration can guarantee a loan. If your agency reaches the second stage of financing, you may need a loan to cover the costs associated with large-scale growth. *In Chapter 7, we will examine the dangers of rapid growth and how second-round financing can help keep you out of bankruptcy.*

If the long-term cumulative cash flow requirements discussed in your business plan call for a second round of financing at some point in the future, get to know a loan officer in advance and establish a relationship with him or her. A loan officer serves as the intermediary between you and the bank. Take the loan officer out to lunch and tell him or her about your business plans. Update him or her regularly on the progress of your business so when you need a loan, he or she will know you, your case, and the cash position of your agency. Loan officers who see business owners as potential clients are usually willing to offer financial advice. They are ultimately the people who can convince the bank that your agency is a worthy investment.

Financial Avenues to Take

Obtaining financing for your new business can be accomplished by requesting financing through banks, commercial lenders, finance companies, and government agencies designed to assist start-up business and small business owners. However, before you start looking at what your options are when considering requesting a loan for your business, you should first be familiar with the types of financing available. By knowing the difference between these types of financing, you will be in a better position to make an educated decision as to what will best fit your needs.

Before you seek financial assistance

If you have all the money you need to start your business, you can skip this section for now. But, eventually you may need to find outside sources of funding to purchase equipment or supply working capital, among other possibilities. The U.S. Small Business Administration suggests asking the following questions before seeking financial assistance:

- Do you need more capital or can you manage existing cash flow more effectively?
- How do you define your need? Do you need money to expand or as a cushion against risk?
- How urgent is your need? You can obtain the best terms when you anticipate your needs rather than looking for money under pressure.
- How great are your risks? All businesses carry risks, and the degree of risk will affect cost and financing alternatives.
- In what state of development is the business? Needs are most critical during transitional stages.
- For what purposes will the capital be used? Any lender will require that capital be requested for very specific needs.
- What is the state of your industry? Depressed, stable, or growth conditions require different approaches to money needs and sources. Businesses that prosper while others are in decline will often receive better funding terms.
- Is your business seasonal or cyclical? Seasonal needs for financing generally are short term.
- How strong is your management team? Management is the most important element assessed by money sources.

Perhaps most importantly, how does your need for financing mesh with your business plan? If you do not have a business plan, make writing one your first priority. All capital sources will want to see your business plan for the start-up and growth of your business.

Lending Institutions

There are four different institutional lenders that you will have to choose from: commercial banks, credit unions, savings and loans, and commercial finances.

Commercial banks

A commercial bank is one of the most common forms of "other people's money" (OPM) that most people are already aware of or have actually used for a loan transaction before. Some people will tell you that bank money is OPM, while others will tell you that bank money is really your own money. This argument starts because they see borrowing money from a bank as borrowing against your own funds. For the purposes of this book however, OPM is considered any money borrowed to use to support your business plan that — if you did not secure it from some outside source — you would not otherwise have.

The general thought is that commercial banking is the best place to get a business loan. One of the reasons is that commercial banks are insured by the Federal Deposit Insurance Company (FDIC) and typically have the largest selection in institutions with which a business owner can work. It is also generally true that you will stand your best chances of getting a business loan through a commercial bank. A commercial bank stands to gain money from a successful business and will not turn away one that they feel will offer a minimal risk with the potential of providing a maximum gain. They are in business as well and are looking for smart deals to take part in.

Commercial banks offer a variety of services that include checking accounts, certificates of deposit (CDs), loans, and fiduciary services in which they will hold something in trust for another, taking responsibility for its care for the other's benefit. They also accept pay drafts and can issue the business letters of credit when they are needed. Beyond these traditional loan services, today's commercial banks also offer credit cards and mortgages to further boost your chances of obtaining funds and allowing you to spend those funds efficiently. The larger of the commercial banks are usually the better option for business. They can offer more perks including reduced fees, more local and national branches, and free ATM services no matter where you find yourself in your travels.

When you are approaching a bank for the first time to ask for a loan, it is almost always better for you to begin with a relatively small deal. You may think that you have found the deal that is going to make you millions, but the bank will see the chance of this coming to fruition as being placed somewhere in the neighborhood of slim to none. Think of your first deal as something that you can easily manage, be successful at, and turn around quickly. It will provide you a foundation of strength for future ventures and give you a lot more negotiating power for those larger deals.

During the preliminary portion of your OPM acquisition, it is also a good idea to take a deal to the bank as a practice exercise. This is especially good because a banker will tell you exactly what he or she needs in order to make the deal happen. There is no ultimate manual out there that can be found to tell you everything about how to put together a package to present to the bank. Sometimes, the best way to learn is through your initial mistakes and the gentle guidance of someone who is hopefully your bank ally. You may have to hear the word "no" several times before you will actually understand how to get to a "yes." Also, the economy and business practices are fluid, changing to keep up with current events as most recently seen with the housing bust that began in 2006.

Regardless of what is going on in the business climate, the best thing you can do is research and create a plan based on what is going on in your market at the current time. There are different market types to be aware of when preparing to approach a bank for a loan: low, high, recession, and recovery. No matter which market you are in, though, banks want to see some basic guidelines met. They do not engage in risky loans simply because it is not their business model. If you or your venture looks to be a risk, they are likely to pass, regardless of the market. The following will increase your chances of securing a loan:

- **Credit:** Banks follow a traditional pattern of loaning money: If they give you a loan, they expect to be paid back with interest. They gauge your ability to pay them back by your credit history. If you have a history of paying back your debts, they will look more favorably on giving you a loan because you have a history of taking care of your financial obligations.

- **Collateral:** If lending guidelines are tightening, you may consider offering up something of value as collateral for the loan. This is a step to consider closely before going through with it, though. You need to ask yourself if you are ready to hand over your house or boat should the business be unable to repay the loan.

- **Cosigning:** Depending on your credit history and any other factors a bank pulls into the equation, they may only feel confident in giving you a loan if you have someone cosign the loan.

- **History:** If you have a history of doing business with a bank, they may feel more confident in working with you. Also, if you have a history of owning a business and can show a track record of success, they may also breathe a little easier in extending a loan to your new business venture.

The tighter the market, the tighter you may find a particular lender's guidelines to be. For example, in a recession, the reins of lending can be pulled in, with loans being issued in a trickle. It may be difficult for anyone to get a loan — even those with excellent credit. Banks have their own goals and bottom lines to protect, and their guidelines will remain fluid to protect their own interests. Lending may become so lean that you may have no choice but to seek OPM from non-traditional means, which we will be covering later in this chapter.

You will find there are generally two views regarding relationships with commercial bank lenders: those who believe in using only one faithful bank and those who believe that you should have no less than three to five good, solid banking relationships in place.

The faithful banker plan

Institutional lenders are one of the most popular forms of traditional OPM, and they can become a strong ally to those with decent credit. The key thing that you must understand about institutional lenders is they expect your full patronage and will work their best efforts for you if you satisfy all of your traditional banking needs through one bank alone. Some banks can be like a jealous best friend; some banks do not like you stepping out with other banks, seeing what types of deals you could get, and borrowing money here and there from a number of different sources. If you want a strong ally on your team, pick an institutional lender that you really like and stick with them. Of course, if a good opportunity comes along, you may want to try to work something out, but in general, your relationship with your bank is like a marriage in that it is best when it is a one-on-one relationship without any third parties stepping in as temptation. Business is business, but you want to conduct smart business with long-term benefits; you do not want to burn any bridges as you grow your venture.

- Advantages
  - Forge a strong relationship with a financial ally who knows you well
- Disadvantages
  - Limits on the amount that one bank may be willing or able to lend
  - High or variable interest rates, making the cost of the loan greater
  - May take time to build a strong relationship

> – Bank may close or be swallowed up by a larger bank, ending your carefully honed relationship and leaving you seeking a new one

The "more the merrier" plan

Not all banks are funny when it comes to sharing their customers with other banks, and if they know anything about smart business, they should probably expect it. The major branches have their own specialties and can offer large sums of money to good clients, but sometimes it is the smaller banks that are more likely to do a deal that the bigger banks would shy away from. It is not a bad idea to have as many options at your disposal as possible.

- Advantages
  - A great source for OPM when all others methods have failed
- Disadvantages
  - Interest rates may be high or variable
  - Limits on the amount that the bank will allow you to borrow
  - Difficult to obtain money for those with a bad or nonexistent credit rating

Credit unions

A credit union is set up as a not-for-profit, and because of this, they tend to offer much better deals for their patrons. It is a cooperative-style financial institution, in that it has members who have partial ownership in the institution. The earnings are actually divided between its members in the form of dividends or reduced interest rates. There are always exceptions to this general setup, but it is common for a credit union to offer higher deposit rates and lower fees. However, to get these better deals, you will have to pay a membership fee and then join the credit union by opening a savings account and "buying in" to a share of the union. Only a member is welcome to deposit or borrow money in any capacity. This is what makes the credit union traditionally have better rates and fees because it is basically a nonprofit organization with lower operating costs than the commercial bank and is content with much more modest returns.

Credit unions are not all the same and most are not insured through the FDIC. However, the National Credit Union Share Insurance Fund (NCUSIF) insures all federal credit unions and many of the state-chartered credit unions. NCUSIF is administered by the National Credit Union Administration (NCUA); this is a federal agency responsible for chartering and supervising all of the federal credit unions, which are basically owned and controlled by their members as a co-op system. Most credit unions will offer the same services as banks, such as checking and credit cards, but do so under a different terminology. For example, where a commercial bank will use the term "checking account," a credit union will call it a "share draft account." Same service, different name. Not all credit unions will have the same services, however, and the ones that have more limited offerings will also not be as likely to offer the perks such as convenient banking hours for those business owners who are working long hours. The best thing to do is look around at the different credit unions available in your area and rate their services and fees in comparison with larger commercial banks.

Savings and loans

Savings and loans (thrifts) are similar to commercial banks in that they are in it for profit. While most commercial banks can only branch by acquisition, the chartered thrift has more freedom and therefore no limits in terms of waiting to find another bank they can acquire. It is actually cheaper for them to branch out nationwide, benefiting the business owner with the lowest cost for services. However, one negative of the federally chartered (savings and loan) thrift is that it is limited to 20 percent of assets in a business loan, a rule that remains in place as of the 2002 Office of Thrift Supervision regulatory bulletin.

Joint Ventures

Sometimes one of the best ideas for accessing a source of money will be to partner with another business entity. This alliance between the two interested parties is not a merger as such because there is no actual transfer of ownership between the two parties. Instead, it is a decision to share assets, knowledge, market shares, and profits. The companies involved are allowed to keep what is theirs, but they combine resources in a common interest to create potentially more profit than what could be generated individually.

Joint ventures have two primary needs: helping the business learn new technology that will make the company function more efficiently and enabling new markets to be opened to their product that they would not have otherwise had access to. If you are partnering with a large company that is interested in expanding in your operating area, this could mean that you have just found a great source of both OPM and other people's resources (OPR). A joint venture can be a great opportunity as long as you are able to find the right company with which to align your company.

A joint venture can create a rather large business out of a very small one. Sometimes a small business can insert itself into a larger corporation in a market it would like to saturate. The larger business can engage in a joint venture with the smaller company and profit through its success, while the small business can become a rather large force in the market in a very short period. Small entrepreneurs need to understand that even they have things to offer that a larger company may want, such as an area of specialty, and if they can convince them of that, it will be as good as obtaining OPM from them.

One problem that can occur is that one of the companies will be afraid to share its technology with a potential competitor, while the other company is afraid to share its market area. If both businesses cannot find a measure of trust between one another, they will not be able to give each other the support they need in order to assure the success of the venture, therefore crippling its potential. Also, a joint venture can mean that while you will be gaining power and OPM within your business-marketing area, you may also lose a portion of the control you have over your business as a whole. In other words, you have to decide whether it is more important for you to own 100 percent of a $1 million dollar company or only 1 percent of a $100 million dollar company.

Not all joint ventures are created equal

Both parties must share equally in order for an initial agreement to work effectively. Such a plan is accomplished with due diligence by checking the credentials of the other business. If both businesses can agree on a fair trade of services, then this is well worth the effort. If the parties cannot agree, then this will only lead to lost money and time — none of which a new business has the luxury of squandering — ultimately defeating the initial intent, which is to strengthen their position.

The key to the acquisition of a successful joint venture arrangement is to find a need that a similar business may have and find a way that you could fill that need for them in a way that can be spelled out within a partnership agreement. Many joint ventures involve the combined efforts of two businesses targeting two different market areas. It is not uncommon for one business in the United States to want to partner with a business in, for example, Asia. This could be a piece of a market that would be very costly to get into without the combined efforts of a couple of businesses that form a joint venture to tackle it.

As good as this can look on paper, it is certainly not a fix-all for a business that is either stagnating or new and looking for an alternative market or technology. Out of 100 such joint ventures, only 40 percent of them will be successful by the end of five years. The other 60 percent would have dissolved long before that five-year period. Do your homework to find a qualified, developed company to venture with, and your chances of success will go up exponentially.

The most important part of any joint venture — besides negotiations — is the contract itself. Every joint venture you consider must have an agreement so that both parties know what is expected and the parameters of what will be involved. These are generally very standard and straightforward agreements. They are fairly easy to come by on the Internet, but in general, there are a few important aspects you will want to cover. The biggest concern is in what form payment will take. Will it be cash? Will it be part ownership of the business? You must also consider who is responsible for making decisions and operating the business day-to-day, who will be responsible for expenses, and under what terms the joint venture will dissolve.

Federal Government

The magic acronym for this section is SBA, otherwise known as the Small Business Administration, which was created in 1953. State and local government are supportive of small business ventures, as they stimulate the economy for a region because they often create jobs. For all the complaints people have against the government and taxes, they can learn to take advantage of the money they have put into the government and let it work for them. It has become a big help over the years because the government has realized that its best chance of getting a return is through the funding of small business programs.

The SBA is not the source for your loan but rather the coordinator for the loan using a participating bank or institution. When an institution sees a business as unfit or too big of a risk, the SBA will step in and make as much as a 90 percent guarantee to the bank that the loan will be paid off by the SBA regardless of what happens to the business. This handy guarantee makes banks friendlier to deal with, especially if you are getting used to being turned down. These loans are not handed over to just anyone, however; the entrepreneur must prove through an extensive application process that he or she will be able to pay off the loan and have collateral to back it up.

SBA lenders are not all created equal. They are separated into three categories, each category participating in the programs with different verve and commitment. The least helpful in most cases will be your participant lenders.

- Participant lenders are occasional participants in the programs offered by the SBA, which would be your average bank's status. These are known to be slow in processing and often impersonal. They are also not highly trusted by the SBA to determine an applicant's qualifications.

For this reason, the SBA checks over each application and will have the ultimate say on whether the applicant meets requirements for the loan.

The next best SBA lender to use would be the certified lenders.

- Certified lenders are considered certified because they are regular participants of the SBA programs. Processing time for these loans are shorter as they are more accustomed to the processing than participating lenders. While they understand the SBA process better and complete the necessary requirement checks thoroughly, the SBA still insists on double-checking the decisions of the bank before qualifying the loan.

The best type of SBA lender is the preferred lender.

- Preferred lenders know the SBA system and have a solid reputation with the SBA as being a good judge of character and risk. Because of their experience, the SBA trusts them and does not get involved in the decision-making process of acceptance. If the bank accepts the applicant, the SBA is 100 percent behind the decision. This is the quickest and most convenient way to take out an SBA loan.

The SBA loan is a good option due to its favorable terms as compared to what you may find with conventional bank financing. SBA programs do not require a large down payment, whereas 20 to 30 percent is common for the conventional lending institution. The typical down payment for an SBA loan is 10 percent, and they have the ability to offer an amortized term of up to 25 years. The SBA also does not carry balloon loans that will drop a large bomb on the business once the loan has reached maturity.

Small businesses fall prey to balloon loans because they are initially attracted to the relatively low payoff amount over the course of the loan. This can be beneficial in terms of managing the cash flow of the business. The problem is if they do not save up for the large balloon payment at the end of the loan, they will be forced to refinance and incur the penalty of several fees on top of their balloon payment. With the typical loan amortization, the time between the initial loan and final judgment day is within five to ten years, which can be a delicate time for most new businesses.

The SBA helps keep money where it is needed — accessible and flowing in the small business — rather than the business depleting all of its own capital, which could potentially result in stifling its growth. These loans are also compatible for small businesses as well as the moderately small corporations. They offer loans starting from the low-end of the spectrum up to $2 million to $5 million. This will not be sufficient for a Fortune 500 company, which works with multimillion-dollar loans; these programs were not designed for the big guns that small businesses have to sometimes compete against. However, these loans can help level the field a bit.

There are eight popular SBA programs available today. To begin with, talk to your bank about applying for a loan through the SBA. Again, the SBA does not extend you a loan directly but works with lenders. You need to supply your bank lender with any paperwork they request in order to submit a loan application, such as financial statements, along with your business plan. If the bank is unable to extend you a loan, ask them to consider your loan under the SBA's guaranty program. Be familiar with the details of all eight of the SBA's programs.

7(a) Loan Program

This is SBA's primary business loan program. While its maximum allowable loan is $2 million, it is the SBA's most flexible business loan program in its terms and eligibility requirements and is designed to accommodate a wide variety of financing needs. Most of these loans are given to serve functions such as working capital, machinery, equipment, furniture, renovation, new construction, and debt refinancing. Commercial lenders are the ones who actually make the loans and the determination for who they will loan to, but the government offers a guaranty for a percentage of the loan should the borrower default. For this particular loan program, the government can guarantee up to 75 percent of the total loan made to the business if it exceeds $150,000 and 85 percent for loans less than $150,000.

The most attractive features of the 7(a) is its low down payment, low interest rates compared to most banks, and an extended loan maturity for as many as ten years for working capital and 25 years for fixed assets. These are great perks. Should a business want to start an early payoff, a very small percentage of the prepayment amount will be charged as a prepayment fee. The early payoff can come in handy when a business is experiencing fast growth and needs to refinance in order to support its expansion, and the small fee required to do this may be more than worth its while.

Microloan Program

This short-term loan offers very small loans up to $35,000 to small businesses that are starting or growing. Funds are made available to intermediary lenders who are nonprofit and community-based, and these lenders typically require some form of collateral for the loan. The loan can be used as working capital to fund the operations, to purchase inventory, supplies, and equipment in order to do business, or furniture and fixtures for the business. There are intermediaries available in most states, the District of Columbia, and Puerto Rico. The states where there is no intermediary include Alaska, Rhode Island, Utah, and West Virginia; Rhode Island and a section of West Virginia are currently accessing intermediaries in neighboring states.

Prequalification Pilot Loan Program

This program allows for small businesses to have their loan applications analyzed and receive a potential blessing from the SBA before a lender or institution takes it into consideration. It covers loan applications in which the business owner is looking for funds up to $250,000, and its deciding factor involves aspects of the applicant's credit, experience, reliability, and to some degree, character. This makes it unique among many of the other loans, which require the applicant to have assets in order to be qualified.

The main purpose for the SBA in this particular program is to help the entrepreneur strengthen his or her loan application. This program can be helpful for an applicant who has relatively good credit and a semi-established business looking for expansion. The SBA will ask to see the applicant's past financial records, ratios, history, and personal credit. The SBA will help determine which sections of the loan request are potential red flags for the bank and then recommend the most favorable terms the applicant should expect.

8(a) Program

This program was specifically designed to help socially or economically disadvantaged people (minority entrepreneur, business leader, or person with a disability). These loans are traditionally used for a start-up or expansion business development. To qualify, a socially or economically disadvantaged person — not just a figurehead in the position — must own and control at least 51 percent of the business. Along these same lines are additional assistance programs that are specifically targeted to veterans, women, and handicapped persons.

Economic Opportunity Loans (EOL)

This program is for the low-income business owner who may be experiencing difficulty in securing financing despite having a sound business idea. As long as one business partner is considered to be living below the poverty level (determined by the federal government and adjusted annually for inflation) and owns at least half of the business, an applicant can qualify for EOL assistance. It is also an option for the small business that has already been declined by a conventional bank or institution. The best part of the EOL program is that the loans are long-term and offer a flexible payback rate of 10 to 25 years depending on the type of loan.

CAPLines

A CAPLines loan is an asset-based line of credit, allowing businesses to manage their short-term needs, such as to continue payroll and purchase equipment. Typically, a business that is unable to qualify for other lines of credit, such as a private investigation agency or other small company, will use this type of loan. The payback terms of a CAPLine are adjusted to fit the seasonality and cash flow of a business, such as a business trying to complete a large project and waiting for payment.

CDC/504 Program

This is a mortgage product that supports local community developments through commercial real estate. The Certified Development Company (CDC) puts up 50 percent, the bank 40 percent, and you come up with the remaining 10 percent. You must occupy/lease 51 percent of the building, and you are free to lease the remaining 49 percent of the building to another business. Also, the business must create jobs, and the more jobs the business creates, the more money will be lent to the business. The terms of a CDC/504 program are attractive, offering a generous 25-year fixed rate.

Writing a Loan Proposal

Successfully securing a loan for your business takes some work on your part because the more prepared you are, the better the chance of a favorable outcome. When you approach a lending institution to request a loan for your business, you need to state your need clearly and provide all the required supporting documentation as to the financial situation of your business. Therefore, the best and most professional way to present your request is by preparing a loan proposal.

A loan proposal is practically a condensed version of your business plan, as you want to provide the lending institution enough information for them to make an informed decision on your loan. Therefore, the information must be concise yet adequate in presenting a full picture of your business, containing all the critical information that presents a full picture of your business. It must be a professional document with up-to-date information on your operation, including any possible changes in the company in the near future. In addition, because not all of individuals who are going to be reviewing your loan proposal will be knowledgeable about the private investigation industry, you should explain any terms or technical information that may not be common to someone not involved in this industry.

When working on your financial projections for your loan proposal, try to be conservative in developing your revenue estimates. Extremely high revenues may be assumed to be unrealistic and out of reach. On the other hand, when estimating expenses, make sure you consider all possible costs and avoid underestimating because you do not want to run short of funds earlier than anticipated. To avoid any questions as to the validity of your numbers, it is good practice to include a narrative explaining how you arrived at the figures for both your revenues and your expenditures.

A solid loan proposal will include a written narrative of the fundamental aspects of the project for which you are seeking the loan, relevant financial information, and all necessary supporting documentation. Each lending institution may have different requirements a loan application.

Professional Advisers

For many business owners who are not involved in a partnership, one of the more frustrating aspects of being the boss is not having someone to bounce ideas off of or no one above you to ask for help. Consultants from the SBA's Office of Small Business Development Centers (SBDC) are one avenue of outside advice. You can find out more about the SBDC and how to contact a consultant by visiting the SBA's Web site at **www.sba.gov/aboutsba/ sbaprograms/sbdc.**

You will want to create a personal network of business advisers, including those with professional credentials. The sooner you can bring experts into your business team, the better for both you and your fledgling business. Be sure to include these professionals on your short list of necessary advisers:

- **A certified public accountant (CPA) or someone of equal ability in accounting.** You will need this person for advice and to provide services on taxes (U.S., state, and local), loan terms, vehicle purchases, and practically anything to do with money. A competent accountant can show you how to get the most profit for each dollar of income. He or she might even have good ideas on additional sources of income you could provide. If you do not know a good accountant whom you trust, get first-hand referrals from a successful business owner or banker.

- **A capable business attorney.** Build a relationship with a good business attorney so you always have someone knowledge-able on hand if you need to have someone to review a contract, legal advice in hiring situations, or an adviser on legal forms and requirements at your state and local level. You will want some-one experienced. It is not good for you to be the guinea pig for a start-up attorney, even if you are running a start-up yourself.

- **A business-banking expert from your primary business bank.** You want a banker who is interested in the growth of your company, someone who is literally "banking" on your success. A good business banker can help you network with vendors, or even find new custom-ers. Often the business banker has a deep reservoir of business knowl-edge that he or she would like to share with you, so ask questions.

- **A solid business insurance agent or broker.** A broker may be your wisest choice because, in theory at least, they check out sev-eral different insurance companies for you and recommend only what they believe is best. Look to a professional insurance adviser to help you analyze and prepare for your business risk.

Perhaps you do not want anything to do with certain aspects of your business, but you do not want to hire employees either. Whether it is weekly bookkeep-ing, or laying a stone walkway, if you do not feel comfortable or competent in performing a necessary business task, it is far better to find the right service to handle it than to neglect the job or botch it. Use your professional advisers — banker, accountant, attorney — as a starting point to find the services that will help you get your worst jobs done right.

Trademarks

A trademark is a word, symbol, phrase, sound, or smell that represents a product to the public. Many trademarked logos and symbols are widely recognized, such as the McDonald's golden arches, the Pepsi logo, and the Master-Card logo. Examples of trademarked sounds are the chimes for the broadcast station NBC and the Yahoo! yodel. Your brand name, logo, or other symbol(s) differentiate your business from a competitor's. To be protected, the mark must either be used in commerce or registered with the intent to use it. While use in commerce is sufficient to establish trademark rights, registration with the USPTO can strengthen trademark enforcement efforts. The letters TM in superscript next to a word, brand, or logo used in commerce is sufficient to designate that the word, brand, or logo is trademarked. The TM is the designation for a non-registered trademark. A trademark that has been registered with the USPTO is designated with the R with a circle around it. Use of the ® for a nonregistered trademark could interfere with the right of an inventor to subsequently register the mark.

Trademark searches can be done professionally for between $300 and $1,200. Nevertheless, you can avoid these charges by using the Internet. Search registered and pending trademarks at the U.S. Patent and Trademark Office (USPTO) Web site (**www.uspto.gov**) and use the Trademark Electronic Search System (TESS). Go to the New User Form Search, type in the name you want to use, and click "Search Term." Be certain that the "Field" term is on "Combined Word Mark." To make sure that your search is comprehensive, be certain to perform the following:

- Enter all phonetically similar names of your company because names that are phonetically similar can cause conflicts in trademark use. For example, if you want to name your company Net-flicks, you should enter Netflix as well.

- Enter the singular and the plural of your company's proposed name.

- If your proposed name has more than one word, enter each word separately.

- Use "wild card" search terms, such as the asterisk (*) to broaden your search. For example, if you are searching for Netflicks, you can enter Netfli* to search for similar names that began with the same six letters.

Be advised that trademark searches are not foolproof. Searches reveal only those names that are registered. There may be unregistered business names that are in use as well. They would be considered valid even if they may not have shown up in the USPTO database. Consequently, after searching there, you should search the Internet for the proposed name. This would probably reveal any current users of your proposed name. If you have reached this stage without discovering any conflicting trademarks or service marks, you should then search the Secretary of State's records for existing corporate names. Most states offer free searches of existing corporate names, generally through the state's Office of the Secretary of State.

If your name passes the previous tests, you may want to reserve it. This step is not absolutely necessary but is recommended as you move to the planning and development stages of your new business. Most states offer a reservation service where you file a short name reservation form with the secretary of state, but there is a fee for this service, which varies with each state. When you have finalized your name, make sure that you have an appropriate corporate suffix to make the public aware of your business entity. These include:

- Corporation or Corp.
- Incorporated or Inc.
- Limited or Ltd.; in some states this suffix can be confused with a "limited partnership" or "limited liability corporation."

Intent to use trademark registration

You can register a trademark with the USPTO prior to use in commerce, thereby establishing priority for the mark, if you plan to use the trademark in commerce relatively soon. Initial registration is good for six months and can be extended (for a fee) for up to three years. If the trademark is not used before the intent-to-use registration expires, the trademark is considered abandoned. It then becomes public and available for others to adopt.

A trademark is a commercial identifier — something that links your company and its products with some (hopefully positive) association in the minds of consumers. These marks of your trade could be brand names, words, or logos. Trademarks are protected because a company that works hard to build a positive reputation and has it associated with a particular mark would be negatively impacted financially if someone with a lesser quality product appropriated that mark and the goodwill that goes with it.

As a result of this goodwill, the mark itself takes on value. Think about the Olympic rings. They appear on all sorts of products licensed by the International Olympic Committee. Consumers relate top athleticism and sportsmanship to these rings. Why would a shoe manufacturer or other company pay big bucks to associate themselves through the Olympic mark? To capitalize on the goodwill that the mark brings up in consumers' minds. Brand identity is an enormous marketing tool, one that should be built up and protected.

Fictitious Name Registration

If your business name is different than your own name, most states require that you file a fictitious name registration, "doing business as" (DBA) registration, or some form of similar registration that specifies that the name you are using to conduct business is not your own. The agency with which the fictitious name or DBA name is filed varies from state to state. In some states, the registration is done with the city or county in which the company has its principal place of business. However, the majority of states require the registration to be done with the state's Secretary of State office. Of all 50 states, the only states that specifically do not require any type of filing when conducting business with a name other than your personal name are Alabama, Arizona, Kansas, Mississippi, New Mexico, and South Carolina. Washington, D.C., makes it optional, and Tennessee does not require such filing for sole proprietorships or general partnerships.

Obtain an Employer Identification Number

All employers, partnerships, and corporations must have an employer identification number (EIN), also known as a federal tax identification number. You must obtain your EIN from the IRS before you conduct any business transactions or hire any employees. The IRS uses the EIN to identify the tax accounts of employers, certain sole proprietorships, corporations, and partnerships. The EIN is used on all tax forms and other licenses. To obtain one of these, fill out Form 55-4, obtainable from the IRS at **www.irs.gov/businesses/small/**. Click "Small Business Forms and Publications." There is no charge. If you are in a hurry to get your number, you can get an EIN assigned to you by telephone by calling 1-800-829-4933.

Also request the following publications, or you can download them via the IRS Web site (**www.irs.gov**):

- Publication #15, circular "Employer's Tax Guide."
- Several copies of Form W-4, "Employer Withholding Allowance Certificate." Each new employee must fill out one of these forms.
- Publication 334, "Tax Guide for Small Businesses."
- Request free copies of "All about O.S.H.A." and "O.S.H.A. Handbook for Small Businesses." Depending on the number of employees you have, you will be subject to certain regulations from this agency. Their address is: O.S.H.A., U.S. Department of Labor, Washington, D.C. 20210, **http://osha.gov/**.

- Request a free copy of "Handy Reference Guide to the Fair Labor Act." Contact: Department of Labor, Washington, D.C. 20210, **www.dol.gov**.

The IRS has developed a Web site called the Small Business Resource Guide, which has been specifically designed to better assist the small business owner and those who are just starting up their new business venture. This guide can be accessed online on the IRS Web site. Through this Web site, new business owners can access and download any number of the necessary forms and publications required by the IRS.

Open a Bank Account

Establishing a strong working relationship from the very beginning with a well-established financial institution is essential in ensuring your financial success. When you are starting a business, it is sound practice to seek the advice of business professionals in their fields of expertise, such as in the banking industry. Taking the time to meet with a bank representative at the time you go to open a business checking account is time well spent, and you will be surprised as to the many services available and the sound financial advice you can receive from bank officials. Information about your business will allow the bank representative to better advise you as to what type of business checking account will best suit your needs. He or she can also provide you with information regarding services provided by the bank, which could benefit you during the early stages of your business and in the future. This is also a good time to find out about the bank's policy on a business line of credit account, which is beneficial to have when starting a new venture. A line of credit account is an arrangement through a financial institution whereby the bank extends a specified amount of unsecured credit to the borrower.

In order to establish a business checking account, most financial institutions will require a copy of the state's certificate of fictitious name filing from a partnership or sole proprietor or an affidavit to that effect. An affidavit is a written declaration sworn to be true and made under oath before someone legally authorized to administer an oath. To open a business checking account for a corporation, most banks will require a copy of the articles of incorporation, an affidavit attesting to the actual existence of the company, and the EIN acquired from the IRS.

Secure an Accountant or Purchase Accounting Software

Deciding whether to secure an accountant or purchase financial software for your business accounting needs will ultimately be up to you. It all depends on the size of your operation, as well as your knowledge of accounting principles. If you feel comfortable enough to keep your accounting records, then purchasing good accounting software should suffice. However, it is recommended that you still have an accountant look over the business records at the end of the year to ensure accuracy when it comes to closing out the year and filing tax returns. There are several accounting software packages available in the market today, but you have to be careful which one you choose. Some are very limited and only include payroll, invoicing, and general recordkeeping. One of the most widely used packages, known for its all-encompassing versatility, is QuickBooks financial software. The basic version of this program, Quick-Books Pro, sells for approximately $199.95 at office supply retailers and has the capability of doing everything from invoicing; tracking sales tax, income, and expenses; and printing checks. QuickBooks' "Premier Edition" is a complete accounting system for your business. You can create forecasts, a business plan, and even do your budgeting, and it sells for approximately $399.95. QuickBooks can also be purchased online directly from the QuickBooks Web site (**www.quickbooks.intuit.com**) or other sites, such as Amazon.com.

If your strengths are not in accounting and recordkeeping, you should secure the services of an accountant, at least during the first year of operations or until you are comfortable enough to do the company's recordkeeping yourself. Accurate recordkeeping is essential in maintaining your company's finances, and sometimes this is something that only an accountant can do accurately.

Knowing exactly where you stand financially at any given time will influence a number of business decisions that must be made on short notice and will either help or hinder your company financially.

Get a Post Office Box

Regardless of whether you started by establishing a temporary office at home or you elected to acquire a location for your business, securing a post office box at your nearest post office is a good idea. As a convenience to its customers, the United States Postal Service has now made it even easier to secure a post office box by providing this service online. Enter the U.S. Postal Service Web site at **www.usps.com** and look under "Products and Services" where you will find "P.O. Boxes Online." The Web site will walk you step-by-step through the process of setting one up.

Having a post office box for your company helps keep your business' correspondence separate from your personal correspondence. Most importantly, it will prevent you from having to reprint any business stationery should you decide to relocate your office later. Continuity in any business means stability, which is what business partners look for when establishing long-term business relationships.

Permits and Licenses

City business license

You will almost certainly need a city business license if you are operating within a city, and you may need a county permit if not located within city boundaries. You can find out more about what licenses and permits you may need, where to get them, and how much they will cost by calling your city hall or county clerk's office. In most cities, the city clerk does not issue business licenses, but can direct you to the correct office if you cannot find it on your own.

You need a city license for several reasons, starting with the fact that you can be fined heavily for running a business without the correct permit. You also need to show your customers that you are legitimate, and you will need a city business license in most states to get your sales tax permit.

When you contact the agency that issues the city business license, ask how long the license is good for, what the renewal process is, whether there are levels of licensing and what level you need, how much it will cost, and whether there is anything else you need to do to be "street legal" as a business within your city or county.

State sales tax permit

Anything you actually sell — such as security cameras or debugging equipment — will be subject to sales tax, and you could end up with a hefty fine by not reporting and paying sales tax as required by your state.

You can contact your Secretary of State's office to apply for your sales tax permit. You will need, in most states, a local business license to do this. Make sure you allow time to get your city license and sales tax permit before you open shop. Ask the agency issuing the permit whether it needs to be renewed annually, how to do that, how and where to file and pay sales taxes, and whether you need to know anything else in order to meet your obligations to the state regarding sales taxes.

In some states, it may be difficult to find information on the Internet about exactly how to apply for your sales tax permit. Calling or sending a written request for information may be the best route to obtain the information you need.

State and county permits/licenses

Depending on where you live, there may be state or county permits or licenses required to start a business. You should call your Secretary of State's office (or ask when you call about the sales tax permit) and your county clerk's office to make sure you are not missing anything you need to apply for.

Setting Up Your Office

Before designating an official office, do not forget to check with you state's division of licensing to determine what remaining business licenses, if any, are needed to officially open an agency. Some states require a detective agency license. The Illinois Department of Professional Regulation, for example, mandates a detective agency license application and fee of $500. Investigators in some states will apply for an agency license through the Secretary of State. In Nebraska, investigators must meet the criteria listed under the Nebraska Private Detective Act, including a minimum of 3,000 hours investigative experience, fingerprint cards, and at least an 80 percent score on a license exam. In Texas, investigators can open an agency with a $350 fee and Class A license application. Given the nature of the work, applications will ask for proof of liability insurance or bond coverage. This is something every investigator should have regardless of whether they work for an agency or own one. Check with the division of licensing to see which policy is preferred. States will vary according to how much you need to carry. The normal range is somewhere between $10,000 and $25,000. If you carry a weapon, the insurance you need will be much more. You must also be sure your permit has not expired. If you are thinking big and have plans to target major corporations as clients, be prepared to carry a $1 or $2 million policy.

When all licensing is in order, the next step is to find an office in which you will conduct business. Where an investigator chooses an office is crucial to his or her success in finding clients. Using the demographic analysis compiled in the business plan, look for an area where a large number of your target clients live or frequently visit. Call real estate builders and ask where they are getting the most business to build residential communities. Contact the local chamber of commerce for information on businesses you want to be located near. If you plan to build business through a network of referrals, and your clients are mostly attorneys, scour the business district for courthouses and note how many law firms are in the area. Keep an open mind to urban communities where public dollars are being spent to revitalize. Heavy commercial areas are also good for business because people on the street are more likely to notice your business and walk in than in areas dominated by vehicle traffic. Does the area provide adequate parking? Nothing scares off visitors more than neighborhoods that do not have any parking space. If parking appears difficult, public transportation services in the area need to be adequate and accessible.

Next, examine the condition of the office space. Does the floor or ceiling need to be replaced? Is the air conditioning, heating, and electrical system shoddy? The best way to negotiate a lease is to first determine what the office space will cost and which costs could be covered by the landlord. When the landlord produces an agreement, look at the terms and conditions. If the terms are completely in the landlord's favor, look for another lease or try to negotiate the terms.

Your ability to negotiate depends on your leverage in the situation. For example, if the office has been vacant for some time or there are plenty of offices in the area, you can use it as leverage to negotiate the lease. If leverage falls in the landlord's favor and he or she recognizes this, you may have to accept the terms, keep looking for another space, or find another area demographic. Be weary of landlords who reserve the right to:

- Pass on building costs without limitation
- Increase taxes if they sell the building
- Terminate leases early
- Prohibit subletting
- Personal guarantees

If you do not go through a broker or real estate agent, ask the landlord to bring the rent down about 10 percent. If the space does not meet your business needs, but the lease is long term, ask the landlord to cover some of the improvement costs. Short-term leases of less than two years should have no improvement costs layered into the agreement. Do not expect landlords to cover any costs. Start-up businesses in the trial period are better off signing short-term leases, but signing a long-term lease is the preference of most commercial-lease landlords and does create more leverage for the renter. If the agency is targeting walk-in clients, make sure the lease covers the right to put up a sign visible from the street. Other conditions to be aware of include property taxes, security deposit, code compliance, option to expand, and termination of the lease.

A start-up agency's approach in furnishing an office should be cost-effective, especially if the lease is short term. Check the paper for going-out-of-business sales, yard sales, antique dealers, and high-end estate sales. The most essential pieces of furniture will include a receptionist's desk (if you hire a receptionist), an office desk, a waiting room couch and coffee table, framed pictures, plants, paint, window drapes, and rugs.

Some investigators designate their home as their office. The benefits here are twofold. First, it allows you to operate from the comfort of your own home. Second, it allows an investigator to claim certain tax deductions. The IRS allows business owners to rent home office space to their corporations, but this must be declared on an income tax return. The tax return must specifically state how many square feet of home office space is being rented by the corporation. It is the owner's responsibility to find out the cost of typical rented office space in your area and multiple that number by the amount of space the corporation is renting from your home. The total cost plus utilities should be charged to the corporation, which will then writes a check to the owner.

If you are planning to operate your business from home, you will need cooperation. Explain to your family that you are going to need to reserve a room; then, plan your workspace. Make sure it is large enough to be comfortable and efficient for everything you will do there, such as writing reports or storing evidence on a computer, as well as the day-to-day aspects of marketing, scheduling, payroll, and more. A tiny desk in a corner will not do. You will need space for a large desk, file cabinets, a computer, a printer, at least two chairs, and an area to spread out information when you meet with clients. You may want to set up an extra place for an assistant to answer the phones or do bookkeeping when you are out if you decide to hire employees. You will need a securely locked storage room for sensitive client evidence. Look to the future. Will you still have room to run your business in that space in a year?

Choose a quiet spot. You cannot work well if there are kids yelling, trains going by, dogs barking, or a television in the background. You will not appear professional if a customer asks, "What's that noise?" You will not be giving your business the attention and focus it needs if you are distracted.

Tools for Operating Your Business

The following items are absolutely necessary for operating a successful private investigation business:

- A desk with a comfortable chair
- A filing cabinet
- A printer/copier/scanner combination
- A telephone with fax and answering machine capabilities
- A laptop computer, allowing you the flexibility to take the information with you should you need to travel as you work toward getting your business started
- Internet access
- CD and DVD burner
- Digital single lens reflex (SLR) camera
- Light filters
- Video recorder
- Medium-sized tripod
- Surveillance vehicle
- GPS tracker
- Binoculars that magnify at 7x50
- Tape recorder

The following sections detail other areas to consider when setting up your office.

Phone

You can start a business with no more than the above essentials, but you will probably do better with a few extras. If you want to be listed in the yellow pages, you will need to have a phone dedicated to business. Some people only use a cell phone, but the dedicated line is preferable. It is more expensive, but you can also receive faxes this way. Use the landline telephone as your official business telephone number and forward calls to your cell phone or an answering machine or service. You also will need a fax machine and possibly a dedicated fax line, which can double as a second business line for calls if necessary. If you choose to use your cell phone as your primary business number, you may regret it when your phone rings constantly at job sites. An answering machine on an office line can be accessed remotely, so you will always be able to check your messages, even from job sites.

A two-line business phone is not a luxury. Line one is typically designated as the primary business line. Line two can be assigned as the fax line and also used to make outgoing calls. Some phone companies offer a "distinctive ring" feature that rings differently if a fax is coming in, so you do not make a mistake and pick up the phone. Telephone prices vary according to quality and features. Find the best one you can afford. Consider models with caller ID and automatic dialing. If you do not plan to use an answering service, consider a telephone with a built-in answering device. Callers will leave messages for you and the device will tell you when they called, so you can prioritize your call returns. You can save yourself some neck discomfort with frequent calls by getting a headset.

Fax machine, copier, and scanner

Unless you plan to use your local copy store for faxes, you need a fax machine. All-in-one machines are used by many small businesses for faxing, copying, and scanning. They are reasonably priced and work well. The higher-priced models have extra features and may be more durable. These are inkjet printers, not laser machines, which cost significantly more.

Point of sale equipment

Credit card processing devices are also known as point of sale (POS) machines. These also provide a wide range of features and prices. Some machines provide receipts; others require a separate printer. Receipts are mandatory, one way or another. Some credit card machines are totally portable and can be used at a customer's home. All that is required is an AC electric outlet and a phone plug. There are other, more expensive credit card devices that use cell phone technology, so you can just swipe the card anywhere, enter the price information, and make the charge. POS software is also available. It works with your computer and costs less than a dedicated credit card machine, but you cannot take it with you if you use a desktop computer and your receipt will come from your printer. This type of POS system is often used at doctors' offices and other professional outlets.

Many companies will want your credit card business. Talk to your bank and check the Internet for credit card service companies. Get the best rate you can, because the fees will come out of your company's profit. Credit card service companies and banks typically charge 1 percent to as much as 3 or 4 percent per transaction. They may tack on monthly "service fees" and other charges. Shop around and negotiate. Be sure to ask the most important questions: How long will it take for your account to be credited with the sale? How often and when will your account be updated? Keep your credit card receipts in your bookkeeping files for later reference if a question should arise. Mistakes can occur. You will want to have backup readily available to reinforce your side of the story.

Office supplies

Standard office supplies include letterheads, envelopes, business cards, and printer ink cartridges. Your letterhead should have a professional look that features your company's name, telephone number, fax number, and your address. If you are working out of your home and do not feel comfortable revealing this to customers, you may prefer to use a post office box for your business mail. You will want a return address where people can safely send payments. If you want a logo or something beyond basic type, you may wish to have a graphic designer create something simple, professional, and easy to read. There are templates in most word processing programs, so you can print a basic letter-head on your own computer.

Envelopes should reflect your letterhead in style and tone. Use business-sized envelopes (No. 10s). If you decide to include a return envelope, it should be a No. 9 to fit inside with your statement.

A No. 10 envelope will accept standard letterhead, folded horizontally in thirds. There are two types: window and closed envelopes. Window envelopes are frequently used by businesses because the mailing address of the intended party on the inside form shows through the envelope's window. Closed envelopes require that the address of the recipient be separately posted, either by printing it on the envelope or using a pre-printed sticker. If you decide not to have envelopes printed, and do not want to run them through your computer printer, you can either print labels with your return address, or purchase a rubber stamp. When you buy rubber stamps, consider getting one imprinted with "For Deposit Only" and your bank account number, to protect checks from being forged if they are inadvertently lost or stolen before you take them to the bank.

Business cards are essential. You will pass them around to virtually everyone you meet; potential customers are everywhere. You never know when a customer will walk into your life. Business cards should be easy to read. There is nothing more irritating than staring at a business card that has so much information you cannot find the number to call or the service being offered. The card should state your company's name, your name and title, a primary phone number, fax number, e-mail address, and possibly your cell number. As you can see, the card is already busy with just the basics. A simple logo, or none at all, is fine. Get the cards professionally printed to give them a professional appearance. You can go to one of the office supply or chain printers for cards, letterhead, and other such items at a reasonable cost. You also may find companies on the Internet that will offer quick turnaround at low prices for such products.

You may also want pre-printed invoices, estimate sheets, and service lists. It is acceptable to print these yourself as long as they look professional.

Computers and Software

Private investigators need computers for two reasons: to keep track of their business ledgers and to store evidence once it has been collected. Investigators must buy an additional computer if they hire a receptionist to keep track of billing and financial ledgers. Another computer will be needed for storing downloadable surveillance photos, video clips, case files, surveillance logs, and reports. When purchasing a computer, buy one with the largest hard drive and memory you can afford. A computer with enough memory eliminates any potential data storage issues with particularly large files. To record photographs on GIF or JPEG files, the computer should come with a CD and DVD burner. This allows evidence from case files to be duplicated and packaged to clients. Look for cable modems that secure a broadband width of four to eight megabytes. T-1 lines upload and download data faster than DSL. A color printer should be purchased for the purposes of case reports and letterheads, which appear more professional.

Personal computers (PCs) and Apple Macintosh computers (Macs) and their variants are both fine for your business. Macs may be less virus-prone, although that is changing. They are considered very reliable, but also more expensive and have fewer specialty business software programs designed to work with them because there are fewer Macs in most businesses.

PCs are often less expensive and have thousands of software programs available for them and more brands to choose from so you can do more shopping around. The price of PCs has come down so much it would be hard to justify purchasing a used one. Some new PCs are in the $500 range, including a monitor. Do not forget that whatever you buy will probably be out of date in a couple of years.

Your first consideration is what you need to make your business run successfully. You are going to access the Internet, probably with a cable, wireless, or DSL broadband connection, so you will need speed and power.

You will be downloading and processing photo files, so you need a large hard drive to store the photos. You will need Adobe PhotoShop or other photo processing software and probably a scanner, as well as a color printer.

Most likely, you will keep your accounting files on the computer and will use the computer to maintain files, create spreadsheets, fax, store documents, and print reports. Use software programs that help with tasks specifically related to your business.

Explain your needs to the computer companies or retailers you are dealing with and compare their responses. If you have friends or family members who are more computer savvy than you are, ask them for their advice.

Desktop or laptop?

It is recommended that you buy one computer with a large hard drive for your office and a laptop for surveillance operations. Storing evidence in two locations is a safe way to ensure the evidence will not get lost. Laptops are especially useful to investigators who use professional software programs, like *Oracle Database Client or Assyst,* which allows investigators to transfer and copy files from a laptop to a master database at the office. Using a remote connection, you can download pictures from a digital camera to a laptop, which can be directly stored into the client database. Client database programs should also have a feature that tracks all the client's details, such as how much they have invested in your services, reports that need to be completed, and money received and expected in the future. Burning footage onto a CD or DVD will make the report appear more professional. The CD or DVD should contain the surveillance logs, photographs, video surveillance footage, and any related public records that can be scanned into a computer file.

Both laptops and destktops have benefits and drawbacks. The desktop computer probably will have a bigger screen and an easy-to-use-keyboard, and external devices, such as your printer and modem, usually are plugged in. A desktop may cost less than a laptop, but you cannot take it into the field to use during surveillance operations. A laptop is portable and easy to use, but it costs more. The cheapest route is to select the most powerful desktop you can afford to get the most computing power for your money. You can purchase a laptop when your business has grown and you have more cash to spend.

You may want to purchase an external hard drive to back up or archive your document files and other essential records at least once a week to avoid data catastrophes. Back up data, such as client reports, invoices, and your financial records, daily or every time you work on a file.

You may also want to consider an online-backup system. Two reasonably priced options are offered by Mozy (**www.mozy.com**) and Ibackup (**www. ibackup.com**). Regular backups protect your data from electrical blackouts, viruses, and other calamities.

Business software

Your new computer will come with the software necessary to operate, whether it is a PC or Mac. It probably will come with a word processing program, Internet browser, an e-mail program, and other programs that the manufacturer includes with the initial purchase.

PCs often come with Microsoft Office, an office suite that includes MS Word, Excel, PowerPoint, and Internet Explorer. You can purchase a similar system for a Mac (the Pages software), but Macs also work well with Microsoft products. There are many other word processing programs, some of them free (check OpenOffice.org (**www.openoffice.org**) for samples). Realistically, at this time, it is a Microsoft world in business, and if you want to easily transfer files to your client's lawyers for official use, you can assume they want a Microsoft Word file (.doc). Beware of word-processing or other programs whose functionality is limited. Some common software programs specifically used by private investigators perform background checks, process digital and image photography, and conduct computer security investigations. Case Management Software is also commonly used to manage cases and to consolidate, track, share, and protect information. For a list of PI software programs, visit the eInvestigator's Web site (**www.einvestigator.com/software/private_ investigation_software.htm**).

Computer security

Firewalls and virus protection programs are essential tools in computer protection. European Union computer security experts estimated in 2007 that viruses begin to attack new computers on the Internet within seconds. Firewalls — whether hardware, software, or a combination of the two — protect your computer from unwelcome intrusions.

Virus protection programs protect your computer against specific, known viruses. Symantec, McAfee, and Norton are among the best-known software providers of this type of protection. Their programs must be updated regularly, preferably every day, to guard against the latest viruses, so you will want a renewable subscription, which should be less than $100 annually.

If you are already familiar with computers, you are probably conscious of spammers, who send out millions of e-mail messages for services you have never requested, and "phishing" schemes. If not, you need to know that dishonest computer hackers constantly try to steal your passwords, bank account numbers, and other personal or business identity information to steal your money or your identity. The simplest way to protect yourself is to never click a link sent by someone you do not know, especially if the person claims to be a "webmaster" at a bank, your Internet service provider, or some other legitimate-sounding source. If you are doubtful, phone the company that is supposedly requesting the information. You want to make sure you have every resource available to help protect your computer against the latest schemes of hackers who want to access your bank accounts, credit cards, passwords, and all of the other information you need to protect.

Accounting software

There are numerous brands of accounting software. Some are so popular that other software providers create "add-ons" that improve the functionality of the software.

QuickBooks is one of the most widely used programs. It is offered in both PC and Mac versions. There are small-business versions that allow you to balance your checkbook, do your payroll, track expenses by category, and create custom forms. You will want to discuss *all* of the accounting details of your business with your accountant *before* you set up your books so you will all be on the same page. There are many accounting terms that he or she may use that you might not understand; for example, your accountant might ask, "Are you on an accrual or cash basis?" QuickBooks takes a little practice to use effectively, but it is not difficult if you take an hour or two to get the basics, set up accounts, and gain some understanding of what it does. QuickBooks offers a contractor edition that allows you to track job costs and profits and to manage progress on several jobs at once.

Other highly rated business accounting program are Peachtree, MYOB Business Essentials, NetSuite Small Business Accounting, and Simply Accounting Pro. They all provide the basic features you need to run your business, and they offer sophiticated business applications besides helping to balance your checkbook and calculate payroll taxes.

Once you have a good accounting program and categories set up correctly, you will not need your accountant every day. Instead, your accountant can do weekly, monthly, or even quarterly oversight and monitoring. If you do not enjoy working with the figures, you may choose to hire a part-time bookkeeper to maintain the numbers and perform data entry. However, if you hire someone else to oversee your financial resources, check the records periodically to be sure everything adds up, or ask your accountant to review your employee's work. Companies of every size have had to grapple with misuse of funds or embezzlement. The best way to prevent this is to keep monitoring the books or have someone you trust do it for you.

Obviously, you will want to start your business financial dealings by using a separate business bank account under the business name. It is confusing and risky to co-mingle your personal funds with the business resources. Deposit all business checks, cash, and credit card payments into that account. If you are operating as a sole proprietorship and need to pay yourself for the work you have performed, write a check from the business account to yourself, then deposit it into your personal account. Run your business squeaky clean to avoid nasty problems tomorrow. The following are some basic accounting terms you may want to discuss with your accountant — together you can decide what will work best for your particular situation:

- **Cash versus accrual**. The cash method is recording a sale when the money is received and an expense recorded when the cash goes out. This measures only what happens in your business, not necessarily when you made the sale. Accrual is recording the income when you invoice the job and recording expenses when they are incurred, not when they are paid.

- **Double entry versus single entry.** Double means every one of your business entries is registered twice: once as a debit, once as a credit. You must be sure that everything balances — dollars are recorded coming in and going out. Single-entry bookkeeping is easier, but it is more prone to mistakes because there is no automatic balance. Your accountant will probably use the double-entry system.

- **Debit versus credit.** Debit is the payout. Credit is where you got the money. For example, suppose your company buys a camera. The camera is a debit. The money to pay for the camera is the credit.

- **Calendar year versus fiscal year.** Businesses operate on a 12-month cycle. If your business operates on a calendar year, that means your annual bookkeeping begins on January 1 and ends December 31. If you operate your business on a fiscal year, it means you begin your 12-month bookkeeping cycle some time after January 1 and end it 12 months after that. For instance, the federal government's fiscal year begins October 1. Some business structures, such as sole proprietorships, are required to operate on a calendar year. Whichever way you maintain your books, your business-year structure is important for tax issues and to anchor your annual business planning and assessment.

There are many terms and systems, but nothing is as important as committing yourself to fine bookkeeping. You must keep track of all accounts, income, and expenses. This is critical to the health and growth of your company. It is the only way you can know how your business is doing and whether you are meeting projections. It is the method by which you will track the effectiveness of your marketing because your record keeping will tell you where your leads come from, what your closing rate is, how much your average customer spends, what services they need (and request), what your materials cost, how much you pay your employees, and all of the other small and large details of operating a successful business. Use the best software that offers the most small business support.

Business planning software can assist you in putting your business plan together, as well as plan its growth and future. Palo Alto Software (**www. paloalto.com**) offers something called Business Plan Pro, which provides hundreds of sample business plans as examples and helps you work through the process of putting your own plan together. Plan Writer Deluxe and Ultimate Business Planner are two other options for planning software. HomeOfficeReports.com reviews business-planning software and looks at aspects such as ease of use, cost, support, features, and compatible software. The cost of this type of software is anywhere from $50 to $1,000. Beware of loading your computer with too many large programs that slow down your operating system. Look over your business-planning software options and pick one that meets your needs. You probably do not need business-planning software that can support a Fortune 500 company. Remember, if you are using QuickBooks Pro or another high-quality accounting program, it will contain some of the planning elements you need, so you do not need to duplicate these features. For a small, start-up business, it is a good idea to keep things simple.

Setting Up Ledgers

Maintaining a private investigation agency requires the ability to track the company's financial progress and to accurately determine its financial situation in the near future. The most efficient way to track your agency's growth is to set up financial ledgers, which give an account of the financial status, growth, and activity of the company. Financial ledgers should be used to track the agency's monthly income and expenses and will help you make informed decisions that affect the future of the company. It will also contain the information that must be provided when filing tax returns and local tax registration papers.

The IRS does not require any specific type of method to organize your financial records, but having an efficient system is key to reporting your income and expenses correctly during tax season. Most business owners use either accounting software or ledger pads to organize their company's monthly income and expenses. Ledger pads are inexpensive and can be purchased at office supply stores that sell stationary items. Ledger pads typical come in six columns that include date, item, folio, debits, credits, and current balance. Most ledger pads will come with pages that have already been hole-punched. If you plan to track revenues and expenditures on a ledger pad, a binder should be purchased to preserve the pages once they are torn out and arranged by fiscal year.

While ledger pads are a good way of keeping records, many businesses have steered away from this arcane method and trended toward electronic record keeping. Accounting software programs like Quicken allow business owners to see their entire financial picture, collecting information from bank accounts, credit card statements, 401(k) plans, and investing accounts.

While many versions of Quicken exist, private investigators renting office space from home may be advised to use Quicken Home & Business 2010 as their personal accounting software program. The Home & Business version organizes both personal and home-based business finances, automatically categorizes expenses, and tracks both profit and loss. Quicken also eliminates the hassle of having multiple passwords by connecting directly to thousands of banks, brokerage firms, and other financial institutions. Not only does the program give you an overview of money coming and going, it captures all deductions, such as mileage and operational costs incurred for specific jobs. Quicken's tax deduction segment shows your deduction status throughout the fiscal year and makes filing a Schedule C easier during tax season. The latest version of Quicken also allows all data to be exported into TurboTax, which has rapidly become one of the most widely used tax preparation software programs in the United States. TurboTax releases a new version each November and helps users complete their tax returns though a step-by-step process. Business owners using Quicken as their financial management tool have the advantage of exporting data into TurboTax because both programs were created and developed by the same company (Intuit, Inc).

If you decide to forgo the traditional method of using ledger pads, keep in mind the drawbacks of using accounting software, which may include the possibility of discontinued support for old versions or problems due to software bugs. While some users reported similar issues related issues to Quicken's older versions, user reviews of the 2010 version have indicated dramatic improvements with respect to its interface.

Keeping a record is greatly aided by keeping invoices and receipts for income and expenditures. This is especially important in the event that you are audited and the IRS wants documentation of your business. Income and expenditure receipts will show the date, amount, and other important details pertaining to your transactions. Income receipts are important for a private investigator because the type of sale will indicate if a sale is taxable by the state. Because private investigators deal in sales of service rather than goods, they may be exempt from being taxed on it. Keep in mind, whether your services are exempt from sales tax or not, the sales totaled from income receipts and invoices must be reported on a year-end tax return. Expenditure receipts include paychecks to employees, money spent on surveillance operations and other investigations, loan payments, and other costs involved in running and maintaining the agency. Always make sure to get a receipt while paying for these costs. Keeping these records is not only important for filing tax returns, it can also clear up any objections your client may have when you bill them for costs associated with investigating their case.

Two types of ledgers should be set up to track the financial activity of a private investigation agency. The first is an income ledger. Income ledgers should only track sales from the business. Loans from outside sources or from personal income should not be included. The income ledger should be divided into three categories: taxable sales, sales tax, and non-taxable sales. Some states will require you to further break down non-taxable sales into smaller categories, which may include services, sales to out-of-state customers, and wholesale sales, so check with an accountant before creating an income ledger. Each table should cover exactly one month. If you make a sale every day, as a process server might, you should have roughly 31 columns across that specify the date, monetary amount of taxable sales, the actual sales tax, non-taxable sales, and the monetary amount of total sales. At the end of every month, your accounting program will automatically total the entries, providing a financial progress report for your business.

An expenditure ledger employs the same process, except the categories are not divided into taxable, sales tax, and non-taxable sales. Instead, each expense will have its own category. For example, investigators who rent office space from a landlord will categorize office rent by itself. The reason expenditure ledgers categorize each expense by itself is because different expenses have different tax deduction rules due to the fact that some expenses are non-deductible, while others have depreciating values, which means expenses that are deductible only after a period of time has passed. Depreciating expenses are calculated by using a *straight-line* or *accelerated-depreciation* method. A straight-line method spreads the cost evenly over the life expectancy of the asset after purchase. For example, if you purchase a surveillance vehicle, the depreciation value would be calculated by finding the average life expectancy of the make and model and then dividing the number of years in the life expectancy by the total cost. The number is expensed in an expenditure ledger each year. An accelerated-depreciation method calculates by expensing most of the cost at the time of purchase or at the beginning of the assets life expectancy.

So which is the better method for tax purposes? The answer depends on what tax bracket you, as an entrepreneur, fall under. Investigators who anticipate being in the same tax bracket over a period of five years might prefer to write-off depreciating expenses immediately because they would get their money sooner — while the business is starting off and needs the savings — so the accelerated method of expensing the asset at the beginning makes more sense. Straight-line depreciation makes more sense for investigators who anticipate moving into a higher tax bracket within a couple of years and giving themselves the opportunity to expense the depreciation later on.

As a private investigator, you will want to give clients the option of paying by credit. Because a credit transaction can take more than a day or so to process, business owners who make and accept payments on credit will need additional ledgers for accounts payable and accounts receivable. Accounts payable will track the amount of money the business owes, such as unpaid utility bills. Accounts receivable are any payments the agency is expecting but has not yet received. Accounts receivable are also payments that have not yet been processed or made. These ledgers are particularly important when an agency is experiencing rapid growth and cash flow is needed to maintain steady growth without crashing the business.

Ledgers for credit transactions bring into light an important method of how expense and income accounting will be recorded. You have two options when thinking about how to record ledgers: by cash or accrual. Accrual accounting shows unearned and expected income in its ledgers. In other words, the money has been paid to you, but the service for that payment has yet to be completed. Or, you have completed the service, but the contract your client signed has not yet been paid. The accrual basis of accounting is only a manda-tory method required by the IRS for businesses with large amounts of inven-tory. For businesses that allow clients to make payments by credit, it is often the preferred method of accounting. However, its employment can sometimes create complications whereby you have less money on hand after paying taxes on reported income before the fees are collected.

Cash basis accounting posts sales and expense payments when the cash is received or spent. The cash basis may be the preferred method of account-ing for investigators who accept only cash for service or who make payments around the same time revenues are collected. Be aware that under accrual accounting, it is possible for a bank account to show more or less money than what the accrual statements show, depending on what money is waiting to be spent or received. The problem encountered by cash basis accounting is deal-ing with clients who pay more than 30 days after invoicing them for a case. To keep track of what clients owe under this accounting method, organize all invoices and put them in a file marked "unpaid." When the client sends money, record the payment as a sale in your income ledger and remove the invoice from the file.

At the end of it all, the ledgers you create will show the bottom line for each month you do business. The bottom line here is the agency's profit/loss state-ment. Up to this point, you have spent all your energy starting a business, getting clients, performing services, and invoicing. The profit/loss statement takes all the information recorded in the ledgers, totals all revenues, and sub-tracts the expense total to reveal whether you have made a profit or you have operated for the month at a loss. An annual income and expenditure ledger takes only the totals for each month and gives you a profit/loss statement for the fiscal year. Measured against your business plan projections, how much you have lost or made in the first year will provide you with your first indica-tion of just how accurate your assumptions about opening a private investiga-tion agency really are.

Sample ledgers can be found in Appendix A of this book.

CASE STUDY: FINDING HELP WITH BUSINESS PLANS AT NO COST

CLASSIFIED CASE STUDIES™

directly from the experts

Michael J. West, president
Arkansas Invesitigations
400 West Capitol Ave, Suite 1700,
Little Rock, AR 72201
www.arkansas-investigations.com
arkinv@centurytel.net
Phone: (501) 605-0360

When I first opened my practice, I thought I knew a lot about business. Time taught me that was not the case at all. The biggest challenge I faced was creating a professional perception, so I learned business strategies from established investigators I knew and considered to be successful. They told me that having a solid business plan was the single most important business guide during their start-up phase. I purchased a software program known from Palo Alto Software and methodically worked out a plan, which I took to the University of Arkansas' Small Business Development Training Center for review. I guess it turned out to be a good plan because they called me back and asked me if they could use it as an example in one of their marketing classes.

I established my company as an S corporation, which allowed me the flexibility of managing and shifting financial resources as needed. When the agency was up and running, I used the business plan as a guide in my daily business. I found that I was able to exceed my year three goals at the end of the first year. I think this was really a result of knowing what my plan was and following it.

To me, one of the most important things is to create an early identity and brand your business. I was also fortunate to have found a consultant who led me through the process. This past year has been my most successful yet. When I first started, I honestly thought that I would supplement my retirement income and be happy with $60,000 a year in addition to my retirement check. I recently received my tax forms and learned that I exceeded the $300,000 mark this year. This far exceeded any goal I ever set for myself. I honestly cannot say I would ever have come close to that without properly marketing, which includes many, many hours of working to make things happen. My goal is another 20 percent increase this year, and it looks like a possibility already.

CHAPTER 4

Finding Clients & Getting Paid

Great business owners understand how to keep up with, or remain ahead of, the curve once they have gone through the rigors of raising a business from the ground up. The first question at this stage should be: How can I find clients? In fact, the smartest business owners ask themselves this question much earlier in advance. Laying the marketing and advertising groundwork several months in advance is critical to the initial stages of an agency's immediate development.

At this stage, you know basic information about your potential clients: what they want and where they are located. The agency has a name, a trademark, and an office. Now it needs a presence on the Internet. The company Web site will act as the face of the agency in cyberspace. What potential clients see there will shape their initial opinion of the agency's professional bearing. It may also decide whether they seek your services or look for another agency.

Maintaining a Web site for your business is crucial. Most people searching for a business in their area will start with the Internet. Give your clients information and a reason to use your services. The following sections outline the basic components of a Web site, how to hire a Web page designer, how to use it to your business's advantage, and the fundamentals of SEO. Remember to continually update your site with fresh information, new pictures, updated contact information, and new design features.

Web Site Design Fundamentals

There are two very basic components to a Web site. They are your Web pages, the compilation of HTML pages you have designed, and the images, content, and other information that will be displayed on your pages. Individual Web pages collectively create your Web site, which can be as small as one page, or it can be thousands of pages. All Web sites have a home page, which is the page that site visitors are taken to when they type in your Web site domain name into a browser. From your home site, visitors can navigate your site and visit other Web pages on your site. All Web sites consistently change as new content and other Web pages are added; so while you may complete your initial design and publish your Web page, typically your site will require further maintenance, updating, and revisions. The most challenging part of creating a Web site is developing a blueprint for how you want your site organized, what pages it will contain, how content will be organized, and how your pages will be laid out as you design your navigation and page relationships. Design your pages individually, formulate what each page should include, and then flesh out the actual content and site design later. You can do this work on a piece of paper or even with sticky notes on the wall, as this will help you visualize the layout.

One of the first things to recognize when building a Web site is that you will either need some type of software program, or you will have to learn HTML coding and build your site from the ground up. .Starting out with the availability of adding interactive content and items to your Web site is the best route to take because even if you do not use them in the beginning, you will most likely use them down the road. When approaching your Web site design, it is usually best to keep colors and fonts at a basic level.

The four main components of a Web site include:

1. **Domain name:** This name is registered and corresponds with where your Web site is physically located on a Web server and is also used for your e-mail accounts.

2. **Web hosting:** This is the physical "storage" of your Web pages on a server that is connected to the Internet. This machine "serves" your Web pages as they are requested by a Web browser, and this machine has an IP address. The Domain Name System (DNS) translates your domain name into your Web account IP address and serves up the appropriate Web pages as requested. Your domain registry will store the IP address of your DNS. The concept may be difficult to understand; however, it is actually quite simple. Your Web site consists of a series of Web pages. These Web pages are files that are stored on a Web server along with images and other content. This Web server has an IP address that is a unique machine name for that server. DNS servers translate your domain name (i.e. "**www.mywebsite. com**") into the IP address where your site is actually hosted, and your Web server then serves your page to the Web browser of your site visitor. Therefore, it is critical that your DNR account (the company where you bought your domain name) is updated with the physical IP address of your DNS (provided by your hosting company). This ensures that anyone who searches or types in your domain name into a browser window will be directed to the DNS, which then translates this to the IP address of your site, ensuring your Web pages are properly displayed at all times.

3. **Web pages**: These are the Web pages you created and published to your Web server. You can create Web pages with programs such as Microsoft Office FrontPage, Microsoft Expression Web, Adobe Dreamweaver CS4, and free design applications.

4. **Optional items**: These might include shopping carts, forms, or databases. None of these are required for Web sites, but your needs may change over time, so keep that in mind.

Hire a Web designer

A professional Web site can cost $3,500 to $15,000. This money should buy layout, design, copywriting, programming, and the first year of hosting. Keep these suggestions in mind if you decide to hire a Web designer:

- You can find a Web designer online.
  - Search for "Web design [your city name]" or "private investigation Web design" for people with experience designing investigation sites.
- Look at other private investigation sites.
  - When you find a design you like, contact the Web master. The Web master is usually listed at the bottom of the home page.
  - Visit sites and take notes about what you like and do not like.
- Review designers' portfolios and samples.
  - Do they grab your attention?
  - Do the links work, and do the graphics load quickly?
  - Is it immediately obvious what the site is promoting?

Designing Your Logo

An integral part of your brand identity is your business logo. The logo must be unique and different from anyone else's because the last thing you want is to have your company mistaken for another. Your agency should have a logo designed to symbolize the services the agency provides. If the agency provides surveillance, the design can be an eye or the shadow of a man in a hat and trenchcoat. Ready-made logos can also be searched for and purchased on the Logo Search Web site (**www.logo-search.com/keyword.php/private-investigator**). For example, if the agency offers executive protection services, click on "Security" and choose from a number of different graphics available for purchase. Logo purchases from this site cost $9.95. Searching the database will at least provide some ideas about what the logo should look like. Graphic artists, marketing agencies, and print shops are excellent places to go to for the design of your logo — make sure to ask them for a high-resolution digital copy so you can reproduce it for all your business stationery and marketing needs. You can also turn to marketing agencies and print shops, which always have graphic artists as part of their staffs. You can find these companies on the Internet, but tapping into your local talent by using local professionals is always a good idea. For that, your local phone book is the best source of information.

Domain Names

You must own your own domain name if you want to have a serious Web presence. Your domain name is your brand name on the Web. It is the address every site visitor will type in to visit your Web site, and it is critical that you choose a good domain name and host it with a reputable provider. There are dozens of companies from which you can purchase your domain name. Most offer convenient control panels that let you update settings, including DNS server IP addresses. If you have your own company exchange server, you will also be able to change IP addresses for your mail servers if you do not wish to use the provided POP, or post office protocol, e-mail accounts with your hosting account. This will also allow you to update your contact information, name, address, and e-mail addresses.

Your domain name should uniquely identify your business. The general rule is that the shorter the domain name, the better, and it should be relevant to your company name, service, or products. If you already have an established corporate name or identity, you should try to base your domain name on that corporate identity, so customers will identify your company name with your domain name. For example, the publisher of this book, Atlantic Publishing Group, Inc, has a domain name at **www.atlantic-pub.com.** We also highly recommend that you secure any similar domain names to protect your identity from others who may use a very similar sounding or identical domain name, with a different extension. Using the example above, you would also want to tab **www.atlanticpub.com**, **www.atlanticpub.net**, and **www.atlanticpub-lishing.com**. Your primary domain name should be the domain name that is "hosted," while others may be parked at no additional cost and pointed to the main domain name URL. This way, you only pay for one hosted domain name but utilize many domain names on the Internet, all directing site visitors to your main hosted site.

It is important that you name your Web site after your domain name. The primary reason for this is so that people know your Web site and business by name. CNN® stands for Cable News Network, but no one calls it that. CNN is simply known as CNN, and the domain name is **www.cnn.com**. Your domain name should easily relate to your company name so your "brand" or company name can be easily recognized or memorized.

Many professional Web designers recommend using keywords in your domain name rather than your company name. For example, the **www.struggling-teens.com** domain name specifically targets the industry of private schools and programs by using the keywords "struggling teens." Therefore, when you type the keywords "struggling teens" into the Google and Yahoo! search engines, this Web site pops up in the top spot under the paid ads. Your domain name may have relevance in how some search engines rank your Web site, so embedding keywords into your domain name may help you achieve better search engine success. Another option you may consider is to purchase both domains names identifying your business and those using keywords. Put your Web site files on the domain name with the keywords and redirect the domain names with the company name to the keywords domain name. This allows you to market the domain name with your company name to help with branding and get the benefits of having the actual Web site located under a domain name with keywords.

Domain names should not be extremely long; this is going to be your URL address for your Web site. The last thing you need is a long address no one can remember. Although some people may bookmark your page in their Internet browser, just as many, if not more, will not. You could lose valuable traffic if your Web site address is too long. If have a long URL address, hyphenating the words will make it easier to read.

There was a time when domain names were readily available, but today you will find that many domain names are already registered. Typically, there are variations of your desired domain name available or perhaps other domain name extensions such as .org, .net, or .us. You can check the availability of a domain name by going to Go Daddy (**www.godaddy.com**).

Search Engine Optimization — Explained

Search engine optimization (SEO) is a marketing vehicle used to increase a Web site's rank among search engines. SEO involves developing your Web site in a way that will give you the maximum visibility with search engines. The more customers who see your products and information listed on search engines, the greater the chance they will click on your business's link. Similarly, the closer your listing is to the top of the first page, the more clicks you will have. Understanding how SEO works is not difficult. Applying it to your site in a productive manner, however, takes considerable work. Web site marketing has become very sophisticated due to increasing levels of available technology. With millions of Web sites competing for potential customers, it has become increasingly complex to ensure your Web site is found by interested buyers.

All Internet professionals have ideas on how to achieve high rankings. Search engines are often called spiders, because they spread across the Internet looking for morsels of information to bring back to eat. In this case, it eats words and phrases, and it prefers the newest, most interesting food it can find. These spiders, or search engines, hunt, retrieve, and collect information based on the keywords requested by users, searching for the most relevant results. Spiders study and rank the content of Web sites by hunting for specific phrases, using two or more related words or phrases to garner the basic meaning of your page. Providing relevant, frequently updated copy with the right keywords and phrases will attract these spiders.

Always keep in mind these two words: "fresh copy." Search engines seek new content. If your content grows outdated or you rarely add new copy, the search engines will overlook your Web site. Your Web site's home page alone is not enough to keep the search engines happy. Blogs or extra pages with additional copy attached to your main Web site are required to rouse the interest of a search engine. Most importantly, you need to integrate the keywords, or those special words pertaining to your private investigation services, into your Web site design, copy, and videos. Use a different title and description with keywords on each page. Remember, the title of the page is the most important SEO factor. Also, do not forget to include a site map on your Web site. The search engine spiders cannot index pages if they are not available. Site maps help search engines understand the layout of your site. Using these keywords will help you "optimize" your Web site and be listed on one of the first two search engine pages. Most users will not go further than this to find the service they desire.

Marketing Your Business

The purpose of advertising is to increase the exposure for your business to the general public. Retailers use certain methods to measure the effect of their advertising campaign, such as coding their coupons. A private investigator, however, should not rely on advertising as the sole method of getting clients to walk in the door. The purpose of advertising is to simply create awareness and deliver a marketing message. A marketing message must make the agency stand out from the competition, but it also must reduce the perceived risk clients will have by appearing similar to the competition's message. What you do in *conjunction* with advertising will contribute to the total impact of your marketing message.

Two types of marketing strategies separate successful businesses from failures. Businesses that adopt a "scattergun" approach send advertising everywhere, hoping the message will land a few hits. This rarely works and can be a waste of time and money. A savvy advertiser is one who identifies a niche, targets clients in the niche, and selectively delivers the marketing message. Internet advertising will also help create more links that direct traffic to the company's Web site. Where should you place ads? Think about your niche and target audience. Where do these people go on the Internet? Attorneys, for example, might use some of the popular legal research databases, such as Westlaw (**www.westlaw.com**) and LexisNexis (**www.lexisnexis.com**), so advertising on these Web sites might increase your marketing position. The trick is to think about where your potential clients are clustering in cyberspace and position your advertising in front of them.

Being listed in the phone book and the Internet yellow pages is vital, but what about radio and newspaper ads? Unless the agency's budget allows for a relentless campaign, it is pointless to advertise in these media outlets because messages are delivered only once and are easily forgotten. Marketing attempts must be repeated multiple times, and this can be expensive.

Cost effective marketing methods utilize creative strategies that maximize exposure for the business without actually paying to advertise. For example, local free press newspapers may find your experiences as a private investigator an intriguing read for its readers and might ask you to write short articles on a particular investigative topic. To find the local free press, check newspaper racks at restaurants, bookstores, and supermarkets. Agencies looking to expand nationally might contact newspapers or magazines with larger distributions. Investigators who offer a specific service should focus on topics that are interesting and relevant to what readers of certain newspapers or magazines expect to read and indirectly serve as an advertisement of your services. If you find your writing skills to be lacking, seek out a freelance writer on Mediabistro.com (**www.mediabistro.com**) or Elance (**www.elance.com**) and offer a small collaboration fee for a 1,500 word article. Provide consultation in the article: Offer advice on how to spot signs of infidelity, how to meet with an investigator, and what the service charges typically are. Do not, under any circumstances, violate any privacy laws by revealing names of people or companies that have been investigated or details of a case, unless it is public record.

Writing an article in this type of magazine may increase your exposure nationally, but if you are a local investigation agency, you want to focus on potential clients in the area. Contact editors from local newspapers to discuss writing stories on why local businesses should do background checks or how to protect against identity theft. Contact the local chamber of commerce. Do they send out a monthly newsletter to members? If you perform background checks for small businesses, create fliers and have the chamber insert the fliers into the publication. Is there a popular local radio station that many local businesses listen to? If so, volunteer to appear as a regular guest and talk about local events in the community, including any real-life private investigation stories the station's listeners would enjoy hearing. Should you prove to be an entertaining guest, the radio host will be more than happy to plug your business at the end of the show.

State Bar Associations also publish monthly newsletters. Find out what their circulation is and consider placing an advertisement in their newsletter. The American Bar Association also provides members with access to its "lawyer locator" and membership directory. Collect their addresses and mail them a media kit. Business collateral in a basic media kit should consist of:

- Letter of introduction
- Company brochure
- Business card
- Stationary with company name and trademark
- Press release
- Recent press clippings
- FAQ sheet

Attend conventions that draw an industry you will be serving. Networking at conventions increases visibility within specific business communities and establishes important industry contacts. For example, investigators who specialize in workers' compensation and insurance liability should look for local insurance industry conventions to attend. Business Networking International (BNI) (**www.bni.com**) is the largest networking organization in the world and has chapters in every state. Membership in organizations such as BNI can substantially increase referrals and is a far more effective way of advertising than placing expensive ads in newspapers. Businesses and law firms that regularly use private investigation services will attend conferences for the private investigation industry. For a complete list of regional private investigator organizations and conferences, visit the Web sites of IRBsearch (**www. irbsearch.com/conferences**) and *P.I. Magazine* (**www.pimagazine.com/ private_investigator_conferences.html**).

Speaking engagements at local community organizations, like Kiwanis or Rotary Club, can also increase the company's marketing position. Community organizations always look for speakers with a unique background and area of expertise. If you book a speaking engagement, blog the date and time of the engagement on your Web site, or have someone film it. If the site has flash capability, post the video afterward on your Web site or to a social networking site, such as YouTube™. Instructional videos on the Internet have become extremely popular. A private investigator's experience makes them an ideal candidate for teaching something people will want to use. For example, posting an instructional video on an investigative technique could pique interest in the social networking community. Uploading an instructional video to YouTube can have a multiplying effect. Social networking can increase your visibility if someone links the video to another social networking site such as Facebook™, MySpace™, or Twitter™.

Increasing brand awareness with social networking is called viral marketing. It is cost-effective and easy because the information exchange from one Web user to the next is similar to the behavior of a self-replicating virus. Another way to create viral marketing is to start an e-newsletter on search directories such as Yahoo! To set up an e-newsletter, purchase software at MyNewsletterBuilder (**www.mynewsletterbuilder.com**).

Develop your marketing plan

Your marketing plan consists of all of the potential customers who will purchase your product or service. It is a study of your target market: who is buying, why they are buying, and how you will surpass the competition and get that market to buy from you. If you are selling investigative services, your marketing plan would also cover how you plan to obtain clients, including your research from area demographics, as well as your networking plan. *A copy of the following worksheet is available in the accompanying CD-ROM.*

Marketing Plan Worksheet

Who are your customers going to be?

_____

_____

Who are your competitors?

_____

_____

How can you compete in this market?

_____

_____

What are your strengths and weaknesses in comparison to competitors?

_____

_____

What can you do better than your competitors?

_____

_____

Are there any governmental or legal factors affecting your business?

_____

_____

What advantages does your service have over the competition?

_____

_____

What type of image do you want for your services?

_____

_____

What features will be emphasized?

_____

_____

What is your pricing strategy?

_____

_____

Is your pricing in line with your image?

_____

_____

Do your prices properly cover costs?

_____

_____

Creating an Effective Brand

As a small-business owner, it may seem that branding your business or yourself may simply be a slick advertising move. However, branding your small business is more about positioning your business and yourself in a positive light so your target market can see it is the best choice out there. When you build a business brand, it is not only about what you do — it is also about the benefits your customer will receive from you that they would not receive from another company. Your goal is to keep your clients coming back and to renew your retainers with them year after year.

A brand helps you to organize the full range of your marketing and advertising strategies. It will convey what you stand for and who you are. An effective brand will encompass the whole business and will include a special logo that will be everywhere in the business: on stationery, cards, packaging, and signs. This brand also will fit right in the pricing of the services, customer services, and your business's guarantees.

A brand can benefit the operation of your business by:

- Building strong customer loyalty
- Bringing more credibility to any project
- Delivering any company message fast and effectively
- Hitting an emotional chord with people
- Separating yourself and your business from the competition
- Positioning a focused message in both the heart and mind of your target market
- Bringing consistency to your marketing promotions and campaigns

Getting started

How do you go about creating a winning brand that will help customers identify your business with everything that will make them feel comfortable and confident with you? Here are a few suggestions to get you started:

- **Identify your personal and business values.** Begin to construct this by listing both personal and business values (honesty, quality, and so on). Then create a "value statement" for your business based on this list. Keep it short. The more condensed your value statement is, the easier it will be for you to recall. In addition, the condensed value statement may be the perfect phrase to use as an advertising tagline that will appear on your marketing materials.

- **Create a mission statement.** A mission statement lays out the purpose underlying your work. A good mission statement is meaningful, but still short enough to remember.

- **Create a vision statement**. A good vision statement will specify how you will know when you have achieved the goal of your mission statement. Setting targets for yourself and continually striving to meet them helps to keep you working smarter and remaining innovative as new possibilities open up.

- **Identify your starting point**. Where are you right now in relation to where you want to be? Write down some of the steps you already know are necessary to make your business dreams become real.

- **Describe your market.** Understanding who you want to reach with branding is critical, as choices of advertising, marketing, and other types of publicity vary depending on the target market(s).

- **Create a positioning statement.** Positioning is your attempt to control the image of the business your customer will see. What is the impression you hope to make in the mind of your ideal customer? In your community, will you aim to be the lowest-cost provider? The highest-quality provider? The most friendly, reliable provider?

Using Social Media and Networking

Social networking is the new "it" marketing vehicle. The main objective is to allow members who have the same interests to interact and exchange information. Many small businesses are finding social networking to be a great way to build and grow, especially in tough economic times when advertising budgets have been cut. Instead of paying for costly advertising, you are spreading information through word of mouth and Web sites that are generally free to use.

Although the exact definition is still being clarified, social networking essentially refers to an online community or group of users where people can connect and communicate with others. Although the actual format may vary from one network to another, communication takes place in many ways, such as blogs, e-mail, instant messaging, forums, video, or chat rooms. Social networking connects people across the world in the privacy of their own homes, and the networking sites are usually free and instantaneous. People can easily stay in touch with current friends, seek old relationships, or establish new friendships. There are thousands of social networking sites, some that are primarily for social use and others that are for business networking.

How it will help

Members of social networking sites are numerous, which creates an excellent opportunity for an individual to expand and promote a business without having to pay for advertising. With social networking, you can build an image and develop your customer base. To increase their Web site traffic, many site owners are quickly realizing the value social networking sites have in drawing new customers. The following are some ideas on how to use social networking site to generate Web site traffic:

- Link from your Web site to your social network profile
- Use social bookmarking to increase your Web site's exposure on social networking sites
- Create and share videos and photos on Flickr and YouTube describing your business, products, and services
- Use social networking forums to promote your business, Web site, and blog
- Promote your business through your profile, with links to your home page

Never underestimate the power of social networking, even for your business. For example, you might post a video on YouTube giving expert tips on how to detect signs of infidelity. Doing so provides you with an opportunity to plug the name and address of the firm by offering free consultation services at the end of your video blog. YouTube is one of the most highly trafficked social networking sites in the world and personalizes the agency in a way that a billboard advertisement never could.

Popular social networking sites

With the ever increasing number of people who use the Internet on a regular basis, these social Web sites have become a must, as this is the best and the easiest way for people to connect with each other and stay in touch.

Orkut is a popular social networking site owned by Google. This social networking site has millions of users; 63 percent of Orkut traffic originates from Brazil, followed by India with 19.2 percent. Like other sites, such as Facebook, Orkut permits the creation of groups known as "communities" based on a designated subject and allows other people to join the communities. Orkut is an online community designed to make your social life more active and stimulating.

Facebook is the leading social networking site, with more than 400 million active users at the time of publication. Initially, Facebook was developed to connect university students, but over time, the site became available publicly and its popularity exploded. The majority of users on Facebook are college and high school students, but this trend is shifting rapidly to people of all ages and backgrounds. On Facebook, it is extremely easy to add friends, send messages, and create communities or event invitations.

MySpace is a social networking Web site that offers an interactive platform for all its users. It allows the sharing of files, pictures, and even music videos. You can view the profiles of your friends, relatives, and any other users; you can also create and share blogs with each other. Users often compare Facebook to MySpace, but one major difference between the two Web sites is the level of customization. MySpace is a large social networking site that allows users to decorate their profiles using HTML and CSS, while Facebook only allows plain text. The most prominent feature that makes MySpace unique among other sites is its affiliate program. If the affiliate product you are selling has a broad appeal, you may want consider using MySpace to market your product, as you will be able to reach the largest crowd quickly. An investigator who specializes in computer security and fraud detection could use a MySpace page to sell his or her services. Investigators can also advertise their services regarding background checks or surveillance, specifically for people who are harassed by other users on MySpace. The site can also be useful in some investigations themselves.

YouTube is another social networking site owned by Google. To become a member of YouTube, go to the "Signup" page, choose a username and password, enter your information, and click the "Signup" button. YouTube is the largest video sharing network site in the world, and it is a great place to do video marketing.

Digg is a place to discover and share content from around the Web, from the smallest blog to major news outlets. Digg is unique compared to other social networking sites because it allows you to directly network with people and directly sell products. Once a post is submitted, it appears on a list in the selected category. From there, it will either fall in ranking or rise in raking, depending on how people vote. Digg is actually what is known as a "social bookmarking" site. You submit your content to Digg, and other Digg users, known as Diggers, review and rate it. Once it is rated high enough, your content may be posted on the home page of Digg, which gets thousands of visitors a day, potentially driving tons of traffic to your Web site or blog.

Twitter is different from other social networking sites, and the popularity of Twitter has grown at an amazing rate. With Twitter, you can let your friends know what you are doing throughout the day right from your phone or computer. When you sign up with Twitter, you can use the service to post and receive messages (known as a "tweet") with your Twitter account, and the service distributes it to your friends and subscribers. In turn, you receive all the messages sent from those you wish to follow, including friends, family, and even celebrities. In essence, Twitter is a cell phone texting-based social network.

Flickr is a photo and video sharing Web site that lets you organize and store your photos online. You can upload from your desktop, send by e-mail, or use your camera phone. It has features to get rid of red eye, crop a photo, or get creative with fonts and effects. Google Picasa is another great photo sharing and storing application.

Popular business networking sites

The following sites offer businesses opportunities to network with other business owners.

- **Bizfriendz (www.bizfriendz.com)**: Make new contacts, promote your products and services, get viral exposure to your business, and earn commissions while you build your network.

- **Biznik (www.biznik.com)**: Their tagline: "Business networking that doesn't suck." This site is geared directly to entrepreneurs and business owners, with a number of different communities.

- **Cofoundr (www.cofoundr.com)**: A private community for entrepreneurs, this site promises to help members build teams and network with other entrepreneurs.

- **Ecademy (www.ecademy.com)**: This site provides extra tools to build your business, such as networking events, Webinars on online topics, and the ability to locate members with specific knowledge.

- **Fast Pitch (www.fastpitchnetworking.com)**: This site reports that it is growing faster than any other social network for professionals. Set up your own profile page to network with other businesspeople.

- **Konnects (www.konnects.com)**: This site gives each member a profile page. Join communities, meet other members, and network with professionals with similar interests.

- **LinkedIn (www.linkedin.com)**: Here you can connect and network with others in your field who can use your abilities and/or services.

- **StartupNation (www.startupnation.com)**: This is an active forum with a wide variety of subjects for businesses.

- **Stumble Upon (www.stumbleupon.com)**: Here you can post any information of value and interest to others.

- **Upspring (www.upspring.com)**: With this site, you can increase exposure and attract more customers. Sign up for free and get a profile page, find and join groups, and increase your networking activities.

- **Xing (www.xing.com)**: This is for active professionals looking for ways to network with people of interest.

One of the most popular professional networking sites for private investigators and businesses who may need the services of an investigator is LinkedIn (**www.linkedin.com**). LinkedIn currently holds more than 65 million professionals worldwide and spans more than 200 countries. Its features allow registered users to maintain a list of professionals they have worked with previously. When your agency appears on another user's site, it lets millions of potential clients know your services are recommended. Clients looking to fill contract jobs are able to offer their jobs to other members, and as a member of LinkedIn, you will be able to bid on them.

IRBSearch (**www.irbsearch.com**) is also one of the leading online professional networks focusing specifically on attracting private investigators, process servers, bail bondsmen, judgment recovery, and repossession specialists. In August of 2009, Pursuit Magazine announced that its social networking forum would be merging with IRB Exchange at **http://irbsearch.ning.com/**. IRB Exchange currently holds over 700 members and is free.

Getting Paid

As discussed in Chapter 1, investigators typically charge between $40 and $150 per hour for their services depending on licensing, specialization, and agency ownership. After completing a job for a client, investigators bill their clients by sending or delivering invoices that break down the service fees and total the number of hours the investigator worked. Before doing this, the investigator must be able to determine what the service is worth. By survey-ing potential clients and competitors in your market analysis beforehand, you should have detailed research on what your competitors are charging for each service. Fees can also depend on risk factors. After reviewing a case and dis-covering that a certain amount of danger is involved, you would be justified in increasing the service fee. In other instances, the client may have fired a previ-ous investigator for mishandling a job. When this occurs, the new detective will be asked to handle a case that has been severely damaged or compromised. Calculating service charges beyond the normal bill rate is based on the case's *perceived value.* In other words, the bill rate should be based on the value the client places on the service. The perceived value can only be known by meet-ing with a potential client and reviewing the case.

Suppose a client requests your services on a case that depended on secrecy and was mishandled by another detective who blew his or her cover during surveillance. The subject under surveillance is now aware that he or she is being watched and is taking measures to conceal his or her activities. Because the subject became aware of the previous investigator's activities, the case has become "heated." A heated case will be extremely difficult for another investi-gator to take over because the subject has likely gone further into hiding. The extra work this case will require is justification for charging a higher bill rate.

Pricing strategies are either cost-based or market-based. An example of a cost-based pricing strategy would be determining the cost to perform the service for the client and then adding another fee that increases the company's profit margin. For example, if you pay an informant $100 for information, out-source a service for $100, spend $60 in gas driving to a surveillance site, spend $50 on film, and work ten hours total, it costs $310 to conduct the service. If you charge $60 per hour and work ten hours on the case, a $600 fee would be added to $310 for a cost-based total of $910. With this strategy, you must know the costs of running the business; otherwise, you could lose money on expenses incurred to conduct the investigation. When an investigator uses a pay database to perform a skip trace or missing persons search, the costs must be recouped by charging the client. Investigators are in business to make money, so expect to charge the client at least two or three times the cost of accessing a pay database. Time is also a cost-based pricing strategy. If you collect evidence that will be used in court, there is a strong chance you will be subpoenaed to testify on behalf of your client. Billing the client to appear in court is routine, even if you are subpoenaed from the opposing counsel.

Market-based pricing involves setting prices based on what competitors are charging for similar services. No matter which pricing strategy you use, never price below the cost. A profit should be made on every job. Market-based pricing is generally believed to be the best way to maximize profits, especially if you are able to find ways to lower the cost of service. Generally, the higher the market need for advanced investigative skills, the higher the fee. Diligent adoption and estate searches are also a niche service that justifies charging two or three times the normal hourly rate. These searches are mandatory by most states during an adoption process and are lengthy to conduct. Cases such as this take a lot of time if you are waiting on information. When investigators know that processing information through certain channels will be slow, but that it only takes a few hours to retrieve the information, it is better to set a flat rate than invoice for the hourly rate.

When your business first opens, it may be wise to price slightly below the competition until a certain level of market penetration is achieved. One might bill the client for the cost of service, but charge a lower hourly rate. However, if a specialized service is offered, and it cannot be obtained elsewhere, it is generally acceptable to charge 20 percent more than the normal rates offered by the agency and its local competitors. Also, if the perceived value of the results is higher than the amount of hours worked, it is justifiable to increase the bill rate. This is commonly known as *results billing*. For example, suppose the police are trying to solve a kidnapping, and several days have passed without finding the kidnapper or the victim. The parents of the victim have become frantic. If a detective is called in and locates the victim within five hours, the result justifies charging more than five hours worth of work because of the perceived value of the results. Not every client may understand that results billing is considered standard practice in the private investigation industry.

To prevent any miscommunication on the matter, simply add a clause in the contract explaining results billing and how the bill may be subject to change. *Contract clauses will be discussed later in this chapter.*

Another way of billing clients is through retainers. A retainer is an agreement between the detective and the client whereby the client pays in advance for work to be performed at some future date. It also acts as a guarantee that investigative services will be required and that the detective will be available when those services are needed. Retainers diminish the possibility of delinquency because the retainer puts the cash up front and allows an immediate draw on services tendered. To accept a retainer, an account must be set up in the name of the client. As the investigator works, he or she earns a draw from the retainer. If a client decides services are no longer needed, the account will close and the remaining unearned funds are not billable. Some clients will have their lawyers draft retainer agreements. If you have not drafted the agreement, be careful to check the fine print in retainer agreements, as some clients forbid you working with their direct competitors or adversaries. This is known as a *pure retainer*. If the pure retainer is substantial enough, it may justify losing potential business elsewhere. Retainers are frequently used at the beginning of an investigation to ensure an agreement between the client and investigator. If a potential client was sent to you on behalf of a company, ask the client for permission to speak with his or her attorney. Attorneys frequently work on retainers and may be in a better position to convince the company they represent to put you on a retainer.

It is important to agree to the terms of a contract or agreement in writing before taking on a case. A retainer agreement should indicate that services will be completed only when the money in the account has been replenished. Otherwise, the investigator may have to continue working the case with associated costs coming directly out of the company's pocket until the money has been received. A basic retainer agreement should include:

- Client's name
- Case description

- Description of services agreed upon
- Services not to be performed
- Time frame for completion of the service
- Legal disclaimer

Clients not on a retainer should be invoiced monthly. Use incentives to encourage clients to pay their bills on time, such as offering a 5 percent discount if they pay their bill within 30 days. Try to keep pricing consistent among clients. Do not charge different rates for the same service unless justified by results billing or some other pricing method. When charging a flat rate, all expenses should be itemized on a time and expense report. Microsoft Excel offers a simple time and expense report template you can download from Microsoft's Web site (**www.microsoft.com**).

Without a retainer, receiving money from customers on time is critical. If you lack money to pay bills associated with operational costs, you may have to borrow money from a lender in order to stay in business. Agencies that experience rapid growth can be seriously harmed by having too many delinquent accounts open at once.

Many private investigators deliver bills by hand, especially if dealing with a business. This increases the chance of being paid on the spot.

Secrets of Job Estimating

Learning how to estimate a job and price it right for both your business and your community is the secret to a successful business. Ideally, you will get it right from day one. More realistically, you will make some mistakes and "eat" some jobs while gaining experience in your new venture. Do not be too hard on yourself if you occasionally under price or overprice your services at the beginning. Keep track of what you estimate for which services and to whom. Also, note when you succeed in selling the job and when you fail. Go over these records every week or two, at first. Once you have gained experience, you may be able to review the records once a month. To operate successfully, you need to stay aware of what you are doing, what works, what does not work, and what you might want to try differently.

Create task breakdowns

Even if your customer winds up seeing a single hourly rate or project rate on the invoice, you need to track what it really costs to do part x, y, or z of any particular job. One helpful way to track these costs is to do a task breakdown on each project. You may not need to go into such detail forever, but during your business start-up period, it is a very good idea.

A task breakdown is an itemized list of all the different parts of the job being performed for a given customer. It starts with the most basic task of all — getting to and from the job site. Tasks may include items like conducting a background check or pulling phone records. For each category, if there is a logical overhead cost, make a column and put your best guess.

If you are using an extra employee or contractor on a particular job, include the cost of these additional people on the task breakdown as well. The goal of your record is to compile a comprehensive view of what is involved on a particular job. It will also help you to see where you may be able to cut costs or when you need to get outside assistance to perform a particular task. At the end of the task breakdown, leave space to write in your actual bid for the job, whether the customer accepted the bid, and when you were paid. Save all the task breakdowns for the first few months of your business. They will be a valuable reference for evaluating what you are doing right in your business management and what areas may need improvement.

Price Strategy and Preparing Bids

Successful private investigation companies tailor their pricing to suit their community. Most communities will not fit the national average numbers precisely. The salaries and costs where you work may vary by substantial amounts, above or below average. You can always double-check your competitors' prices by doing a little price sleuthing.

You will find out quickly if your fees are within the normal range for your area by the responses customers give you when they receive your bids. If every bid is accepted without hesitation, you may be charging too little. If you are being turned down regularly, ask why. If the answer is usually "too expensive," either you are contacting the wrong customers for your business plan or you have priced yourself out of the market.

However, let us get past a great myth: You do not need to be the cheapest in town to do well. If you plan to run a successful business, your goal must be to keep your company profitable. Once you are running smoothly and making the money you require, you can donate your time and energy to those less fortunate. Until then, you must screen out customers who cannot afford your fees.

Your people-skills are critical to succeed in this business. Look and listen, then repeat back to the customer what you hear to make sure you grasp the nature of what he or she wants. Pay attention to what the customer tells you, and read between the lines. If you are alert, you will probably sense whether this person will be easy or difficult to work with by the way he or she talks about his or her needs. This is more than "small talk." For future up-selling, you will benefit by knowing what he or she wants in the short run and over the next couple of years. Ask what it will take to meet this person's expectations and about his or her likes and dislikes. Write it all down, as completely as possible. Be certain you make note of any promises you give the customer. Then politely ask for time to prepare your pricing for the job and give yourself one or two days. Factor all of the knowledge you have gained in your evaluation and interview into your bid or price. Type it up neatly or print it on a form legibly, and then print out a clear, clean copy to present to your customer and keep an identical copy for yourself.

Do not forget there is a major difference between an *estimate* and a quote or bid. An estimate is what you think the cost to the customer will be, based on your best guess given the facts at hand. The *quote* or *bid* is a commitment to do a particular type of work or set of tasks for a specified amount of money.

You always can change your figures if the customer changes his or her specifications, but a bid must be honored within its specifications. Be sure of your numbers and your commitment for the work before you give the customer a locked-in contract price.

Negotiating Contracts

A contract is an essential legal document for any type of case an investigator agrees to take. When drafting a contract for an individual, ask for a legal form of identification and photocopy it. Some lawyers exploit loopholes when the proper name of the client has not been submitted on the document. If the client is a company, make sure the contract lists the exact name of the business that is registered with the Secretary of State and includes the name of the state the company is registered in. You can find this information by visiting your state's Secretary of State Web site. Clauses are important because they verify understanding of the terms and conditions of the agreement. Some examples of clauses in contracts are:

- Merger and integration (pertains to party understanding)
- Choice of law and forum (pertains to laws of state)
- Statute of limitations (pertains to litigation)
- Indemnification (pertains to liability)
- Time of performance (pertains to time expectancy on a case)
- Arbitration (pertains to resolving disputes)
- Savings (pertains to enforcing contract)
- Attorney fees (pertains to the loser paying attorney fees in the event of litigation)
- Non-waiver (excuses temporary non-compliance of terms)
- Liquidated damages (pertains to late fees)

When negotiating a contract, the client may be interested in refining the language of the contract as it pertains to his or her situation. The contract may be revised several times before the agreement is signed. An investigator's contract should include the date the contract was signed, when investigations will

171

formally begin, retainer amount if provided, and hourly rate. Make clients aware that any information obtained during the course of an investigation will remain confidential unless disclosure is mandated by a court order. A photocopied or carbon copy contract is considered original if the signatures are authentic. Be sure to save all contracts in a fireproof safe, and do not throw them away after the agreement ends.

Some business owners will play it safe by hiring a lawyer to initially draft their contracts. If legal action needs to be taken against a client who has breached a contract, the first step is to resolve it through direct negotiation with the client. If the dispute is not resolved through negotiation, the next step is mediation. A mediator is a legal expert who hears the arguments of both parties and then offers advice on how to solve the dispute. A mediator's advice is non-binding. If a mediator is needed, a local chapter of the Small Business Administration can assist with finding one. If the mediator cannot negotiate a mutually agreeable resolution, an arbitrator can be sought. An arbitrator acts like a mediator, except an arbitrator's ruling at this stage is binding, and both parties must adhere to the ruling. Before seeking an arbitrator, consult with a lawyer to see if arbitration is recommended. If the dispute reaches arbitration or litigation, significant expenses can be incurred. An arbitrator's ruling should take less than six months. Litigation incurs lawyer fees and could last up to a year or more. To find an arbitrator, contact the American Arbitrator Association (**www.adr.org**).

CASE STUDY: NETWORKING TO INVEST IN LONG-TERM CLIENTS

Robert Hessee, president
Hessee & Associates
Investigative Services
229 Vernon Street,
Roseville, CA 95678
www.hesseeinvestigations.com
rob@hesseeinvestigations.com
Phone: (916) 295-9997
Fax: (916) 787-1991

Finding clients can really hurt your business if you do it the wrong way. Some see the scattergun approach as a way to increase business when the service offerings are more generalized. I targeted a certain market based on my experience. I have training to provide service to a specific area of private investigations and always believed that a scattergun approach would attract work I was not prepared to adequately provide. Over the years, I noticed that the most successful private investigators limit themselves and their business to specific areas of expertise.

I also market with the goal of establishing long-term relationships with clients. For me, obtaining short-term clients is a waste of my marketing efforts because the return on investment is much smaller. When I began my business, I created a one-page flyer and faxed it to all the local attorneys working in the criminal defense field. I found their contact information on the local Bar Association Web site, made phone calls, and mailed personal letters to attorneys that I had prior relationships with. Joining an industry association has been very useful for networking and getting referrals for new business.

When you get clients, you obviously want to make sure they pay the bill. One of the benefits of establishing long-term relationships is that you have a working relationship with professionals and not fly-by-night clients. You also know they will pay if they plan to use your services in the future. Luckily, I have only had a few delinquent payments. One case was with a Hollywood actor who simply chose not to pay his bill. The amount of the bill was not worth the time and effort to pursue the payment.

The other non-payment came from an attorney who suffered a stroke and has not returned to practice. I chose to not pursue payment because he had other financial problems, and I did not want to add to them. I do have slow-paying clients from time to time, but I employ my wife in the business, and she is in charge of tracking payments, processing invoices, and sending late notices. By using someone else to do my billing, I can always be the "nice guy" and maintain a positive working relationship with the client.

CHAPTER 5
How to Investigate Different Cases

The first thing to establish at the beginning of every client-investigator relationship is a set of expectations and guidelines pertaining to the case. In Chapter 3, we discussed the importance of geographically selecting an office in close proximity to the targeted demographic. Many clients will approach your office in secrecy. Therefore, the best office is one with a parking lot in the back of the building, as well as a back entrance so customers can enter discreetly.

When meeting with a prospective client, read the person's body language. Do they appear nervous or at ease? Greet them warmly. Use nonverbal cues to convey you are someone they can trust. If you do not have time to discuss the general facts of their case that day, a general office associate should schedule a date and time for a meeting. The first meeting may be informal. If the client feels comfortable being seen with an investigator, schedule a lunch date. At the meeting, listen closely to the facts of the case and explain your objectives, including your role as an investigator. Discuss how you will conduct the investigation, how you will communicate with the client during the course of the investigation, and what information or resources the client may be asked to produce. The role of an investigator is to be impartial and document facts, whether those facts are to the client's liking or not. It is not to fabricate evidence or perform illegal activities.

Confidentiality is expected unless otherwise stated by the client. The client wants to know that everything the investigation uncovers is not subject to public disclosure. In specific cases, be upfront and ask what circumstances surrounding the case may require confidentiality. Make sure he or she understands that all documented evidence is confidential. However, if subpoenaed to testify in court, you may be required by law to divulge any information pertaining to the case.

If the case is being funded with a retainer fee, mention that expense reports will be submitted as the case unfolds. This allows the client to know exactly how much they are spending and whether they can afford to add more money into the retainer account. When dealing with individuals, collecting a retainer is a standard policy. It is reasonable to assume that individuals who balk at retainers may not have enough money to pay in the future. If you feel that this is the case, seriously consider rejecting the case. Tell the client that once the retainer fees are exhausted, more money will need to be added to the account to continue working the case. If a case involves a lot of traveling, discuss travel expenses with the client. If the case calls for a flat or hourly rate, discuss your standard service prices.

Ask the client if the case is time sensitive. This is especially important for cases that require locating a skip to serve a subpoena. If the case is time sensitive, the contract should reflect the timeframe in which you expect the job to be completed. Also, explain what the client can expect if you are subpoenaed to court as an expert witness in their case. In court, the investigator must report his or her facts impartially. Make sure the client understands the consequences of reporting evidence or bringing a case to trail. Infidelity cases are notorious for producing adverse affects. The client should be prepared to accept the consequences and how this will affect his or her family and relationships. Most clients come to an agency uncertain about what they want from the truth, so you have to guide them. Ask what they will do if you discover the evidence they are looking for. Doing so gives the client an idea of whether he or she really wants to proceed. Taking a vested interest in the client also gives him or her an indication that you are worthy of his or her trust.

Clients must understand how confidentiality may come in conflict with state law. For example, if a client wants to find out her husband's true financial worth, a detective working the case would need access to records of former liens, judgments, or bankruptcy filings. While an investigator can legally obtain some records, other records will require the power of subpoena. Because financial records are protected by state law, detectives cannot access the information through creditors and credit bureaus. Therefore, the wife may need to have the records subpoenaed. The records cannot be subpoenaed without the owner of the records — in this case, the client's husband — knowing. In other words, if the wife does not want the husband to find out about the investigation, the investigator must find another legal way of obtaining past financial records. A detective well versed in state laws can provide counsel to the client and save him or her the trouble of making a mistake that breaks confidentiality. If you need to coordinate with other agencies, let the client know you will not be breaking the confidentiality agreement in doing so. For example, if you need to notify a local police department regarding the time and date of a scheduled surveillance, the client should know that you are not are not required by law to provide reasons for the surveillance.

Once the client has agreed to proceed with the investigation, tell him or her you will need every piece of information he or she can gather relating to the case. In a missing persons case, the client should provide you with a photograph of the person in question. Ask the client what the person was last seen wearing. When tracking a runaway teen, ask the client if the subject has done this before. If so, find out if other friends were involved. Collecting personal and professional information will build a profile of the subject and provide a starting point for the investigation. Collect names of friends, family members, coworkers, available bank accounts, social security numbers, and forwarding addresses. Make sure the client understands that leaving out even the smallest detail might impede the investigation.

In a surveillance case, you need to know if the case is heated — whether the subject knows he or she has been placed under surveillance. If so, get details on when and how the case became elevated. A case becomes elevated when the subject is made aware of surveillance activities and documenting evidence has become more difficult. Ask for the previous investigator's reports. Get permission to interview certain people associated with the subject, if appropriate. Apprise the client of state laws. Specify which types of investigative activities are legal and which are illegal. If the client unwittingly suggests a method that is not legal, suggest a few legal ways to obtain the information. Using this meeting to build the client-investigator relationship is important because it may be the first and only face-to-face meeting. The impression you make in this meeting will be the basis for getting referrals when the client recommends your services to others.

Investigating Infidelity & Divorce Cases

The U.S Census Bureau estimates that between 40 and 50 percent of all marriages end in divorce. While the increasing trend cannot be explained by one reason alone, infidelity is one of the leading causes of divorce. According to the American Journal of Sociology, 85 percent of women who believe their husband is having an affair are correct in their assumptions, while 50 percent of men who suspect their wives of cheating assume correctly. These numbers are reflected in the large number of cases that licensed investigators receive every month. In some infidelity cases, the client will contact the investigator directly. In some divorce cases, the client's attorney will hire the detective. If the client suspects infidelity, you will be hired to confirm and document evidence of the activity. If infidelity has already been confirmed and the client is preparing for a divorce, you may be hired to uncover any hidden assets for the purposes of a divorce settlement. If the client is fighting for custody of the children, they may need to document evidence of the spouse's negligence as a parent.

During a consultation, it is important to ask questions about the spouse's behavior. If the answers fit the profile of someone who has committed infidelity, begin collecting personal and professional information about the spouse. If the client's lawyer has not already done so, advise the client about divorce laws in your state. Most cases are settled as either fault based or no-fault based. Forty-nine states allow no-fault divorce filings, which means divorce can be filed on the charge of irreconcilable differences. New York is the only state that requires proof of fault in a divorce. In fault-based cases, the client needs documented evidence of infidelity, unfit parentage, or some other clear indication of marital fault. Roughly 5 percent of all divorces involve a contested situation where both parties are unable to agree on the terms of property, asset allocation, and child custody. Regardless of whether a case is filed as fault-based or no-fault based, divorce settlements tend to rule in favor of the party that has documented evidence of marital infidelity prior to separation.

The easiest way for a detective to investigate spousal activity is to obtain cell phone records. However, cell phone records can only be obtained by subpoena. Subpoenaed cell records are more common *after* a divorce has been filed, as secrecy is no longer required by the client at this stage. In divorce proceedings, phone records can be used to show phone calls placed to a number before a divorce filing. If the client is still married and wishes to maintain secrecy, he or she may request a run on cell numbers found on the spouse's electronic or paper billing statement. Cell phone records will reveal numbers dialed, including the date, time, and duration of the call. Using the records, the detective should run a *reverse search* on any numbers the client identifies as unrecognizable. A reverse search is a search performed through a private directory that sorts names and addresses by entering a telephone number. These search directories are available as publications at local libraries. Some online reverse searches are free for landlines, but some may require a fee. Check WhitePages (**www.whitepages.com**) and AnyWho (**www.anywho.com**) before consulting private directories available in libraries. Online pay databases, like Master-Files (**www.masterfiles.com**), offer more advanced searches that could save time. Any search result returned as "unlisted" in these databases is normally an indication of a cell number. To validate the number as a landline or a cell, run it through Phone Validator (**www.phonevalidator.com**). Charge the client approximately $25 per number for a reverse search on a listed number. If the number is unlisted, charge the client more for work involved in finding more information. Breaking an unlisted number can be done by paying an *information broker*. Information brokers are companies that specialize in advanced searches. However, be careful about going to an information broker, as some states have begun to outlaw the activity.

Doing a reverse search on a billing statement or subpoenaed list of cell phone numbers should yield the name, number, and address of the person contacted from the cell phone. After doing a reverse directory search, the investigator collects each name and address attached to the numbers in question and prepares to put the spouse under surveillance. Using single lens reflex (SLR) and video cameras, the client will expect undeniable proof of adultery in the form of photographs and recorded video. Setting up surveillance near the subject's home will require the use of vantage points and knowledge of the subject's daily activities. Tracking a subject would be easier if detectives were legally allowed to wiretap cell phones, but doing so is considered an invasion of privacy and is restricted by law. Therefore, knowing where the subject is going when he or she leaves the house may require sitting in your car for long hours observing the subject's residence. When the subject eventually leaves the home, you will note the time of departure in your surveillance log, wait until he or she has turned out of the neighborhood before following. You will tail him or her in such a way that avoids the suspicion of the subject. After arriving at the location where the subject has stopped, you will note the address and verify whether it matches the address your client noted during your preliminary meeting. You will set up another vantage point and wait until the subject is seen leaving the address.

The opportunity to capture his or her departure on film will come and go in one fleeting moment, so you must stay alert. When the subject leaves the residence, you should catch it on film and file it later in the evidence report. You will follow the subject until he or she reaches his or her own home address.

You may also need to follow the subject for the next few days to his or her place of employment and when the subject leaves for lunch. You will photograph each person the subject interacts with and log the date, time, and location of the surveillance.

Conducting Background Checks

Background checks are relevant in any situation in which two or more people are doing business with each other. For example, landlords might conduct a quick background check to verify the potential renter's personal or financial past. If a background check indicates a clean credit history, the landlord most likely will consider renting to the potential tenant.

People interested in a premarital investigation might also request background searches. More than ever, people are seeking to protect their fortunes from professional con artists by digging up information from their fiancé's past. In many premarital cases, the client has become suspicious of certain behaviors. Clients in premarital investigations may also be family members concerned for their inheritance after a suspicious stranger has agreed to marry their widowed father or mother. An investigator has no way of knowing if this person will con his or her spouse, but a thorough background check should at least verify if it has been done before.

Background searches are also requested by employers when considering whether to hire a new employee. When employers post jobs over the Internet and in newspapers, they receive hundreds of résumés and must select a handful for an interview. Background searches can help narrow this field. New hires can prove to be an expensive mistake if the employee turns out to be unreliable, incompetent, or even criminal. To avail themselves of the misery, employers routinely run background checks with investigators.

The first step in running a background check is to run a directory check on a Web site such as 411.com (**www.411.com**) for the phone or address provided on the individual's application. Running a search here can yield information on previous numbers and addresses, the subject's phone carrier, as well as the address corresponding to a phone number if it is a landline. An employer may run a credit report to confirm the individual's accountability. If a credit report is requested, the investigator will need a signed affidavit from the individual as permission to run the check.

When pulling a credit report in a premarital investigation, investigators should be cognizant of the laws created by the Fair Credit Reporting Act (FCRA), which regulates how and why credit reports are accessed. If you need financial information for a premarital case, and do not feel comfortable pulling a credit report, contact the property appraiser's office at a local courthouse in the subject's county. The property appraiser's office is a local office that keeps real estate records of all properties purchased and sold in the county. If the subject has bought, sold, or rented property in the county, phone and social security numbers should be listed. The records can also have a landlord's contact information. Investigators comfortable with pulling credit reports should associate themselves with credit bureaus. Experian, TransUnion, and Equifax are the three major credit bureaus that report credit information and sell personal credit reports. Databases such as Lexis/Nexus, Westlaw, ChoicePoint, and eFunds are not credit bureaus, but also gather the same types of information. If a report is pulled for reasons not permissible by the FCRA, you risk permanently losing access to credit reports from credit bureaus. What are permissible purposes? Section 604 of the FCRA states that a report can be pulled with an individual's written permission and for reasons pertaining to:

- Court orders
- Employment purposes
- Insurance underwriting
- Eligibility for a license
- Investment purposes
- Legitimate business need
- A business transaction (initiated by the consumer)
- A review of the terms of a business account

In child custody cases, the FCRA allows investigators to pull credit reports to determine the subject's eligibility as a care provider. Under this allowance, a savvy detective may be able to justify pulling a subject's credit score in pre-marital cases if the client has children. The investigator should contact their state agency handling child support issues, which has permission under FCRA regulations to pull the report. Credit reports do not always give an exact credit score unless purchased, but the report will contain any negative items reported on the account, such as tax liens, missed payments, bankruptcies, and outstanding debt. If the subject has a tax lien or bankruptcy filing on their credit report, the investigator should look for the court case, which should be available in public records at the local courthouse. Finding the court case may lead to more information, such as other parties who may have been involved. The credit report will show that you or the agency you have contacted has made an inquiry on the account. However, if the subject does not check his or her credit report regularly, it may be overlooked.

The next step is to investigate arrest and convictions records. To run a criminal record check, you need the subject's date of birth. At this stage, you may have the name of your subject attached to one or more addresses, but because there could be another person by the same name, you might have to cross-reference the information to be sure you have the right person. Cross-reference the information by asking your client for the subject's license plate number or by following the subject via mobile surveillance. Be aware that obtaining a driver's license plate number is becoming more difficult due to the Driver's Privacy Protection Act (DPPA), which carries stiff fines and penalties for violations that include obtaining and reselling the information. Access for investigative purposes to licensed detectives is permitted under Section 2721 (8) of the DPPA, provided they meet the permissible uses listed under the section. Accessing license plate information is also permitted in connection with skip tracing, process serving, and ongoing civil or criminal cases in which an attorney hires a private investigator to do a background search on a witness or plaintiff.

With a name, list of addresses, and license plate number in hand, visit the voter registration or county clerk office to get the subject's date of birth. Using the name and date of birth, you can access public records through the county clerk for information on felonies or misdemeanors connected with the subject. Unless the subject has a criminal record in the FBI's national database, only local courthouses in the county of residence will have a record. If the subject has moved frequently, contact every courthouse or county clerk's office surrounding all previous addresses. If the subject is connected with too many addresses, tracking the subject's movements may be virtually impossible. If the subject has frequently moved, search a national database of local courthouses, such as National Background Data (**www.nationalbackgrounddata.com**). If you are unable to find a record of convictions, it is safe to assume that the subject does not have any.

Past divorce records are also filed at the local court level. Divorce records frequently contain lurid details and allegations, so checking these records will potentially divulge information about past behaviors. For more information on a subject's background, you can also check police records for charges that may have been dropped or contact a neighbor from past addresses. If a neighbor remembers the subject, they might know something about the character of the subject in question and his or her activities or relationships.

Investigating Personal Injury Cases

In personal injury cases, a prosecuting attorney may hire you to investigate a company for unsafe or negligent practices. In another case, you may be hired to investigate a possible phony insurance claim made by someone suing for damages. If these opposing ends of the legal spectrum seem ironic, remember that a detective's line of work calls for unbiased, impartial conduct. Adherence to this standard not only builds a solid reputation, but also increases a detective's job opportunities. Personal injury lawsuits can involve:

- Factory or office mishaps
- Car crashes

- Product defects
- Property liability
- Medical malpractice
- Battery

Factory or office mishaps frequently occur when a worker is using potentially hazardous machinery. After an accident has occurred, investigators representing both sides are dispatched by attorneys. The attorney representing the plaintiff or injured person will attempt to uncover signs of negligence on the part of the company. Negligence can be proved in cases where certain safety protocols do not meet the minimum requirements under law. The investigator will represent his or her client in this endeavor by attempting to uncover any possible signs of unsafe practices or preventative measures that the company failed to install. The attorney representing the company and/or its insurance carrier will dispatch an investigator to prove that all safety measures were in place at the time of the accident and the accident occurred due to recklessness of the worker. The investigator's report should include interviews with accident witnesses and the area supervisor, an examination of the police report and company policy documents related to safety, and a thorough investigation of the accident site, which may include the use of forensics.

Personal injury cases can also involve car crashes between two or more motorists. Detectives who take on auto accident cases will often begin their investigation by conducting an accident reconstruction. Being an expert in this particular niche can generate a lot of business. In 2008, there were over 34,000 fatal crashes reported in the United States, according to the Fatality Analysis Reporting System. Each year, approximately 2.5 million motorists are permanently injured. Roughly 40 percent of fatalities occur due to drunken driving, 30 percent from reckless driving, and 30 percent from speeding.

Automotive forensics is a good niche industry due to the frequency of accidents as well as the degree of training and specialization it requires. Accident reconstruction involves recreating the event through a computerized simulation. Specialists in this field visit collision sites, take photographs, note the location and frequency of traffic signals, record measurements, and use simulated physics programs to determine the sequence of events during the crash. Most cars have event data recorders or air bag modules that can be extracted. If a speedometer is jarred loose in a frontal crash, it may indicate the car's speed when the accident took place. Examining light bulb filaments may also determine if the headlights were on or off at the time of the crash. Tools used by the collision investigator include drag sleds, crush jigs, brake-testing computers, and crash data retrieval systems. Investigators use this equipment to perform vehicle autopsies and make speed calculations. This allows investigators to forensically reconstruct the accident scene at the time of emergency medical assistance arrival. An investigator revisiting the scene of an accident will use a drag sled to calculate the friction of the road and determine the car's velocity at the moment of impact, taking into account external factors, such as road elevation or road conditions. He or she then measures the distance of the longest skid, subtracts the wheel base number, and adds a break efficiency number. This calculation gives an accurate number for how many miles per hour the car was traveling. The evidence is then paired with toxicology results and background checks on the drivers involved.

Personal injury cases can take on a criminal element when they involve hit-and-run accidents. Perpetrators of hit-and-runs usually leave behind clues, such as vehicle parts, paint chips, or blood. When investigating a hit-and-run, locate the witnesses and take statements. Afterward, contact local repair shops to determine if any vehicles that match witness descriptions were repaired or repainted since the day of the accident.

Battery is another type of personal injury case often investigated. Battery includes any form of unwanted touching. Most battery cases involve domestic disputes between couples. Personal injury as a result of physical battery can also become psychological. Battery involves unwanted physical contact, whereas child abuse may simply involve negligence. In battery cases, a subject's prior history of violence should be investigated. Contact lower civil courts to find information on previous instances of less serious infractions. For more serious cases, contact the state criminal courts. If a divorce case involves a restraining order, the record will be listed in public record. Get addresses of the previous wives, girlfriends, or neighbors and interview them to find evidence that a subject has a history of violence. This may be used in court if the plaintiff decides to press charges for battery.

When investigating a child abuse case, pulling a credit report may be allowed by the FCRA if the investigator documents abuse. The state agency handling child support issues might be able to use this as justification. If a parent demonstrates negligence while caring for a child, a credit report may reflect the parent's financial viability. The credit report will then be used to determine the parent's capacity to make child support payments. Not all child abuse cases involve doing background searches on deadbeat parents who skip their child support payments. Some involve neglectful parents who may need to be stripped of their custody. While the investigator must document signs of child abuse, it helps to know how to spot the indicators of child abuse in order to properly investigate and document it. Parents who continually blame or criticize their child, seem unconcerned by the child's condition, miss appointments with doctors and teachers, and exhibit controlling behaviors are all signs that the parent may be abusive or negligent. A good detective can also spot signs of sexual abuse by noting the child's behavior and interaction with the parent. While detectives are not paid to qualify expert opinions in human behavior, they must be trained to know what certain behaviors indicate.

Personal injury cases are either about preventing or proving liability. In premise liability cases, a tenant will a hire an investigator if they believe the landlord has neglected to provide a safe environment after an injury has been sustained. Standard lease provisions state that renters who are harmed by a landlord's failure to provide a safe or habitable environment have the right to recover damages. Some negligent activities, such as failure to install a handicap ramp, will not require investigation because they are obvious. However, if the landlord was informed of a potential problem before it occurred, a detective will be sent in to collect evidence indicating the landlord had prior knowledge of the problem before it caused an accident. Collecting evidence means being unbiased in one's approach. If a tenant hires you to gather evidence, and the evidence strongly suggests the landlord was not at fault, the landlord cannot be held liable for damages. Even if a landlord is found guilty of negligence, he or she may not always be liable. If evidence or eyewitness testimony proves that a crime shifted from the landlord's premise to another location, the landlord may not be liable.

Investigating Malpractice Suits

In cases of malpractice, the investigator must be able to draw a line between a poor result and professional malfeasance. Malpractice can take two different forms: medical or legal. In medical malpractice cases, doctors who act outside the established rules are subject to liability if the practice causes an injury. Doctors should have a consent form signed by the patient or the patient's power of attorney for health care related issues showing acknowledgment of any potential outcomes that may occur as a result of completing the procedure. The consent form proves the patient knew the potential consequences and agreed to the procedure. A detective's job is to investigate whether the subject was made aware of the specific injury that actually occurred prior to the procedure. Investigators should begin by checking the higher courts for civil action records involving malpractice cases filed against the subject. Interviewing previous patients may also lead to the discovery that the doctor had previous issues with the procedure and failed to tell current clients about the results.

In recent years, malpractice suits have been brought against thousands of doctors who performed breast augmentation using implants that have lead to infections, cancer, and various autoimmune diseases. In cases such as this, it can be difficult to prove malpractice when little was known about the effects at the time of the procedure.

Do not be surprised if you find yourself investigating another detective. Legal malpractice suits are most commonly brought against attorneys or detectives who may have harmed their clients via breach of contract. The rules for licensed investigators are strict. If you are found to have violated a confidentiality agreement or privacy law or charged exorbitant fees after failing to properly investigate, you are subject to legal malpractice. A malpractice suit can be brought against an agency if the licensed firm contracts an unlicensed investigator to perform a specific duty he or she is not legally allowed to perform under state laws. It is possible for an agency to contract a licensed investigator without realizing his or her license is not fully in order. When contracting a freelancer, always check with the division of licensing to make sure the person is licensed to do what you contracted him or her for.

For example, suppose a client hires an agency to find out about her husband's financial situation. If the agency contracts an unlicensed investigator to pull a credit report, the agency will surely be fined by the FCRA and will likely have its license revoked. Now, suppose the husband checks his credit report and discovers that his report was examined by his wife. Two weeks later, he files for divorce. If the agency failed to warn the client that the activity may be discovered, the agency can be sued for causing personal injury. The client came to the investigation agency in confidence and told the agency she did not want her husband to find out what she was doing. Knowing this, the agency withheld a critical piece of professional knowledge, deeming it impossible for the client to make an informed decision. A prosecuting attorney will argue that the uninformed decision directly caused the client's divorce.

Investigating Workers' Compensation & Insurance Fraud Cases

Workers' compensation cases differ slightly from personal injury cases. In workers' compensation cases, the employee has been injured on the job, but is not suing the company for negligence. Rather, he or she is collecting disability insurance and being paid by the company while recovering from the injury. Workers' compensation claims cost insurance companies roughly $5 billion a year, so they want to verify the all claims are accurate. Detectives working insurance claims should begin by checking the claimant's previous hospital records. If the records indicate a history of suspicious injuries, it may be the first sign of fraud. Next, check the higher courts to see if the claimant has filed personal injury cases in the past.

The insurance may also want to put the subject under short-term or periodic surveillance. Short-term surveillance is employed by insurance companies as a routine verification of the new claim and usually lasts a day or two. However, if suspicious activity is uncovered, the insurance company will request long-term surveillance. Insurance companies are privy to doctor appointments and will ask the investigator to take video of the subject before and after the appointments. If a claimant is faking an injury to collect insurance, any evidence proving fraud must be recorded, not photographed. A photograph does not decisively document physical factors such as strength, mobility, or a specific movement the claimant has sworn he cannot perform. A video recording shows indelible evidence of continual physical movement. The video surveillance should also indicate the time and date on the film; otherwise, a smart defender will cast doubt on the currency of the footage. If the subject is cautious about being seen in public, you may have to set up hidden cameras that can be replayed at a later time. If a stationary surveillance can get the job done, set up the cover and make sure your vehicle is parked somewhere near the subject's residence. In a typical insurance fraud case, you will have perhaps 20 seconds to record the comings and goings of the subject. Surveillance on an insurance claimant is almost always obtained during daylight hours.

Heated insurance fraud cases are much more difficult because the subject knows he or she is being recorded and will be more careful to avoid being caught on film. Some guilty subjects may expect surveillance operations outside their home and fake the injury until they get indoors. If possible, check the vantage points for a window or tail them into a store with a handheld camera. Whatever legal method of surveillance you employ, remember that a jury will expect to see the claimant's face clearly on film.

Aside from tax evasion, insurance fraud is the second most common type of fraud committed in the United States. Because many insurance companies staff their own investigators, detectives pursuing this field might look for employment with an insurance company rather than a private investigation firm. To network in this industry, see the National Insurance Fraud Investigators Web site at **www.nafraud.com**. For workers' compensation laws by state, visit WorkersCompensationInsurance.com (**www.workerscompensationinsurance.com**).

Fraud may also include cases handled by a certified fraud examiner, such as identity theft or accounting fraud. Other types of fraud may include jobs performed by auto mechanics or technical repair shops.

Investigating Theft Cases

Many private investigators are hired to track down traditional burglars after police investigations have fizzled out. These detectives should know how to collect evidence from a crime scene, whether it involves lifting a fingerprint or examining an object left behind by the thief. When investigating a burglary, statistics may help to construct a list of possible suspects. For example, most victims know the burglar or they have had the burglar as a guest in their residence just before the burglary. The best way to begin a theft case is to revisit and examine the scene to make sure the police did not miss evidence. If nothing substantial turns up, visit local pawnshops in the area. Pawnshops are required by law to inventory all pawned items for police inspection and private investigators can ask the police for stolen items discovered. Check the inventory tickets for any items that match the description of the stolen property. If you find a pawnshop the police have not checked, notify the police of a matching item immediately. If you are asked to investigate a stolen purse incident, ask the client which direction the thief ran, locate the alleyways, and look for dumpsters. In most cases, the thief will unload the contents of the purse into a garbage disposal unit, keeping only the money. For items with serial numbers, such as cars, television sets, guns, stocks, or bond certificates, the National Crime Information Center should be notified in order to track the item. Information entered into the database also helps investigators coordinate with local police.

Bounty Hunting

Another common type of private investigator is a bounty hunter. The basic tenets of bounty hunting were first established in the 1872 Supreme Court case *Taylor vs. Taintor*. Under this ruling, criminal defendants who ran out on bail bonds were considered fugitives who waived all constitutional rights to their bail bondsman. When a defendant is sent to prison, a judge sets bail. Criminal defendants who make bail are released until their court date. A bail bondsman sells bonds to help the criminal defendant post bail and secure his or her release. By offering a bond, the bondsman is making a monetary guarantee to the court that the defendant will show up for his or her court date. When a defendant runs out on his or her bail bond, he or she becomes a fugitive of the law. The guarantee and rights waiver in the bond means the bondsman has the right to track down and apprehend the fugitive on their property without a search warrant. The bondsman will not go after the fugitive himself or herself, but will hire a bounty hunter instead. The bounty hunter, acting as an agent on behalf of the bondsman, can essentially track down and arrest the fugitive.

Investigators working as process servers may consider working in this particular field, as most states allow bounty hunters to operate without training or an investigator's license. However, states tend to vary on their procedure guidelines. In California, a license for bounty hunting is required. Check your state's laws regarding bounty hunting if you are thinking of pursuing this career.

Many investigators who work as skip tracers also work as bounty hunters. Unlike bounty hunters, skip tracers are more likely to have an investigator license. Also, skip tracing does not give the investigator the power of arrest. *Skip tracing is discussed further in the following section within this chapter.*

Bounty hunters have different levels of authority depending on the state in which they are operating. What may be deemed a permissible act in one state may not be permissible in another. In states that restrict bounty hunting, if the fugitive is caught in another state, he or she may have to undergo an extradition process. However, when a defendant waives his or her constitutional rights to a bondsman, extradition is waived from states that permit bounty hunting. For each state's bounty hunting laws, visit HowStuffWorks Web site on bounty hunting (**www.howstuffworks.com/framed.htm?parent=bounty-hunting.htm&url=http://www.bailyes.com/bounty-hunter-recovery-agent-laws.htm**).

Bounty hunters who attempt to apprehend and arrest in foreign countries may be arrested for kidnapping because they are not licensed to operate in that country. Bounty hunting investigations are time sensitive. Some states require the fugitive be returned within an allotted period of time or the bondsman forfeits the bond.

Investigating Collection & Repossession Cases

Collection and repossession cases also require locating a skip. In collections cases, a skip is typically someone who owes money on a bill and is trying to avoid paying that bill. Companies have several options in this scenario: They can take the loss, try to collect the money due, or repossess the item that has not been paid for in full. Most companies will wait until the bill is 90 days past due before contacting an investigator. If the company decides to pursue repossession, it must first make sure the contract they signed with the individual allows it to repossess the item in question. A detective who takes on a repossession case should be apprised of the clause. States vary on laws relating to trespassing and repossession. If the law is not followed, the company may not be able to recoup their losses.

Suppose your client, who owns a car dealership, has stopped receiving monthly payments from a customer who is leasing a car. The client gives you the name and address the customer used to lease the car, only to find the skip has moved without leaving a forwarding address. Using a combination reverse searches, public records, and/or pay databases, you locate the skip, follow him or her to work and uncover the skip's new place of work. You contact the current company and arrange an agreement between the employer and the client to dock the skip's salary for the money owed.

Most collection and repossession cases do not go that smoothly. If the skip cannot make the payments, you must repossess the car and try to recoup any late fees that may have been written into the contract. Collection and repossession can be a hard field to succeed in because the skip will have to produce the money or relinquish possession if you want to be paid. A skip may attempt to avoid and deceive and, in some cases, will become hostile. You may also have to repossess the vehicle against the skip's will.

Investigating a Missing Persons Case

The criteria for locating a missing person depends on whether the person is alive, wants to be found, or knows he or she is being looked for. Missing persons cases are among the most common cases received by investigators.

In estate search cases that involve missing heirs to large, unclaimed estates, clients and lawyers who need to locate these heirs may not know whether the missing person is dead or alive. An investigator's skip tracing methods will help make that determination. If the missing person is presumed alive, profile the subject. This involves obtaining the most recent photograph available and interviewing those who may have seen the individual last.

If the missing person is a runaway, talk to the runaway's friends or extended family members. Children who run away from home invariably seek refuge with people they trust. Cell phone records can be subpoenaed in missing person cases. If the records show a list of phone calls, visit or call each person and ask about the missing person's whereabouts. If he or she does not know, ask when the runaway was last seen or find out any information that might help your search, such as the subject's behavior, the company he or she kept, or anything the subject may have said about running away.

When dealing with a possible abduction, contact the police and file a missing persons report. The first 48 hours of any disappearance are crucial. If the missing person does not surface within that timeframe, the trail may grow cold. Many people believe that someone cannot be reported missing until 72 hours after their disappearence — this is a common misconception. If the missing person is suspected to be the victim of a kidnapping or violent crime in the presence of supporting evidence, a missing persons report should immediately be filed with the police. Evidence of an unusual absence is also grounds for immediate filing. If the missing person is believed to be driving in a known vehicle, it may be possible to track by GPS. The investigator should also contact all local radio stations, as well as state missing person databases to report the incident.

Skip Tracing & Public Record Searches

For skip and other missing person searches, an investigator's greatest resource is public records. Public records may be free to access, but others may cost money. Learning how to search public records is just as important as knowing where to look. The uniqueness of each case may require different methods and, in some cases, a little creativity. Knowing how to search public records helps the detective narrow the list of names to an exact match. The information must be correct and current, or you will waste time tracking a skip or missing person to an old address. For example, suppose you have been hired to find a man by the name of Joe Smith. In any given city, there may be at least 50 people named Joe Smith. The list will be longer if you do not know Joe Smith's middle initial. So, how do you know which Joe Smith is your Joe Smith? How do you know whether he still lives or works at a given location? Information gleaned from free or paid databases may provide only pieces of the puzzle. Your goal is to search and cross reference enough databases so all the information forms a total picture. Always begin a search with a free database before going to a pay site. Free databases include:

- WhitePages (**www.whitepages.com**)
- Argali (**www.argali.com**)
- AnyWho (**www.anywho.com**)
- InfoSpace (**www.infospace.com**)

To locate the subject through a free database, start with information provided by the client. In most cases, the client will have at least some intimate knowledge of the subject, such as the subject's middle initial, phone number, or last known residence. Enter this information into a free database online. Doing so may yield several pages worth of names and each will include estimated age, telephone number, address, and list of relatives. If the client can verify at least some of the information on a search result, you have identified your subject.

If Joe Smith's middle name is Robert, use the telephone numbers for each Joe R. Smith and visit Phone Validator (**www.phonevalidator.com**). The search results will provide the name of the phone carrier and whether the phone is a landline or a cell. If the number is a cell, submit a court order to have the phone records subpoenaed from the carrier to find out who the subject contacted recently. Doing a reverse search on each number will provide names and addresses of the people who most likely have knowledge of the subject's whereabouts. If the subject is not intentionally hiding, you may have to call or visit the people with whom he or she is associated. If the subject does not want to be found, you may have to tail him or her.

Next, cross-reference the free databases by searching county property appraiser records. Go to an Internet search engine and execute a keyword search, typing "property appraiser records" and the name of the county you are searching in. If the subject owns property within the county, his or her information will be registered in the county property appraiser records. Information is updated monthly, so if you find Joe R. Smith in this database, the information is likely to be current. Free sites may not contain current information, so cross-referencing them with property appraiser records will validate the results. Genealogy archives, such as Ancestry.com (**www.ancestry.com**), are also great online resources when looking for birth and death records, marriage records, veteran records, and family relatives. If the client provides an old address, request a forwarding address from the post office. The post office will most likely have the information if the missing person is not intentionally trying not to be found. If the subject is a skip, the forwarding address most likely will not be available.

When relatives of a missing person have been located, speak with them. If the missing person is a skip, the case may become heated if the relative attempts to contact the subject regarding your inquiries. However, some investigators will intentionally heat a skip case if they believe the relative's actions will lead directly to the subject's location.

Pay databases are necessary in cases in which the missing person does not want to be found. Pay sites sometimes require proof of licensing. Some will charge monthly subscription fees for unlimited access, others simply charge for one-time access. Either way, money spent on accessing pay sites should be billed to the client under operational costs. Pay databases include:

- Tracers Information Specialists (**www.tracersinfo.com**)
- IRBsearch (**www.irbsearch.com**)
- Skip Smasher (**www.skipsmasher.com**)
- Merlin Information Specialists (**www.merlindata.com**)

Due to FCRA regulations, credit bureaus will not sell credit information to investigators. However, they do sell credit header information to information brokers, who resell the information to investigators. Credit header information is anything not related to a person's credit score, including a subject's name, date of birth, social security number, current and previous addresses, telephone numbers, and a list of relatives. Some information brokers may only have part of a social security number available. Getting Joe R. Smith's social security number will separate him from the other Joe R. Smith's in the county. If you get a partial number, obtain the remaining numbers by plugging the known digits into one of the pay sites. If that fails, visit the county clerk's office or division of motor vehicles with the partial number, and they will supply it. The Driver's Privacy Protection Act allows government agencies and licensed investigators access to driver's license information, but may restrict unlicensed investigators. If access to these records is denied, search the Social Security Death Index to determine if the missing person in question is still living. The Death Index provides:

- First and last name and middle initial
- Date of birth
- Month and year of death
- Social security number
- Year social security number was issued
- Last known ZIP code

The Social Security Administration has been recording deaths since 1962. If the missing person died before 1962, the subject's information might not be found here. In estate cases, ask the client for the missing person's social security number and enter the number into the Death Index. The database contains information on over 86 million people and can be accessed from many online genealogy archives that use the site to track their own records or directly on the Social Security Death Master File Web site (**www.ssdmf.com**). Genealogy archives are Internet databases that trace family pedigrees and can be used to find missing heirs or owners of unclaimed property. Some detectives use the archives to prove kinship evidence or locate someone for DNA testing.

If the missing person is not be dead or in hiding, he or she may be incarcerated. Search a federal prison database such as FederalInmateSearch.net (**www.federalinmatesearch.net**). If Joe R. Smith does not show up, try a state or county jail search such as Ancestor Hunt (**www.ancestorhunt.com/prison_search.htm**). If the subject has a military background, write to the military department under which he or she served to locate the subject.

A public records search frequently leads to the courthouse where official public records tell the story on divorces, alimony and paternity suits, mortgage loans, property transactions, bankruptcy cases, criminal cases, malpractice suits, and even small claims cases. In many of these, you can to read testimonies from the plaintiff, the defendant, and the witnesses involved, as well as any judgments levied. Information in these records often reveals past behaviors or secrets the client hired you to find in the first place.

There are three types of court systems you should contact when conducting a background or public record search. Property transactions, including information on purchases, loans, liens, and judgments, are recorded in the local court system. State courts deal with divorce, alimony, and malpractice suits. State records will contain information on any case in which the plaintiff is suing for a significant amount of money. However, the information that is accessible through the state court system varies. Federal courts handle bankruptcy proceedings. You should check county courthouse records online at CountyRecords.com (**www.countyrecords.com**) before going to a federal courthouse. Defendants in some felony cases will have their cases pleaded down to misdemeanors, which will not show up in federal records, but will most likely appear in county records instead.

Pretexting for Information

Pretexting is the act of inventing a false scenario with the intention of persuading someone to release information without causing him or her harm. Investigators use pretexts for the purpose of obtaining information that informants might not normally give if they knew the truth. What constitutes pretexting varies in the eyes of some investigators. For example, some investigators believe pretexting relates only to the act of obtaining personal or non-public information from individuals or financial institutions under false pretenses. For other investigators pretexting is more broadly defined as any deceptive act, such as calling someone under false pretenses to verify the name of the person they are speaking with. Under the laws that govern its legality, a pretext should not be used for personal gain or harmful intent. This is commonly referred to as *permissible deception.* Financial institutions are very serious about protecting consumer information due to the fact that consumer protection is strictly enforced by federal law. Investigators should never pretext to gain financial information. Remember, a private investigator's license granted to you by the state awards the privilege of accessing information from financial institutions such as credit bureaus without having to lie or explain why you need the information. The state expects you to know the proper uses of pretext and the consequences of violating the Gramm-Leach-Bliley Act, a law that will be discussed further in Chapter 9.

To avoid violating the law in any type of situation, it is better to change the reasons for wanting the information rather than changing your identity. Even though it is legal, never put the use of a permissible deception in your reports. If the case goes to trial, any lawyer looking to cast doubt on the investigation may try to call your evidence-gathering methods into question, even if the pretext falls under the category of permissible deception. If a pretext both allows and requires you to change your identity, call the subject from a spoof telephone line or pretext in a way that allows him or her to fill in the blanks based on information you provide. Methods for spoofing a caller ID include hitting *67 before dialing the number, using a Voice Over Internet Protocol system (VOIP), purchasing a prepaid phone, or buying spoofing technology from a private investigation store. Be aware, however, that spoofing methods may not work for long distance calls.

For more information on pretexting and the Federal Trade Commission's authority to ensure consumers are not subject to unfair or deceptive business practices, read PIMagazine.com's article The FTC on Pretexting at **www. pimagazine.com/ftc_article.htm**.

How to Spot a Bug or Wiretap

Private investigators are not always hired to spy on someone. In some cases, they are hired to perform a countermeasures sweep for clients who believe they are being investigated. Companies who are direct competitors may spy on each other, as may spouses who become suspicious of one another. It is also important to know the difference between a bug and a wiretap. Wiretapping is the method of recording phone and Internet conversations through intercepting lines. When a room is bugged, a transmitter has been planted to pick up conversations between people inside a room.

Prior to performing a countermeasures sweep, detectives should ask their clients to think of anyone who might be inclined to spy on them. A detective performing a sweep will not find physical evidence of a wiretap if the phone company is cooperating with the authorities. When law enforcement issues a warrant to use a wiretap, they ask the telephone company to reroute a telephone line directly to their offices. With the advent of digital switching technology, police and government agency wiretaps have made it difficult to tell whether a line is being tapped because the phone company can simply copy the digitized bits in a phone conversation to a second line. Digital switching makes it nearly impossible to tell whether a line is tapped. Digital switching is also why countermeasures sweeps have become a highly specialized service. However, wiretaps created by anyone beside federal or law enforcement agents are more likely to be illegal, low-tech, and easier to spot in a countermeasures sweep.

Detecting a phone that has been wiretapped requires a different effort than examining a room that may be bugged. Detecting a wiretap will involve the use of a lineman's handset, a small device with a keypad and alligator clips that allows a technician to monitor active calls. If a landline is wiretapped, the detective will look for a handset hidden somewhere inside a room. Once the handset is located, the detective will examine the wires. If the wires are connected to a phone jack, the client's line may be tapped. If no handset turns up, the countermeasures sweep should lead the detective to the junction box located outside the living unit. A junction box is a small box that connects several lines in a neighborhood or apartment complex and should be located on the property. To examine the junction box, open the terminal, find the client's line (which should be labeled), and examine the line for any signs of tampering. If the client's line looks different from the other lines, the phone may be tapped. If the lines are not labeled, attach the alligator clips from a lineman's handset to each line. By dialing the line's Automatic number announcement circuit at 1-800-444-4444, a programmed voice will announce the identity of the line.

When scanning for bugs, detectives use receivers to pick up devices that emit radio waves, such as ultrasonic or radio frequency bugs. Hi-tech bugs can be remotely controlled to switch on and off, as well as emit short bursts that store conversations in a buffer. Therefore, detectives who specialize in countermeasures sweeps should have only the most advanced equipment to counter the possibility that hidden surveillance equipment may be more technologically advanced. Investigators commonly find bugs in lamp shades, behind desks, and in fixtures that are not visible but put the recording within earshot.

CASE STUDY: THE TECHNICAL ASPECTS OF PRIVATE INVESTIGATION

Jeffrey Jones, president
Jones Forensic Collision
Investigations
P.O. Box 5021, Lancaster, PA 17606
jonesforensics@comcast.net
Phone: (717) 575-8839

In my private investigation business, my cases usually begin by reviewing reports that have already been written. I review police reports, as well as other expert reports, insurance reports, and medical records if any are involved. I then visit the scene of the collision, take photographs, and measurements. I may look at the geography and road design and then visit the vehicles if they still exist. I mechanically inspect them and then take photos and measurements of them.

If they have "black boxes" or data recorders, I will download them. Some of the best data comes from the airbag modules in cars and event data recorders in tractor-trailers; although, these devices were only made available in tractor-trailers after 1999. I depend much on road evidence recorded at the time of the investigation by police or insurance. Speeds of vehicles can be determined by the crushing of vehicles, the length of skid marks, and the distance recorded as how far a vehicle or pedestrian falls, flips, or vaults. We can also study angles of collision and distance traveled after collision to determine speeds. After all the measurements are taken, I interview any drivers and witnesses listed in the police report.

The most common type of cases I work involve injury or fatal collisions. I have had a few cases that were just fender benders, which is unusual. Each is profitable in its own way, as my fees are based on time. Time in court testifying is more profitable than investigating because I charge higher fees for expert testimony. That is the payoff. It also feels rewarding when I can prove someone is not guilty of reckless endangerment or manslaughter as a result of a collision.

I once showed a woman how she mathematically could not have avoided running over a motorcyclist that fell into her path after being struck by another car. She ran the man over and he was killed, but the physics showed there was no possible way she could have avoided him. I think this gave her the peace of mind she needed.

CHAPTER 6

Working a Case

The truth about working cases is that some will require stealth activities designed to avoid arousing the suspicion of subjects, and others are conducted with the knowledge of many, including the subject, who has already been identified and located. Some cases considered "open" will not require the use of surveillance because they do not require the use of a fake identity, pretext, or hidden agenda. In other words, people are sometimes aware of you and that the investigation is being conducted. For example, an automotive forensic specialist hired to determine the cause of an accident needs no reason to spy on the subjects involved in a car crash because the evidence extracted from the measuring techniques will provide it. The authorities may also require the parties involved to cooperate with the specialist when taking statements to compile a full report.

On the other hand, covert operations may involve subjects who have yet to be identified and cannot be located or they may involve investigative activities that only the client is aware of. In the case of an auto accident, the investigation is considered covert if the case involves a hit-and-run and the detective has been hired to track the offender. In covert operations, a pretext may be necessary if the detective is unexpectedly confronted by someone who threatens to make the case known to the subject under investigation. After locating the subject, the detective should begin surveillance preparations that include a checklist of items necessary to effectively complete the job. A pre-surveillance checklist should include:

- Checking the surveillance vehicle's tire pressure
- Cleaning the car windows
- Water bottles
- Batteries
- Flashlights
- Pen and pad
- Jumper cables
- Spare tire
- First aid kit
- Vehicle registration documents
- Surveillance equipment
- Film
- Cell phone and charger
- Laptop
- Loose change for tolls
- Weapons check (safety locked, cartridge loaded)
- Change of clothes for foot surveillance
- Updated address of surveillance location
- Studying map of surveillance area using MapQuest or Google
- Notifying dispatch of the operation
- Studying neighborhood activity and vantage points

The first step is to scout the surveillance area one or two days in advance. Scouting the location allows the investigator to assess what items he or she will need to conduct the surveillance. It also establishes the entry and exit points he or she will use for mobile surveillance once the subject leaves the area. Lastly, it allows the investigator to establish critical vantage points without being noticed by the subject.

Always make sure the video cameras are clean, reloaded, and recharged a day before a covert operation. Smudges on the lens of a camera will distort the clarity of a picture, rendering it useless to the client. Bring power chargers and make sure your cell phone is fully charged. Check the weather forecast for the day of the surveillance. If the weather is going to be cold, the camera may need a lens defogger. A backpack should contain essential items, such as binoculars, night vision equipment, a change of clothes, towels, laptop, and money for gas and tolls. A tape recorder will be necessary to keep a surveillance log going while tailing the subject on the road. Make sure the recorder has a memory card if the recorder is digital or a new tape loaded and a fresh set of batteries. When using a tape recorder, fast-forward several seconds into the tape so you do not lose the beginning of a recording. Also, test the video recorder to make sure the proper date and time is running.

Assess the subject's daily schedule by talking to the client or gleaning information from a previous investigator's file. To determine the best time to conduct a surveillance operation, learn where the subject goes in the morning, afternoon, and evening. Pre-surveillance logs should be included in your report because you want to bill the client for time spent prepping and scouting. Pre-surveillance operations should include identifying the subject and any vehicle that may be at the location. The report should also include pre-surveillance photos, which may include photos of the neighborhood or general area and all possible exits. When photographing a location, include identifying aspects that make the location unmistakable, such as the address number of the house or building or a sign showing the name of the community. Discretely walk around the location, take short and long shots of the location in a 360-degree circle, and make note of which observation points appear clear and blocked. Observe other homes or buildings in the area. Neighbors who participate in a neighborhood watch are usually on alert and extremely suspicious of individuals who walk around their neighborhood for no apparent reason.

To assess the level of activity or nosiness in an area, create a pretext and knock on doors around the area to talk with the subject's neighbors. In fixed surveillance operations, neighbors involved in community watch programs may approach unknown vehicles. The suspicious neighbor may not be a direct threat to the operation, so driving away as they approach may only cause them to gossip or have a squad car sent in to patrol the community. The best approach with a neighbor is to simply remain calm, roll down the window, and have a cover story ready. Or, you can tell them you are conducting an investigation without giving specific details about who or what is being investigated. Some investigators will set up pretexts to justify their extended presence in a neighborhood, like offering to paint someone's house or posing as a telephone repairman.

The next step in pre-surveillance is to determine and make note of the vantage points. A vantage point is the line of site that will provide the best view to observe the subject. Some vantage points will be selected to get the best shot of the subject in progress. Others should be selected to prevent the operation from being compromised. Everything rides on selecting a safe vantage point. If the subject becomes aware of your presence, you may wind up losing the case to another investigator.

Some vantage points will be strictly used for specific times of day and depend on where the light is hitting the camera. On particularly bright days, a closer vantage point is necessary to avoid a glare. Long-distance vantage points should be chosen to factor in the level of activity in the area. For example, if the surveillance operation begins in the morning, a detective should choose a location where glare is not an issue and that is a safe distance from the location to avoid arousing suspicion of neighbors. The investigator will then wait until the level of activity in the neighborhood has dropped to its lowest level before moving into a closer vantage point.

The purpose of establishing multiple vantage points is to remove your presence from the neighbor's consciousness. An unknown vehicle parked in one spot all day will eventually be noticed by someone. Moving the surveillance vehicle around several times diminishes the presence of a vehicle that residents are not accustomed to seeing. If the vantage points allow for a complete 360-degree circle, find the vantage point that allows for the use of binoculars.

A clear view of the subject's backyard may give the investigator a vantage point that allows him or her to see what is going on inside. When operating at night, choose the closest surveillance point possible, such as the sidewalk directly across from the front entrance of the house. If another vantage point allows you to observe activities through a lighted room or window, make sure the front door is within your scope.

Be sure to test equipment at each vantage point. If an optical zoom camera can get a clear visual shot from a mile away, mark the vantage point on your log as usable. Gathering all the details about the case from the client beforehand may influence which vantage points you choose. A "heated" file means the subject is on high alert, making the closer vantage points unusable. Knowing the file and using the information to scout an area gives the detective a tactical advantage when the real surveillance takes place.

Vantage points are classified in short-, medium-, and long-range. A short-range vantage point is an aggressive tactic because the investigator's position and line of site will be directly in front of a home, office, or public entrance. Short-range vantage points will have the best view of the subject, but are almost impossible to set up if the file is heated. If a case is not heated, you may still have to move to the next location after a few hours to avoid suspicion. Another risk with short-range vantage points is that the subject may be able to perform a counter-surveillance operation, noting the make, model, and license plate number on your vehicle. Dressing your vehicle with a fake license plate to avoid blowing cover can get you in trouble with law enforcement if the vehicle is parked in a public area during mobile surveillance. Instead, buy magnetic business signs using a fake company name and stick them to both sides of the vehicle. The sign should include a telephone number to act as an information decoy. If the vehicle comes under counter-surveillance, the subject will be more inclined to write down the number than the license plate number. The benefit of a medium-range vantage point is that counter-surveillance is made less possible because the subject will not be able to see the vehicle as well. While the detective still has a clear visual of the front entrance, it may be more limited. If the file is heated, the subject may become less aware of an undercover presence. Establishing a long-range vantage point will require the use of long-range equipment. Extremely heated cases will call for the use of long-range vantage points only.

Observing activities will be most limited with a long-range vantage point, and detectives who use long-range vantage points may have trouble tailing the subject if he or she suddenly leaves the area. As a rule, investigators will spend most of their time in medium-range vantage points and occasionally switch to short- or long-range vantage points.

Lights inside a residence are an investigator's early warning signal that some-one is either home, going to bed, or about to leave the premise. If a bedroom light is turned off, the investigator may be free to move into short-range sur-veillance. It may also mean the subject is preparing to leave the premises, and the investigator must be prepared to follow. The subject may leave for another location at some point, and when he or she does, the camera should be ready.

To shoot video footage, make sure the lens is zoomed in on the subject. Begin recording by slowly zooming out as he or she walks to the car. Zooming out will establish a close-up of the subject and give the viewer a clear shot of the premises. Avoid zooming too frequently, as it may temporarily throw the video off-focus, making it appear unprofessional and hard to follow. When using a camera, make sure the proper light density filter is being used to elimi-nate sunlight that can ruin a snapshot. A shot should never be taken in the direction of sunlight, so try to position the vehicle away from the sun. You should have already determined which filter to use during your surveillance prep work. During nighttime surveillance, a white flash on the camera may alert the subject to your presence. To avoid a white flash, place red tape over the filter. The picture will change color, but the clarity will be the same.

Tailing the Subject

Masking light filters are of no use if the vehicle is not properly customized. The best type of surveillance vehicle should have tinted windows, a dark paint that blends in easily with other vehicles on the road, and no flashy features that could be used to identify it. White is a common color that will be overlooked during the day, but it becomes easy to spot at night. An investigator's surveillance vehicle should also have enough horsepower to keep up with those subjects who tend to drive fast. The vehicle should be insured and membership with a roadside assistance program is recommended. The vehicle should have enough room to store all the equipment, plus a bike if you plan to conduct short-range sweeps from long-range vantage points. Stock the vehicle with additional surveillance essentials, such as batteries, flashlights, jumper cables, a first-aid kit, and glass cleaner. A medium-sized tripod will keep a camera steady during mobile surveillance. It should be easily accessible within the vehicle.

Transitioning from fixed or stationary surveillance to mobile surveillance requires the ability to tail the vehicle out of an area without being noticed. The best way to follow a subject is to find an alternate exit during pre-surveillance that puts you moving in the same direction as the subject. If the subject leaves while the vehicle is in short range, wait 20 seconds before starting the vehicle. Without a GPS tracker, tailing the subject in mobile surveillance requires the ability to maintain cover and drive safely while filming the subject in route to another location. If the client requests evidence of mobile surveillance, mount a camera on a medium-sized tripod and place it in your lap while tailing the car. The pursuit vehicle should always remain in the middle lane until the subject exits onto another road. Staying in the middle lane also gives the driver the option of discreetly changing lanes. The temptation to change lanes with the subject should be resisted unless necessary. If the subject becomes suspicious of your vehicle, he or she will test his or her intuition by intentionally changing lanes to see if your vehicle mirrors the movement.

To reduce the risk factors involved in mobile surveillance, equip the pursuit vehicle with side mirrors that reduce blind spots. Losing the subject as a result of a wrong turn, traffic congestion, or traffic light will happen occasionally. Subjects who believe they are being followed may become reckless in their attempt to lose you. Never take the bait by engaging the subject in a high-speed chase. Doing so is dangerous and will only confirm the subject's suspicion that you are an investigator. If the case becomes heated, calm the subject's suspicion by exiting the road. Investigators who are identified, or "made," in their vehicles by the subject will no longer be able to use short-range surveillance in a future operation because the subject will be on the lookout for a vehicle that matches your vehicle's description.

Mobile surveillance can be an extremely tense engagement, particularly if the subject is known to be dangerous. To counteract tension during an operation, turn on the radio to keep any jangling nerves under control. Traffic may be the biggest impediment in keeping up with another vehicle. The pursuit vehicle must maintain a minimum safe distance from the other vehicle, but as a result of maintaining separation, you will occasionally lose the vehicle to a red light. By anticipating the second or third traffic light ahead, a trailing investigator reduces the amount of times he or she will have to stop at a red light and wait for the light to turn before trying to catch up. For example, if the light three or four blocks ahead has been green for a while, it will most likely turn red before you get there and after the subject has moved beyond it. If you anticipate this, speed up until it becomes certain you will both make the light, and then create separation. A driver is more likely to notice a vehicle in the rearview when it continues to maintain the same amount of distance, especially if the driver has changed speeds several times. Investigators who run a one-person operation will have to deal with the difficulties of juggling safety, anonymity, and surveillance. The amount of distance necessary in mobile surveillance will also depend on the environment. If the operation is in an urban environment, the minimum safe distance will be shorter, taking traffic and the number of stoplights into account. Mobile surveillance operations that occur in rural areas may require separation of greater and more varying distances.

Agencies that operate as a partnership or employ six to 12 investigators have the luxury of using two- or four-person surveillance teams. The use of multiple vehicles increases the level of deception by allowing a lead vehicle to stay ahead of the subject, while the other vehicle remains 1,000 feet back. Communication between vehicles is usually aided by a two-way radio. If the rear vehicle loses the subject in traffic, the lead vehicle will slow down until it is safely behind the subject. When the rear vehicle catches up, the lead vehicle increases speed until it has moved back into position. One-person operations may also employ these methods by occasionally turning right at an intersection, then making a U-turn back onto the road. If the driver is frequently looking in the rearview mirror and sees the vehicle turning, he or she may refocus attention on the road instead. Non-congested traffic areas provide the best opportunity to turn off-road. Turning at the wrong time puts the entire operation at risk if the pursuit vehicle fails to reestablish its target in heavy traffic.

While in pursuit, use a tape recorder to dictate where the target is going. Dictation will be important when writing a report later. Dictation is also a good way to complement the video footage recorded during mobile surveillance. In a two-person surveillance operation, the vehicle with visual confirmation of the subject should always dictate the target's activities over a two-way radio, as well as alert the team to any changes in the subject's movements if one part of the surveillance unit loses visual. Two types of radio backup should be carried in any situation in which the team may be separated.

Every mobile surveillance operation will have an endpoint. Sometimes, the endpoint will be known, other times it will not. When the endpoint of a mobile surveillance operation is a public area, you have to decide whether to drive off or tail the subject on foot. Foot surveillance tends to be the most dangerous type of surveillance because the chances of being detected increase. Means of escape also become more limited if the vehicle is beyond the investigator's immediate reach. If the subject gets into a car and drives off, you may be left stranded. If the endpoint takes you to a public area, such as a mall, park, or restaurant, the subject is more apt to have his or her guard down because public areas come with a diminished level of privacy. If the subject is observed meeting with another person, take photographs, use binoculars to make note of the other person's license plate number, and have someone at the office run it through a database, if possible.

If the driver turns into a gated community, enter the neighborhood directly behind the driver when the gates open, but only do so if the driver has not exhibited any awareness of your presence. If the case becomes heated, pull back and wait until another car pulls up with an electronic key. Look for the vehicle once you are beyond the gates and move the vehicle into a short-, medium-, or long-range vantage point opposite the building the subject has parked in front of. It may be embarrassing and perhaps detrimental to the operation if confronted by the leasing office as a trespasser. To avoid being confronted, note the name of the gated community upon entering. After setting up in the new location, use a laptop or dial 411 information to get the number of the leasing office. Dial the leasing office and ask whether a courtesy officer patrols the residence and whether he or she is available. If the leasing office provides a number, contact the courtesy officer, identify yourself, and give him or her a vehicle description and tag and license number for him or her to verify. If no courtesy officer patrols the premise, get the number for the local police department, notify the department of the operation, and ask them to notify the leasing office that you are working on their premise.

Without having knowledge of the target's exact whereabouts at the location, medium vantage points are ideal. While most incriminating activity takes place indoors, trips to certain locations may be incriminating enough. If the driver turns into a gated home, set up a vantage point from behind the gates, note the time, and wait for the car to leave the property.

Establishing foot surveillance in an urban area may require the use of long-range optics to obtain a direct line of sight because you may be dealing with a gorge of high-rise buildings. If you have scouted an urban area in pre-surveillance, find the best vantage point in a 360-degree angle and set up before traffic makes parking more difficult. If a vantage point from the street cannot be accessed, try another building that affords a direct line of sight. If the subject's hotel is adjacent another hotel, count the floors, walk into the neighboring hotel, and ask for a room facing the target. Always remember to hang the "do not disturb" sign over the door. If a maid walks in and catches you shadowing someone, the front desk might call the police.

Rural environments may require the use of camouflage, as observations may have to be made through wooded areas. Keep the camera lenses free of dirt or smudges when trekking through a rural area. Tan nylons can be used to keep the lenses clean and prevent lenses from glaring. If you establish a long-range vantage point in a rural area, any glare from your equipment may be spotted by an observer. If walking through a wooded area is anticipated, bring a hat and clothes that will cover all areas of the body to avoid being bitten by ticks or insects. A backpack should have insect repellent, water, and storage containers for food if you plan to be there for a long period of time.

Whatever public area the target arrives at, never engage him or her at any point, and always evaluate the objective before tailing the person on foot surveillance. If the subject of an infidelity case heads into a shopping mall, and you believe he or she is there to meet or shop with his or her accomplice, you have incentive to follow. If the person remains in the parking lot for a long time, the case may be heated, which means the subject is waiting for you to make a move. Resist the impulse to act casual by getting out of the vehicle because he or she may either follow or write down your vehicle's license plate number. If the subject approaches the vehicle, be prepared to leave before he or she knocks on the window. The target will not be able to identify you if the windows are properly tinted.

Always remain behind the target during mobile foot surveillance. To avoid looking suspicious, walk casually. Act busy, and do not loiter or drift around. If you follow the subject to a jewelry store, go to the nearest kiosk, pretend to window shop, and take a few pictures.

Investigators who enter restaurants should always pay their bill in advance to avoid having to settle the bill after the subject has left. Getting into an elevator with the subject is risky, but necessary if you want to see what floor he or she is getting off on. Instead of choosing the same floor, note the button he or she presses, and press the button for the floor above it. Never get in front or in view of the subject. Sit behind the subject on a bus. Change clothes as soon as possible if the target sees you. If he or she heads into a shop, use the public restroom and quickly put on a different outfit. Following a target into a secluded area with no exit points is a serious mistake. In heated cases, if the target has military training, he or she may try to corner you. If approached by the target on foot, never admit for whom you are working. Act innocent if he or she accuses you of spying and immediately attempt to leave the premises. If he or she looks around and suddenly heads in the reverse direction, do not panic — keep walking in the same direction until the target passes.

Counter-surveillance

When the evidence has been collected, pack up, review the footage, and prepare to make a final sweep of the area for any suspicious activity that might be worth adding to the report. The post-surveillance phase is about making sure your position has not been compromised, which means detecting any counter-surveillance activity the client may not have been aware of. For example, a vehicle trailing in the rearview mirror for too long and changing lanes at the same time you do may be a sign that someone is attempting to identify you and document your activities. In the post-surveillance phase, always try to leave the site from a different exit. If counter-surveillance is believed to be in the area, they may attempt to follow your vehicle.

Counter-surveillance poses a serious threat to an operation in progress. Vehicles that stay in the rearview mirror for a long time should be noted if they arrive with you at the subject's endpoint. Early detection may warrant the decision to get off the subject's tail before any evidence is collected. An unsuccessful operation will at least offer another opportunity, allowing you to make tactical preparations for dealing with counter-surveillance. However, the effort may not be completely wasted, as the surveillance log will provide confirmation to the client that the case is heated.

When engaged in post-surveillance, focus on the road ahead, but be aware of any vehicles following you. Trained professionals hired for counter-surveillance will be using the same tailing techniques that you use, so try baiting him or her into a mistake that compromises his or her operation. Never drive straight home. Instead, take the other investigator to a public area and get the license plate number. The client will be extremely pleased if you manage to confirm a heated case and identify the other professional. Whatever happens, do not confront the counter-surveillance.

Creating the Surveillance Log

Following post-surveillance, the investigator will immediately work on the operation's surveillance log. A surveillance log should start with a header titled, "General file information." General information should include:

- Case number
- Date assigned
- Completion date
- Subject profile (physical description)

Each section of the surveillance log should be broken into headers. The next header should itemize the date and time of each operation, including the number of hours you worked on the case. In the header below surveillance dates, write the name(s) of the investigators involved and add another header for the type of equipment used. A property assessment header should have a physical description of the surveillance areas, including directions to the area from major roads and the names of any databases that listed the property registration. Following the property assessment, a header should be created to verify vehicle information, such as the make, model, license plate number, and registration of the subject and/or any counter-surveillance vehicles. The next header should have an investigative summary. The investigative summary should be a summary of everything that was observed during the operation. A video summary will include how many minutes were recorded, as well as a narrative account of everything that appears in the footage. Under a final header titled, "Surveillance details," write extensively about the details observed, including the exact time the details were observed. The surveillance details should be as descriptive as possible. Should the investigator's description be too generic, it may leave out important evidence. Surveillance details in an insurance claims case, for example, should not merely have a written statement saying the subject went into his backyard and barbecued steak. It should record every physical movement, noting how he bent down and moved a heavy object or the way he chased a stray cat away from the grill.

When the report is finished, write the words "end of report." The surveillance log will then go into the overall surveillance report, which is submitted either periodically or at the end of the case. Writing a report requires good writing skills. Any report that looks sloppy or is poorly written could diminish the agency's professional appearance. To avoid clerical mistakes, run a spelling and grammar check before submitting the documents.

A professional investigator report should include a title page, introduction, body, and conclusion. The name of the client/subject case should be typed on the title page (example: Johnson/Johnson Infidelity Case). The introduction should state the case's background and the hiring date. The body of the report will include the surveillance logs. The conclusion should provide an assessment of the situation and any recommendations for further action. Additional information can include photographs, official records, and information gleaned from a background check. Supporting materials can also be obtained from police reports and hospital records.

CASE STUDY: THE IMPORTANCE OF PLANNING FOR A SURVEILLANCE OPERATION

William S. Ellis, President
Tactical Investigations
2701 N. Mill Ave. Suite 72, Bowling Green, KY 42104
www.tacticalinvestigations.net
tacticalinvestigations@hotmail.com
Phone: (270) 202-4200
Fax: (270) 846-3746

One of my more memorable surveillance cases involved an insurance claim in which the subject sustained an injury and his doctor claimed he would never be able to walk again. We set up pre-surveillance operations in front of the subject's house and for two days saw no activity. On the afternoon of the third day, our cameras documented a garage door opening and a car that matched our client's vehicle description. The driver looked like the guy we were hired to watch. The image behind the windshield appeared muddled from our vantage point, and we needed clear identification, as well as concrete evidence of him in the act of walking, standing, or doing anything that refuted the injury made on the insurance claim. At that point, we still had no evidence that it was a false claim. For all we knew, he could have been going to the pharmacy to get prescription painkillers.

Knowing everything that you can about your subject can pay big dividends, and it certainly did in this particular case. When we started tailing the subject, we lost him due to heavy traffic conditions. To try to guess where he might be headed, I checked my case files and found an interview we conducted with a colleague who claimed the subject was an avid golfer. On a hunch, we ran a check on the number of golf courses in the area and found two locations. When we arrived at the first location, we found his car parked in the lot. We shot footage of his car, zoomed out to get a panoramic, and then zoomed in toward a sign that showed the name of the golf course. I always keep my golf clubs in the surveillance van for mobile surveillance operations, so I was able to rent a cart and drive around the course. I started following the subject and obtained video of him playing golf for several hours.

We typically shoot our surveillance video in Hi 8mm tape, mix down to VHS tapes for our clients, and save the original 8mm tapes for a period of seven years. Our reports and digital photos are stored on the company computer. Our computer has two internal hard drives and one external drive. Automatic back-ups are performed many times per day. Every case detail is dictated into a micro recorder in real time. These tapes are also preserved for over seven years.

CHAPTER 7
Maintaining Your Business, Avoiding Pitfalls, and Reaping Benefits

If you have determined who your clients are, you probably have a good idea of where your income is going to come from. You need to look at your costs and what you expect to bring in each month and fill out a projected cash flow statement, so you can see how your expenses are going to relate to what you expect to make. It is easy to get caught up in how much you will eventually be making, but many businesses have been killed by inadequate cash flow. It does not matter how much money you will make next month if you cannot pay the rent this month.

The Forms You Need

- **Projected cash flow statement:** This statement serves as a projection of cash coming in and going out, month by month, for the first year of business.

- **Fixed costs estimate:** This estimate looks at the fixed expenses on a month-by-month basis — for instance, rent, telephone, insurance, and fixed loan payments.

- **Variable costs estimate:** This estimate looks at the fluctuating costs of doing business — such as automobile fuel, office supplies, utilities, or equipment maintenance or repair — on a month-by-month basis.

- **Income projection:** This projection addresses how much you expect to make in income.

- **Pricing structure worksheet:** This worksheet helps you calculate how much it costs per day for you to be in business and determine what you need to build into your fees, beyond fixed expenses, in order to make a profit.

Business success is directly connected to sound money management: keeping careful track of the amount of money that comes in, where it comes from, how much money goes out, and who receives it. Sound money management begins with knowing your costs. Ideally, you will calculate your best estimate of operating cost *before* you start your business and build in regular reevaluations to be sure your estimates are on the mark once your business is underway.

You will want to know your basic cost of doing business — the amount you need to meet just to remain solvent — *before* you add on products that customers are purchasing from you. If that number is $5,000, and there are 30 days in a month, you must make an average of $167 for each day of the month just to pay your basic expenses. In other words, you do not make any money until you exceed that amount.

Start this process by estimating what it costs you to be in business for one month. Add up fixed costs, such as rent, phones, vehicle payments, ongoing marketing expenses, and the costs of your equipment spread out over their expected working life. For instance, if your surveillance equipment costs $1,000 and you expect it to last three 8-month seasons, the equipment cost is $41.67 per month. You can expand that to a 12-month season if you like, for a monthly cost of $27.78. Do not forget to add in the monthly cost of film and film development or memory cards and software needed for downloading images.

You will also need to figure employee wages and benefits, and many other costs. An accountant may be able to give you a more detailed approach to determine your costs. That is another benefit of working with a professional expert. The point is to have a realistic method of determining costs so you will know how to factor them into your pricing. Your cost of doing business should always be borne by the customer, not your business.

Taxes

Taxes are a critical factor in sound money management. It is essential to maintain records of all sales and expenses, down to the last penny. The IRS will want to see what came in and what went out, especially if your business is ever audited. Clear, up-to-date records show that you are a responsible taxpayer, and help avoid any suspicion of shady policies. Keep your company above board and financially transparent to the parties that have a legal right to see the numbers.

Also recognize that keeping accurate books is not a favor to the government. Your financial records are an ongoing map of your business's life. If you do not keep accurate and detailed numbers, you will not have any idea how your company is doing financially. You must have the numbers and understand them to know whether you are meeting your goals and have a decent profit margin.

You will want to make sure your federal, state, and local taxes are filed on a timely basis. In some places, you may be required to collect sales tax on services, and periodically pay it to the governing body. Verify these requirements by contacting your city or state tax department. They will tell you what licenses or tax filings are necessary, as well as the schedule and appropriate ways to file. Many taxing entities are converting to online tax filings for businesses. You will need to set up a special account on the related government Web site to use online filing and payment methods.

Controlling Costs

Controlling costs is the most challenging aspect of business. You are not in business as entertainment or to just occupy your time. You are in business to make money. You must accomplish two things: find customers who will pay you fairly for your services, and control your business spending to enable you to make a profit. Many small businesses, especially new ones, find that their cash flow is out of control and, even though accounts receivable is healthy, they do not have the money on hand to pay bills or payroll on time. This is where budgeting and cost controls become critical.

Your company's cost controls begin with the first item or service you pay for, whether it is a law firm to help you legally establish your business or accounting services to guide you through tax preparation. It is to your advantage to shop around, determine the going rate for your target purchase, and look for discounts on that rate. A small law or accounting firm that specializes in small businesses may offer lower rates than a large firm that demands higher rates to cover the overhead costs of a fancier office and numerous employees. You may also find the service is more personal when dealing with a small law firm or accounting practice.

Never blindly accept any price. Ask yourself how any product or service can be obtained for less money. You may not get as low of a price elsewhere, but you do have the ability to move to lower cost suppliers who will deliver the quality you expect. As you put together your monthly, quarterly, and annual budgets and cost estimates, plan to spend as little as possible. When you start out in business, it is wise to stick to the basics and save the luxuries for a later day. It may be tempting to be a bit extravagant here and there: a nice leather chair for your office, a fancier desk, a warehouse for your equipment, but you cannot make money if you are spending it all. Develop a frugal mindset.

Hiring Employees

After your business is underway and you start going out to quote jobs or work in the field, you may decide that a phone answering machine is not enough. If too many hours of the day are spent investigating for your clients, it may be time to hire a secretary to take calls from potential clients interested in obtaining your services. There are definite advantages in having someone in the office to answer the phones, call the vendors, and do phone marketing or set schedules for bidding. Having a secretary allows you to get your messages and reach would-be clients faster; otherwise, you might risk losing those who called other investigators in the time it took you to return their message.

You may want to tiptoe into the role of employing an office worker. Part-time help is usually easy to come by. You may simply ask around among friends or relatives. Or, if you are reluctant to take a chance on a friend's recommendation, and you live in an urban or suburban area, place a classified ad in your local paper or online publication or on a local/national site, such as Craigslist (**www.craigslist.org**) or Monster (**www.monster.com**). You will probably receive more job applications than you can handle.

Start the selection process before you place the ad by describing exactly what you want this employee to do, what experience he or she will need before starting, and what software programs or equipment skills the person will need to have. Also remember that your office helper may well become the "face and voice" of your business, so the person you choose should be able to get along with the public, in person and especially on the phone. You may want someone who can also do cold calling to solicit business for an extra bonus if an appointment is actually set. Or, perhaps you would rather have a bookkeeper to take over some of the data entry responsibilities. Whatever it is you want, write it down, read it over several times, and picture the kind of person you would feel comfortable with. Personality counts.

Discriminatory practices

Under Title VII, the Americans with Disabilities Act, and the Age Discrimination in Employment Act, it is illegal to discriminate in any aspect of employment, including:

- Hiring and firing
- Compensation, assignment, or classification of employees
- Transfer, promotion, layoff, or recall
- Job advertisements
- Recruitment
- Testing
- Use of company facilities
- Training and apprenticeship programs
- Fringe benefits
- Pay, retirement plans, and disability leave
- Other terms and conditions of employment

Discriminatory practices under these laws also include:

- Harassment based on race, color, religion, sex, national origin, disability, or age
- Retaliation against an individual for filing a charge of discrimination, participating in an investigation, or opposing discriminatory practices
- Employment decisions based on stereotypes or assumptions about the abilities, traits, or performance of individuals of a certain sex, race, age, religion, or ethnic group, or individuals with disabilities
- Denying employment opportunities to a person because of marriage to, or association with, an individual of a particular race, religion, national origin, or an individual with a disability
- Discrimination because of participation in schools or places of worship associated with a particular racial, ethnic, or religious group (Title VII)

Employers are required to post notices to all employees advising them of their rights under the laws that the Equal Employment Opportunity Commission (EEOC) enforces and their right to be free from retaliation. Such notices must be accessible to persons with visual or other disabilities that affect reading.

These guidelines should be followed by all business people, even small, start-up businesses like yours. Once you select a person to hire, you will need to set up a personnel file for him or her, prepare the appropriate government paperwork for tax withholding, and other new-hire policies. If you are not sure what is required, your accountant, your state tax officer, or your local chamber of commerce can point you in the right direction.

You will also want to set aside some concentrated time to train your new employee in the way you want business to be handled. He or she may be spending a lot of "alone time" in the office if you are out in the field. You will want to closely monitor the results of the office work you assign to be sure the job is done. With any luck, there will be no problems, but if there are, you will have to retrain or fire the individual. Neither of these tasks is much fun; it is much easier to pick your employee carefully at the start.

Finally, because you hired an office worker to take the burden off yourself, you will want to see some payback in terms of increased revenue within a fairly short period of time. Be sure you do a cost analysis of your hiring experiment to see if it is bringing you more income or costing you more money than you expected.

Ideally, you need to find someone who is licensed to work as an investigator if you need employees to handle caseloads that require state licensure. Hiring a secretary means finding an employee with knowledge and experience in clerical or administrative services, who can handle activities such as bookkeeping and office management. If you come across that type of individual, find out why he or she is not employed. Experience alone is not a good indicator of a satisfactory employee. After all, this person might have been fired because he or she was not dependable or competent. Successful business managers recommend zero tolerance for any bad behavior, whether it is showing up late, laziness, or constant complaining without getting anything done. Make your policies clear from day one and put them in writing, so there will be no misunderstandings if you must fire the employee.

So where do you find employees for your business? It is common for prospective employees to contact businesses looking for work. They may see your vehicle and offer their services. Eager, experienced workers may drop into your lap, especially when the economy is not doing well. When times are good, you may have to be a little more proactive in your search.

Newspaper or Internet ads are effective — put one together outlining exactly what you are looking for. Specify the work and hours, but consider whether you want to put the hourly pay in the ad. In some areas of the country, help-wanted ads for private investigation companies contain the starting hourly wage. In others, a wage range is listed, and in other places, words such as "competitive hourly wage" are used instead of specific numbers. Get to know the pay scales in your area for the work you want done, check the ads being placed by your competitors, and use those standards as guides. Also, be sure to state in your ad that applicants must be currently eligible to work in the United States for any employer.

This is the only "pre-screening" you can legally do to make sure you are not hiring an ineligible worker. If you live in a large metropolitan area, you may get better results from community papers than from the large dailies that cover areas 100 or more miles. Online services such as Craigslist and its local competitors may be a cost effective form of advertising. Just be sure your applicants are local. It is not wise to employ someone who lives two hours away and drives an old car that may or may not start on any given day.

Keep in mind that it is illegal to place an ad that discriminates against anyone because of race, sex, age, religion, or other factors. You are looking for someone who can do the job, no matter what other qualities the person has or does not have. List your telephone number and/or e-mail address in the ad rather than an address or post office box number. If you list your address, and you are working out of your home, you may have unexpected visitors at your door at all hours. Using a post office box will delay response time, so it is not desirable for hiring in a rush. Hiring another investigator to handle additional caseloads requires patience and good judgment. So, what do you look for when interviewing someone for an investigative position?

Interviews

The interview process begins on the telephone, as you are setting a time for a personal meeting. The first thing to consider is the attitude of the person on the other end. Is he or she friendly or surly? Any private investigator worth hiring should sound articulate and composed; this is a good indicator that he or she will be able to handle situations that frequently go wrong during an investigation, such as being confronted by an angry subject or the police. What is the overall demeanor of the person you are talking to on the telephone? Does this sound like a person you would like to be around? If you need someone to regularly handle activities that do not require a license (such as process serving), then experience does not matter as much as professional demeanor. Otherwise, their experience and qualifications will play a major role in your decision to hire the person.

Why do they want the job? Do they have an interest in private investigation, or do they just need some money? Select the most suitable applicants before you schedule face-to-face meetings. You will want to know whether they have experience with the tools and equipment they will be using as your employee.

During the personal interview, apply the same standards you would expect your customers to use. How is this person presenting himself or herself? Is the person clean? Is clothing torn or dirty? Does he or she look you in the eye? If the prospective employee claims to have experience, ask them two or three questions that require some knowledge to answer. You do not have to be challenging or harsh in your questioning. You can be friendly, even funny. You simply want to determine to the best of your ability whether this person is being honest with you. You might want to present a scenario and ask how the applicant would start, perform, and finish the task you describe.

Review the applicant's résumé and ask questions about gaps in work history or lack of recommendations or past employers. Someone who tries to turn that work history into a major qualification to work for you might not be as desirable as an employee. If you have the sense that your candidate is lying, be cautious about hiring him or her. It is easier to not hire someone in the first place than to fire him or her after the fact.

Before you interview anyone, read up on rules about discrimination in hiring. Some questions are forbidden. You may not ask about a person's religion, politics, or sexual preference. Your questions should track the qualifications for the job, not outside interests or qualities the prospect has no control over. That same standard would not apply to an office worker whose most challenging physical effort will be moving paper from one side of a desk to another or using the telephone.

It is not out of bounds to ask "what if" questions during a job interview. The answers should reveal much about how the interviewee would handle delicate situations. For example, an appropriate question is, "What would be your response to a client in a two-party state who asks you to secretly record a phone conversation without the other party's consent or knowledge?" Because two-party states deem it illegal to record phone conversations without consent of both parties, the investigator should have knowledge of the state's laws and refuse to record any such conversation. Discuss the job with the applicant, describing in detail what you would want that person to do. Check the person's reactions. If the candidate responds in a way that is completely unreasonable, smile, thank him for his or her time, and end the interview. Also, avoid the applicant whose interview style is to present a list of demands he or she expects you to meet.

With each job applicant, try to objectively see the person. Is this someone you want to be around every day? Someone a customer would like and trust? Someone you believe can help your company grow? All of these things matter.

Hiring people you can promote is important because it gives employees reassurance they can grow along with your company, and it provides incentives for superior performance. Ambition can work for you. Do not be reluctant to hire the smartest people you can find.

Once you have narrowed your list and found the person or persons you would like to hire, check them out. Call former employers to inquire about their work histories and performance. Be aware that many former employers will be reluctant to offer bad news about someone. Know the qualities you want to inquire about and ask specific questions. If you just ask, "What can you tell me about Bob?" you will probably get an answer as general as the question: "He was alright." You want to know if Bob showed up on time, did what he was supposed to do, and caused any problems. Listen for what Bob's former employee is not telling you. If his former employer is distant or does not seem as though he has much to say about Bob, this may be a warning sign. On the other hand, if he says, "I would hire him again in a minute," you have the answer you need.

Once you have made a decision, call your new employee, and give him or her the good news. Tell him or her clearly, as you should have done during the interview, that you have a probationary period of 60 or 90 days (longer or shorter as you choose) during which he or she can quit or you can let him or her go with no hard feelings and no obligation on either side. Send the employee a confirmation letter outlining your work policies and what is expected. This can be a separate document if you like. Again, as with customers, it is best to have all requirements and expectations in writing.

Contact everyone else you have interviewed and explain that you have made a decision to hire someone else. Wish everyone well and thank them for their time. Even after you select a candidate, keep the other appropriate résumés and contact information. You never know when you may need another employee, and if someone who applied previously happens to be available, you will save yourself time in finding your next hire.

Some communities restrict how many employees a home-based business can have. Check your local zoning and other regulations before you commit to a number of people parking their cars and doing other business-related activities in the neighborhood. If you face such restrictions, you will be forced to either rent business space or arrange to meet all of your workers at job sites or other locations.

New employee paperwork

No matter whom you hire, you will have to fill out and send in or retain certain government documents. These include W-4 forms, the Employee's Withholding Allowance Certificate, and the W-5, for employees with a child, if they qualify for advance payment of the earned income credit. Check the IRS site or **http://business.gov/business-law/forms** to download forms.

Application of Federal Law to Employers

A number of factors may cause an employer to be covered by a federal employment law. These include the number of employees employed by a business; whether an employer is a private entity or a branch of federal, state, or local government; and the type of industry an employer is in.

The following chart shows how the number of workers a company employs determines whether a specific federal statute applies to the business:

Number of Employees	Applicable Statute
100	WARN — Worker Adjustment and Retraining Notification Act
50	FMLA — Family Medical Leave Act
20	ADEA — Age Discrimination in Employment Act

Number of Employees	Applicable Statute
20	COBRA — Consolidated Omnibus Benefits Reconciliation Act
20	OWBPA — Older Workers Benefit Protection Act
15	ADA — American with Disabilities Act
15	GINA — Genetic Information Nondiscrimination Act
15	Title VII of the Civil Rights Act of 1964
15	PDA — Pregnancy Discrimination Act
1	EPPA — Employee Polygraph Protection Act
1	EPA — Equal Pay Act
1	FCRA — Fair Credit Reporting Act
1	FLSA — Fair Labor Standards Act
1	IRCA — Immigration Reform and Control Act
1	OSHA — Occupational Safety and Health Act
1	PRWORA — Personal Responsibility and Work Opportunity Reconciliation Act
1	USERRA — Uniform Services Employment and Reemployment Rights Act

Creating an Ethical Environment

The most effective fraud deterrent is a corporate culture that does not tolerate fraud. Creating an ethical culture in the workplace is a process that takes time, investment, and continual education. For an ethical culture to become established, both management and employees must be committed to it and willing to live by it every day.

Ethics policy or code of conduct

Every organization should have a formal ethics policy, not only because it deters fraud, but because it also legally supports efforts to enforce ethical conduct in the workplace. Employees who have read and signed a formal ethics policy cannot claim they were unaware their conduct was unacceptable. Recommended codes of conduct for various types of organizations are commercially available, but every organization should tailor its own ethics policy to suit its business and its needs. A good ethics policy is simple and easy to understand, addresses general conduct, and offers a few examples to explain how the code might be applied. It should not contain myriad rules to cover specific situations, or threats such as "violators will be prosecuted to the full extent of the law." In a legal trial of a fraud perpetrator, it is the judge and not the company that will decide the sentence. An ethics policy or code of conduct should cover:

- **General conduct at work**: Explain that ethical and honest behavior is expected of all employees, and they are expected to act in the best interests of the company.

- **Conflicts of interest**: Employees may not understand what does and does not constitute a conflict of interest, so some simple examples are appropriate.

- **Confidentiality**: Company policy on the sharing of information among employees and departments or with people outside the company.

- **Relationships with vendors and customers**: Company policy regarding doing business with a relative, friend, or personal acquaintance.

- **Gifts**: Policy regarding the types and amounts of gifts that may be accepted or given by employees during the course of doing business.

- **Entertainment**: The types of entertainment activities considered appropriate for vendors and customers that will be accepted on expense accounts.

- **Relationships with the media**: Company policy regarding who should communicate with the media about company affairs.

- **Use of the organization's assets for personal purposes**: This section should cover personal use of the Internet while at work and use of copy machines, telephones, and company vehicles.

- **Procedure for reporting unethical behavior**: Employees should be encouraged to report any ethical violation, large or small. This section should explain how and to whom reports should be submitted, and the use of a tip hotline if one exists.

- **Consequences of unethical behavior**: Discipline options should be clearly communicated and consistently enforced.

An ethics policy will not be effective if it is handed to each new employee and then forgotten. The ethics policy should be reviewed with employees every year, ideally as part of an antifraud education program.

Deductions

The goal of every business is to maximize profits while minimizing the amount of taxes to be paid. Understanding how to make deductions from operational expenses is the key to helping business owners accomplish the latter. You will pay taxes on three levels: federal, state, and county. Federal collects on corporate income. State collects on sales and payroll taxes. County may collect based on certain criteria, such as the number of employees you have. As a taxpayer, making deductions on expenses incurred by the agency eliminates a certain amount of income from being taxed. To make these deductions, it is important to understand which expense deductions you are allowed to write off as taxable income. Understanding the process means following certain rules set forth by the IRS when filing a federal tax return. According to the Internal Revenue Code, any business expenses deemed necessary to run the business can be subtracted from income tax. These expenses include office rent, supplies, surveillance equipment, office computers, office utility bills, bond or liability insurance, and payroll taxes. As long as you can prove the expenses are business-related, they are subtractions to be made. The IRS has special rules for other expenses that fall into a gray area between personal and business expense, such as traveling. Because travel expenses may be seen by the IRS as a personal expenses, the trip will have to be justified as work-related. If you have an expense that is used for both personal and business-related reasons, it is best to divide the cost between business and personal. For example, if a case requires traveling a great distance, and you book a flight to arrive there, the cost of the flight, hotel, and meals can be deducted from the expenses because they are business related. If you happen to vacation there for an extra few days, it will not be considered business related and whatever personal expenses incurred are subject to taxation.

Investigators who operate from a home office may make deductions on mortgage interest, home office utilities, home office repairs, insurance, and depreciation. The easiest way to qualify for a home office deduction is by renting home office space to the agency and declaring the rental on your personal tax return. Rent is a deductible business asset that the IRS considers to be any amount of money paid for space you do not own. An agency established as a corporation does not own your home office. If you rent your office space to the corporation, it is considered an allowable deduction. Home office deductions can be made with two precepts. First, the home office must be used regularly and exclusively for business purposes. Second, it has to be considered a principal place of doing business if you do business outside the location. For example, if you rent office space just to maintain a professional appearance when meeting with a client, but spent a lot of time at a home office writing reports, a deduction can be made. Because rent is considered an allowable deduction, you can also deduct the rent you pay at your secondary office where you meet with clients.

Health insurance can be deducted if it is purchased for yourself and family members. Keep in mind that sole proprietors must pay taxes to social security and Medicare by paying self-employment taxes. Self-employment tax can be completed on a Schedule C or Schedule SE. To make deductions on health insurance, take the self-employment income, subtract 50 percent for the self-employment tax and subtract any retirement contributions. Whatever is left is the allowable deduction on health insurance expenses. If the company employs workers and pays the insurance premiums of all its employees, it must be reported on a Schedule K-1, which allows the owner to deduct the payments in his own personal tax return. Other insurance costs related to the private investigation industry, such as bond or liability, can also be deducted.

If you have borrowed a significant amount of money, you may be wondering if interested accrued on your loans money will be taxed. The answer is no. The IRS understands that the welfare of small businesses depend on loans and being able to repay the banks. Business interest is considered the amount lenders charge for money borrowed to directly fund business activities. Deducting interest on loans is especially important for entrepreneurs who borrow large amounts of money with high interest rates during their start-up phase.

Employee pay is a deductible expense, but it is important to file payroll taxes monthly using the Electronic Federal Tax Payment System created by the IRS at **www.eftps.gov**. At the end of every quarter, report the deductions from payroll and file an IRS Form 941. If you hire an independent contractor, the subcontractor will be responsible for his or her own taxes. Business owners must first make sure their independent contractors do not fall under the category of an employee; otherwise, they will be held accountable for past payroll taxes. The IRS defines an employee as someone who regularly performs a service that is controlled by an employer. The best way to establish an employer-contractor agreement is to set up a contract that defines their liability in the partnership. For a complete list of IRS criteria, go to IRS Publication 15-A, *Employer's Supplemental Tax Guide* at **www.irs.gov/formspubs/ index.html**. To determine if someone qualifies as an independent contractor, ask yourself:

- Do they have other clients?
- Do they provide their own equipment and work space?
- Do they set their own business hours?
- Is the work performed by them?
- Do they have a business phone and company stationary?
- Do they rent office space?
- Do they advertise?
- Do they carry their own insurance?

To further know how deductions are made, it is important to understand the difference between current and capital expenses. Current expenses are expenses incurred by doing everyday business, such as utilities, rent, and so forth. Capital expenses are business assets that are not fully deductible at the time of the expense. Business assets include things such as office furniture and your surveillance vehicle. Regarding business assets, you must spread out the deduction over a number of years. However, depreciating assets may be the exception to the rule because some business assets vary in their level of depreciation. Business owners should examine Section 179 of the IRS Code, which allows an option to deduct assets purchased in the first year of purchase instead of being capitalized and depreciated. To know which business assets apply to the rules of deduction, go to the IRS Web site at **www.irs.gov/form-spubs/index.html**.

Compensating Yourself

At this stage, the business has begun to accumulate income, and now comes the part every business owner likes: being paid. In order to receive money as a business owner, you must first devise a compensation structure. Whichever structure you choose, it is important to weigh the impact it will have on the financial stability of the business, as well its benefit within the type of business structure you have created. The five compensation structures to consider include compensation through bonuses, dividends, draw, income shifting, or straight salary.

Awarding a year-end bonus is a good way to increase compensation after profits have been totaled and is usually paired with draw as compensation. Any well-designed bonus plan will award a bonus without hurting the financial health of the business. Entrepreneurs in partnerships or LLCs should consult their accountant for tax implications that may arise as a result of creating a bonus plan. C-Corps must treat bonuses as wages and may be required to pay Medicare, social security, state, and federal taxes on it. Rather than waiting until the end of the year to see if any money is left over, examine the issue month-to-month by paying expenses each month and creating a reserve ledger. If the reserve money has not been used for operational expenses by the end of the year, it may be awarded as a bonus.

Generally, treating a bonus as a profit distribution (otherwise known as a dividend) has better tax implications for owners of S corporations. C corporations face double taxation on dividends and should therefore treat the money as a bonus. Dividends work for S corporation owners because, as a business structure, they distribute money via wages and profit distributions, and dividends are exempt from self-employment tax. To avoid taking risks in this compensation strategy, create safeguards by documenting profit distribution plans ahead of time and consult an accountant before acting on the plan.

Another compensation structure is by draw. Owners of sole proprietorships typically pay themselves through an "owner's draw," which should be reported on a Schedule C during tax season. On the other hand, LLCs and S corporations are organized to have their profits automatically "flowed through" from the business to the owner and are taxed once on an annual tax return.

Owners of C corporations may be able to compensate themselves through income shifting, which shifts profits to a lower tax bracket and avoids some payroll taxes. The best way to use an income shift is to employ family members who may not be subject to the Federal Insurance Contributions Act (FICA) or the Federal Unemployment Tax Act (FUTA), depending on their age or relation. If you decide to use a straight salary, you are receiving a fixed income paid at regular intervals. A straight salary is important to owners of C corporations who want to avoid double taxation. The size of your salary must be determined after considering whether the tax benefits are greater if transferred from the corporation to your personal account or simply left in the corporate account. If you anticipate the corporate tax rate being higher than your personal tax rate for the year, increase compensation coming from straight salary.

If you need money beyond what you already make from the business, it is feasible to execute a loan agreement. Simply treat it as you would any other loan and make incremental repayments to the company as they have been outlined in the agreement. Consult with an accountant on how to structure the agreement to the company's best possible financial and tax advantage.

How Sudden Success Can Put You Out of Business

Is it possible to go out of business if your agency grows too fast? Oddly enough, unless you take measures that will safeguard against this cruel fate, it is entirely possible. Many business owners operate under the assumption that they will pay off their debts, pass breakeven, and reach profitability once the agency becomes backlogged with cases. However, if you offer credit as a viable payment term to your clients, and too many clients pay their bills more than 30 days out, the business has no money to pay off its operational expenses and could begin to accumulate large debts that could put you out of business.

While offering clients the option of paying by credit is a necessary competitive strategy, some payments will most assuredly be delayed. For example, suppose the agency is doing work for a handful of clients without securing a retainer. Over the course of the month, not only does the agency incur operational expenses to handle the cases, it also has to pay its operational expenses to stay open, such as paying rent, utility, and employees. Because these clients have delayed their payments, the agency does not have enough money to pay off this month's expenses. You know the money is coming, so you execute a loan agreement and lend the business the cash it needs to get through the month. When the clients make their payments, the agency simply uses the money to pay off the loan. Crisis averted, right? Sort of.

Executing a loan agreement whereby you lend the business money works if you have the cash to lend, but what if the agency is suddenly taking on more clients than it can handle? To keep pace with the work, the agency will have to expand by hiring more employees and buying more equipment, including two or three more surveillance vehicles. Also, what if travel expenses triple when these clients begin to request your services overseas? Now the business is growing too rapidly, and suddenly, the cost to maintain the agency has tripled, making it less likely that you will be able to front the immediate cash necessary to keep the business afloat while it waits for the delayed payments to roll in. Then it gets worse. After tripling the agency's operational expenses to complete the work, some of your clients begin paying their bills 60 to 90 days out. Not only has the agency tripled its debts, it stays tripled over a two or three months span, and now there is not enough money to execute a loan agreement. Unpaid employees begin to quit, shorting manpower. You begin defaulting on loans, causing high interest rates to kick in. The energy company shuts off the power in your office. Before you know it, your success has ruined the business and crippled its ability to stay open.

The best way to avoid this nightmare scenario is to make sure the agency's collection policies guarantee prompt payment. As previously mentioned in Chapter 4, establishing a retainer or using a written agreement that offers discounts for prompt payment will ensure the agency has the money it needs to stay open and achieve true profitability. By no means should this caveat prevent you from making as much money as possible, but if you plan to maintain a successful business, it is important to understand the risks of success. To be forewarned is to be forearmed.

If you do find yourself in a cash-crush as a result of rapid growth, factoring can provide a short-term solution. Factoring allows you to receive money immediately to cover business expenses by putting down the payments that are owed to you as collateral. Here is how it works: A company that specializes in factoring lends money to a business. In turn, the business gives the lending company the receivable from a contract that has already been fulfilled. When the client pays his or her bill, the money goes straight to the company that lent the money. In the end, you receive your money on time, and the lending company receives the money from the original invoice. Factoring is a good way to get out of a bind, but it should be used piecemeal because this method of receiving money quickly comes with certain transaction fees that could wind up costing a lot of money if used too much. When searching for a factoring service online or in the Yellow Pages, keep in mind that rates tend to vary between 1 and 5 percent and advances between 80 to 95 percent of the receivables value.

Understanding Bankruptcy Laws

One of the hardest decisions a business owner can make is the decision to file for bankruptcy. The cold hard truth about business is that no matter how well a business is prepared to succeed, nothing is ever assured. If you find yourself in a position where the company cannot continue to sustain itself, filing for bankruptcy may be a necessary decision that is best for you and your business. Despite appearances, bankruptcy laws have been designed as a form of financial protection. Without bankruptcy protection, creditors would be able to sue an individual or corporation into financial oblivion. Bankruptcy protection not only protects individuals and corporations, it provides options that allow the individual or corporation to seek a fresh start without being permanently ruined.

Bankruptcy is what business owners declare when the company becomes insolvent and can no longer pay creditors who have lent money to finance operational expenses. Creditors in turn will usually file a petition against the owner to recoup what is owed or attempt to restructure the debt agreement. The entire process is governed by the Federal Rules of Bankruptcy Procedure enacted by the Supreme Court. The rules cover how creditors file bankruptcy petitions, duties of the debtor, and filing motions for bankruptcy. All motions must be filed in a local bankruptcy court near the debtor's residence, business, or principle location of his or her assets. The three types of bankruptcy cases relevant to private investigation businesses are:

- Chapter 7
- Chapter 11
- Chapter 13

Under Chapter 7 bankruptcy protection, a company agrees to liquidate (sell off) its assets as a way of reducing or eliminating debt without incurring any further legal action. For example, if creditors seek repayment for $1 million, and the corporation filing for Chapter 7 sells off its assets for $500,000, the creditors will get $500,000 and lose the rest. Creditors are not allowed to go after the remaining sum by seeking collection through the owners personal income or assets. The stipulation for companies under Chapter 7 is that they must halt operations permanently in order to avoid further legal action by creditors. Chapter 7 bankruptcy forms must include a schedule of assets and liabilities, current income and expenditures, statement of financial affairs, contracts and leases, and the most recent tax return. The official forms for all Chapter filings can be found at **www.uscourts.gov/bkforms/index.html**.

Individuals or companies who file Chapter 7 are also allowed to file schedule of exempt property, which protects some properties from creditor petitions. Property exemptions can vary, as some states have replaced exemptions in federal bankruptcy code with their own exemption laws. To know which properties are protected under this filing, consult the local bankruptcy court. Total fees collected for the bankruptcy filing process cost roughly $300.

Bankruptcy is a serious situation for business owners and lenders, but other motions have been specifically designed to protect a business owner's assets from being liquidated by lenders. Chapter 11 is a bankruptcy motion that gives the business time to reorganize its operations while receiving protection from creditor petitions. A business owner can file for Chapter 7 to settle his or her debts with creditors while jointly filing a Chapter 11 to protect the company's existence. Dual applications are necessary for some business owners depending on the type of business structure they operate. For example, corporations are considered separate entities from the individuals who create them, and therefore, the company, not the individual, is held responsible for repayment. In business structures such as sole proprietorships, the business is not a separate entity from the owner, and so creditors may be allowed to go after an individual's personal assets. In this type of situation, jointly filing a Chapter 7 with a Chapter 11 protects both entities. A Chapter 11 application requires almost the same processing information as a Chapter 7, except the owner must also prepare and submit a reorganization plan to the bankruptcy court with details on how it will correct its operational problems as well as its strategy to repay creditors. Chapter 11 application fees cost roughly $1,000.

A Chapter 13 bankruptcy filing allows individuals with an income to repay their debts through a three- to five-year plan. Instead of liquidating personal assets through Chapter 7, the individual can prevent home foreclosure by filing Chapter 13. It also allows owners to restructure their debts over a longer period of time, which can result in having to make lower incremental payments. An individual's Chapter 13 eligibility depends on unsecured debt totaling less than $360,475 and secured debt totaling less than $1,081,400. Filing a Chapter 13 application requires almost the same processing information as a Chapter 7 and 11, except the court must have a copy of the debt repayment plan, evidence of income, including income statements, and evidence of any anticipated raises in income. Total application fees for Chapter 13 cost roughly $275. For more information on bankruptcy laws, go to: **www.uscourts.gov/bankruptcycourts/bankruptcybasics/process.html.**

CASE STUDY: HOW ACCURATE BOOKKEEPING CAN SAVE MONEY

Danny R. Smith, President
DRS Investigations, LLC
1533 Milwaukee Street, Suite 136,
Boise, ID 83704
www.drsinvestigations.com
admin@drinvestigations.com
Phone: (208) 452-4159
Fax: (866) 401-1821

Vehicle expenses are typically the most substantial cost deductions for investigators on their tax return. I also deduct the cost of and maintenance fees on computers, optics, cameras, GPS tracking devices, recording devices, office equipment, and files. There are also substantial deductions for ongoing training costs. Any journals, publications, or books purchased to keep up with the ever-changing nature of the industry can be deducted. I claim deductions for membership to private investigation associations as well as travel expenses incurred from attending industry conferences. Marketing materials and costs, database subscriptions, and other business-related incidentals are also deductible. Collectively, it saves my agency a lot of money. If you want to deduct these expenses, you have to accurately keep track of finance and operational costs. I personally use three methods. First, I have a daily planner for notes in the field, which I use for tracking any mileage I put on the van. Second, I use QuickBooks Online, which my accountant and I can access anywhere from any computer. Third, I file all my invoices and receipts in case my accountant needs a business expense verified.

The savings that come from making allowable deductions are especially welcome when cash flow tightens during an economic recession or troubled business period. Having a pension when times are tough is also helpful because you always have money in reserve to maintain operations if need be. Many law enforcement people become investigators after they have drawn a pension. My pension with the Los Angeles County Sheriff's Department allows me the flexibility to operate without worrying if I can pay my employees or office rent every month. Plus, I have found that private investigation does have some recession-proof aspects that offset some of the negative effects caused by an economic slowdown. Our research has indicated that the number of divorce cases has declined during the recession due to the threat of increased financial hardship that comes with marital separation. Quite simply, couples are working harder to make their marriages work. That means investigators are seeing a reduced caseload for infidelity and child custody suits. On the other hand, the rate of insurance fraud cases has increased substantially during this same period, as people have become more inclined to steal money. As such, the increased number of workers' compensation claims has offset the loss of business from other areas in the private sector.

CHAPTER 8
Working with Law Firms & Enforcement Agencies

Evidence is anything that can be used to support a theory or assertion as being fact or fiction. It is also perhaps the single most important part of working with law firms and law enforcement agencies. Before an investigation begins, a client has a theory or assertion he or she believes to be true. The investigator's job is to collect anything that proves or disproves the client's initial theory or assertion. If a client believes his or her spouse is cheating, the assertion is proved true by evidence that reveals unfaithful behavior, such as pictures of the spouse holding hands with someone else in public. If evidence disproves the client's theory, they may feel relieved to know they were wrong.

At the beginning of this book, we said evidence must be unbiased, untainted, and most importantly, it must be fact. Following all three requirements is the only way to ensure that evidence is admissible in court. So how does an investigator make sure the evidence collected is unbiased, untainted, and factual? As previously discussed, your responsibilities and objectives as an investigator should be clearly outlined and explained during your initial meeting with the client. Lawyers are professionals who should already know this. What you provide as evidence and what they choose to submit as evidence is not your responsibility or concern. Your responsibility is simply to provide evidence and let the client's lawyer deal with the evidence as he or she chooses. If you are subpoenaed by the opposing counsel, you will be required to answer all questions truthfully, even if the answers damage your client's case. Lying simply to maintain a good rapport with lawyers and get work in the future is not worth the severe penalties that come with committing perjury. And besides, no good lawyer wants to deal with an investigator who is known for showing bias. If an opposing counsel can prove you conducted the investigation with bias, the evidence you collected is suddenly worthless and the lawyer's entire case is ruined. If the opposing counsel can prove the evidence was tainted, the evidence is also no good to your client's lawyer. As we will discuss later in this chapter, the best way to ensure evidence stays untainted is to follow the chain of custody rules.

The types of evidence you will be asked by lawyers to collect for courtroom presentation can be *direct, indirect,* or *circumstantial.* Direct evidence supports a theory or an assertion without question. For example, suppose a female client asserts that her husband lied about his whereabouts on a specific day and time. Upon further investigation, you go to the location, discover a lingerie shop that still has a receipt of the husband's purchase from last week. The store also has video footage from that time showing the husband buying a nightgown for another woman, who is also seen on the tape. The receipt and the film are both pieces of direct evidence that prove the client's assertion that the husband was indeed here at a specific time and, therefore, lied about his whereabouts.

Indirect evidence is commonly based on witness testimony that cannot actually be produced as direct evidence. Due to the fact that the evidence came from hearsay, it can only be used in limited ways. For example, if a witness in your client's divorce proceeding testifies that he heard the husband say he was unhappy with his marriage and thinking of having an affair, this is indirect evidence that can be offered to show the husband's intent to have an affair. However, if this type testimony is given, the court will note that it cannot be offered as proof that the husband actually *had* an affair. The opposing counsel may also attempt to discredit the witness and the testimony by introducing indirect evidence that shows the witness has motive for lying. For example, if someone else heard the witness profess his love for the husband's wife, the hearsay can be offered as indirect evidence to show the witness has a motive for lying about the husband.

The third type of evidence is called circumstantial evidence. Here is where direct evidence can be cast into some shadow of doubt. Although the receipt and film from the lingerie store show direct evidence that the husband lied about his whereabouts, it does not directly prove that the husband is having an affair with the woman on film. While the receipt and film are direct evidence of the husband's lying, it exists as circumstantial evidence of an affair. Circumstantial evidence only provides a logical indication that the client's assertion is true. In the court of law, the evidence can be used by opposing counsel in an attempt to prove or disprove the client's assertion. For example, your client's lawyer may claim the evidence shows the lingerie purchase was intended for the mistress. The husband's lawyer, however, may argue that his client claims the woman on film is a friend who was simply there to assist him in picking out a surprise gift for his wife. The argument may go back and forth, but until direct evidence of philandering can be produced, the affair exists as hearsay — unless, of course, you produce enough indirect or circumstantial evidence. Let us now suppose both indirect and circumstantial evidence shows that:

- The husband lied several times about his whereabouts and met the other woman every time at a different location.
- The husband's wife said she never received the gift.
- The witness heard the husband say he was thinking of having an affair.
- Surveillance logs and video footage show dates and times when the husband entered and left the woman's apartment.
- The wife said she smelled perfume on his collar when he came home.

By now, you should have a clear indication of what your job as an evidence collector should be. When you take a case, the main objective is to find the truth by collecting direct evidence that either supports or negates the client's claim. If you cannot collect direct evidence, you will have to collect enough indirect or circumstantial evidence that leads everyone to the belief that no other conclusion is possible. In essence, if you collect enough circumstantial evidence, it may be just as good as collecting one piece of direct evidence that supports or disproves the client's claim altogether.

Chain of Custody

During an ongoing civil or criminal investigation, it is entirely possible that evidence will change hands among investigators, the police, and crime labs. Opposing counsel is aware of this process and may attempt to challenge the admissibility of evidence by looking for mistakes in how the evidence was handled, claiming the evidence at some point became unprotected, possibly tainted, and should thus be considered inadmissible in court. In the new age of advanced forensic science, any evidence that has been responsibly collected, preserved, and analyzed by a lab — such as blood type or a packet of heroin — can make its authenticity extremely difficult for opposing counsel to refute.

To ensure admissibility of evidence in court, those who handle and possess evidence during an investigation must follow a protocol in order to preserve what is known as the *chain of custody*. The chain of custody refers to the chronological documentation of seized evidence, including who first collected it, how it was itemized, who received possession of evidence, where it was transferred, and details of analysis.

Between most agencies, states, and even countries, guidelines for the chain of custody remain fairly consistent. They require that evidence should not be changed, examiners be professionally competent to handle the evidence, authorization is granted to receive the evidence, evidence logs are created to track all handling, and the person in charge of the evidence is held responsible for ensuring the guidelines are adhered to. Keeping an accurate track of the evidence creates a "road map" from beginning to end and holds each handler in the chain of custody responsible for the evidence while it is in his or her possession. Most importantly, it helps to ensure that evidence is protected from being tainted by someone through deliberate or unintentional means.

As a private detective, the chain of custody begins when you find yourself in discovery of evidence that no one has seen yet. When collected, you are the first person to assume custody of something that could later be used by lawyers in a courtroom or by police to assist in their investigation of a crime. Most investigators keep track of evidence in the chain of custody by marking each item with a serial identifier that allows investigators to locate and track it. If a blood sample has been taken from a crime scene, the item could be marked by the year, the name of the case, a letter, and a number. For example, if Joe Smith has been murdered, and the investigator collects a blood sample, the item could be marked as "10 Smith A.2." The number "10" would mark the year of the case (2010), the name of the case (Smith), the letter "A" relating to what group of items the blood sample was categorized under (DNA items), and the number 2 would be the actual item in the grouping (the blood sample).

To preserve the chain of custody, evidence should be sealed and locked away in a safe location designated specifically for storing evidence. Private investigators should at least have a fireproof safe or a storage room protected under lock-and-key for such a purpose. When the evidence changes hands in the chain of custody, it must be recorded on a standard evidence log and signed by the parties involved in the exchange. Maintaining an evidence log for each handler proves the chain of custody. Each log should provide answers to questions regarding:

- The identification of the item(s)
- The date it was originally collected
- The date the individual or agency received it
- Why the individual or agency is currently handling it
- How they received it

- Who they received it from
- Who handled it previously
- Where it has traveled and been stored

If documentation to one of these questions cannot be provided or a gap exists at any juncture in the chain of custody, opposing counsel may ask for a motion to declare the evidence inadmissible in court. When evidence is handed to another individual or agency, the chain of custody form should be updated with a new form attached to the top of the stack. In today's world of digital technology, many forms of forensic evidence can be stored electronically. Digital storage has broadened the scope of collecting evidence because it can be used to trace and obtain an endless host of electronic items, such as deleted e-mails, banking records, or Internet activity. It has also made the chain of custody easier to preserve.

For most private investigators, the evidence they handle and collect may come in the form of video recordings, photographs, court records, or written statements. A smart private investigator may even contract a computer forensics expert to review and document the electronic algorithms before and after copies of the digital evidence are passed on to other individuals or agencies.

When handing off digital evidence, always make a copy for the individual or agency requesting permission to handle it. Doing so prevents the inadmissibility of evidence in the event that a copy becomes tainted or appears to have been tampered with in the chain of custody. The chronological record will also show who possessed the evidence when it became tainted if the algorithms do not match. Also, keep the original in a safe or locked storage room. When an investigator testifies in court, the investigator's testimony is usually more important than bringing the actual evidence into the courtroom. No original form of evidence should be used in court if it can be properly copied or officially represented in some other way. In fact, many judges will allow an affidavit to stand in place of the evidence and may even eliminate the need to subpoena the investigator for testimony. For example, if an investigator signs an affidavit that identifies who they are and what they found, it can be submitted as a sufficient form of evidence or testimony. Doing this can sometimes cut down on the amount of subpoenas investigators receive or evidence that must be copied and presented to the court.

Working with the Police

There are several situations in which private investigators might find themselves working with local police departments. When conducting a background search, check local arrest records. Gleaning information over the phone from local law enforcement is generally easier than obtaining records from state agencies. As we previously discussed, arrest records pled down to misdemeanors will show up on file in either the county court records or the local precinct. Most police departments are amenable. If they refuse to give out information over the phone, try to fax or mail a records request, but expect to be charged a small fee for information.

Locating teenage runaways

When taking a teen runaway case, it is recommended that a missing persons report be filed immediately with the local police department and the National Crime Information Center. Do not expect much assistance from the police when conducting a skip search. At best, the police will assign an officer who handles juvenile offender. Get the name of that person and communicate directly with him or her during the skip search. By registering the teen's name, birth date, and physical description with the National Crime Information Center, you expand the search nationally in case the teen has moved cross-country. The police do not have the time or manpower sustain a long-term search due to the sheer number of people reported missing every day. Regardless, filing a report on behalf of the parents alerts the local and state police to the case. It also prepares them for the possibility that they may have to apprehend the subject if located.

In some cases, the runaway teen may have already been picked up for loitering and is being held at a juvenile detention center. Filing a report covers the possibility that the teen has already been apprehended by a state or local agency. If so, the police will interview the teen in conjunction with a social worker to make sure the situation at home is not dangerous. If they determine the situation to be safe, they will award custody to the investigator working for the parents. Because teens are minors and the teen's parents have hired the investigator, the police will turn the child over to the investigator. By hiring the investigator, the parents have given their permission to the investigator to act on their behalf.

Should you successfully locate a runaway teenager at a boarding house, a friend's place, or some other public or private residence, note the location, call the police, and ask to have a squad car sent for the minor at that location. If the teen leaves the location, use the tailing techniques described in Chapter 6 and notify the precinct that the subject is on the move. Do not attempt to apprehend the teen yourself; you do not have the authority to do so. You must call the police and ask to have the teen picked up and then retrieve the teen from police custody.

Coordinating with police during surveillance

Surveillance operations will also require some kind of limited coordination with the police. Just before you begin an operation, call the local dispatcher with a request to alert all patrol units of your intention to conduct an operation in the area, providing your name, license number, vehicle description, and tag number. Notifying the dispatcher beforehand avoids the embarrassment of explaining yourself to the police after a neighbor becomes suspicious of your vehicle and reports it. Attracting unwanted attention may also cause the case to become heated if the subject sees a police car outside his or her window. Follow the same protocol when conducting an operation around an apartment complex by asking the front desk if they have a courtesy officer on premise. Some officers even live there under reduced rent in exchange for keeping watch to scare off criminals. The courtesy officer may even assist you by providing a vantage point if he or she believes the subject poses a threat to the safety of the community.

Examining crimes scenes after a police investigation

When dealing with a law enforcement agency, always be courteous, professional, and appear easy to work with, even if they behave rudely. Doing so increases the chance of establishing working relationships and valuable contacts when needed. Never do anything to intervene with a police investigation, even if that investigation is relevant to your own case. Investigators who get in the way of a crime scene before the police have processed it may be charged with tampering with evidence. Should you be the first to discover a crime scene, do not touch any of the evidence. Instead, report it to the police and wait for them to arrive. Once they have processed the scene, you are free to examine the area for yourself.

Taping off the area is the only permissible action for a private investigator to take when arriving first at a crime scene. Cordoning off the area prevents people from entering the space and contaminating the evidence left behind. The police process crime scenes for two main reasons: to determine what happened and to collect clues that lead to the perpetrator. When the police have finished their work, try to obtain a copy of the report to see what they found and have concluded. They begin the process by starting with the exterior, checking for pry marks at the entrance or broken glass. Using latex gloves, crime scene investigators work their way to the interior of the scene, looking for pieces of evidence, such as blood, cigarette butts, fingerprints, or anything that might contain traces of DNA. No investigator should attempt to collect evidence without proper training in forensic science. Most of the time, the police report alone should provide enough information without having to visit the area personally. Putting in a request to enter the chain of custody should give you everything you need to conduct your own investigation.

Subpoena and Courtroom Testimony

Investigators who close cases for their clients know that their involvement in the case may not end once payment for the final invoice has been received. Although it may be necessary to work with law enforcement *during* an investigation, you are likely to spend time working with lawyers *after* the investigation has concluded. In cases pertaining to legal matters — such as infidelity cases that lead to divorce trials or adoption and estate searches — clients may have their lawyers present when meeting you for the first time. If not, the investigator should ask if he or she has an attorney. If the client has an attorney and the case is likely to wind up in court as a criminal trial, the attorney will want to protect what is known as the *work product rule*. Work product simply refers to evidence or materials prepared for litigation that does not have to be legally shared with opposing counsel. By law, protecting the work product rule means the investigator must deal with the lawyer rather than the client. *We will discuss work product more in depth a little later in this chapter.*

When a case is headed to court, private investigators should prepare for cross-examination by opposing counsel. Being called for cross-examination means the opposing counsel has requested your presence in court to answer questions regarding the investigation. The opposing counsel's questions may be aimed at contradicting your testimony, revealing mistakes in your methods to cast doubt over the evidence, reducing your credibility as a witness, or asking questions designed to hurt your client's case. Properly using all the investigative techniques in this book will ensure the credibility of the evidence and the methods employed. However, any question that opposing counsel asks must be answered truthfully, whether it hurts your client's case or not. Falsely answering questions under oath is perjury and not worth the penalties faced if found guilty. Once the cross-examination is over, your client's attorney will have the opportunity for a redirect, which means he or she can counter by asking questions designed to support your credibility, the evidence, and ultimately, the client's case.

Investigators who receive subpoenas should immediately notify their client's lawyer. The lawyer will then prepare you for any questions the opposing counsel may ask. During cross-examination, opposing counsel will look for visible signs of uncertainty or hesitation in the testimony. Review all the details of the case before taking the stand, including dates and times, surveillance logs, video files, photographs, and anything that will make details of the investigation easier to recall. A private investigator's testimony must be truthful, but it is your calm and cool performance on the stand that makes lawyers comfortable with calling you as a witness. Other than investigative competency, it is the best way to get referrals to work with other lawyers. To prepare for cross-examination in a civil case, your client's lawyer may apprise you of the Federal Rules of Civil Procedure, which govern how courtroom procedures work. In a criminal case, he or she may review the Federal Rules of Criminal Procedure. The rules in both types of cases explain procedural terms such as "discovery" "leading the witness," "hearsay," "relevance," and what it means to "overrule" and "sustain" an objection. Some lawyers will assume these procedures to be known and understood, so to read up on the rules by visiting the U.S. Courts Web site (**www.uscourts.gov/rules/civil2007.pdf and www.uscourts. gov/rules/crim2007.pdf**) civil and criminal procedures.

Taking Depositions for Attorneys

Besides being subpoenaed for cross-examination, taking depositions or written statements from witnesses is the second most common reason you may find yourself working with an attorney. A deposition is a statement taken by a witness in written or recorded form. While attorneys will schedule the date and time of the deposition, investigators are usually hired by the client to facilitate the recording because they typically charge less than attorneys to get written statements from witnesses. During a deposition, a court reporter will be assigned to record the conversation between the investigator and the witness.

The key to conducting a successful deposition is having the interpersonal skills that will set the person at ease and make him or her feel relaxed enough to answer your questions truthfully. In some cases, informants will agree to answer depositions. Informants are those who have intimate knowledge of something relevant to a case and have decided to cooperate without the knowledge or consent of others. The key to taking written statements from witnesses and informants is to establish a level of trust during the interview. To get the answers you are looking for, emotional incentives are more effective than logical reasoning. If the witness genuinely likes you, he or she will be more inclined to help you.

The best way to establish a rapport with a witness or informant is to become his or her friend and show that you share his or her point of view. Before swearing them in, smile, ask them about their personal life, find some common ground to show you can relate to them. Use the first five minutes to get a feel for his or her beliefs, opinions, and motivators. Even if you must pretend to think like the witness, do so, and he or she will begin to trust you with information in his or her possession.

Once you have earned the witness's trust, mask your intentions by maintaining a casual manner and asking broad questions at the beginning. Doing so allows you to segue into the questions you really want answered without putting that person on guard.

When a private investigator begins a deposition, he or she will begin by using an audio or video recorder to state his or her own name and occupation and the date, time, location, and purpose of the recording. In addition, he or she will introduce the witness by verbally announcing his or her name, including the names of those present during the deposition. Next, the investigator should require the witness to take a formal oath acknowledging the fact that his or her statements are being recorded.

Depositions are not always used as evidence, especially if the testimony damages your client's case. Rather, it is used primarily to find out what a witness knows, so the lawyer will know in advance what the witness plans to say if called to testify in court. In court, if the witness says anything contrary to what has been written in the transcript, he or she will be held accountable and may be guilty of committing perjury. When initiating a deposition, it is important to make sure the witness verbally acknowledges the purpose of the deposition on record.

Depositions are usually scheduled in an attorney's office. By law, the witness is allowed to have his or her attorney present during the questioning. Always remember to bring a copy of the witness's subpoena to the deposition in case the witness fails to show up, and his or her absence needs to be documented. Depositions vary according to their length. Some are no more than 15 minutes, others can last several sessions and span more than a week. When taking a deposition, it is important that the investigator ask questions that are both precise and relevant to the witness's involvement in the case. Speak slowly so the conversation on the recording is clear and the witness can understand what is being asked. If a question or response needs to be eliminated from record, you can ask the court reporter to "strike" it from the transcript.

If the attorney of the witness is present, he or she may form an objection to a question and advise the witness not to answer. Objections may be raised if the question is incriminating to his or her witness or biased. Questions in depositions should also be designed to determine whether the witness's testimony is favorable or unfavorable to the case. Questions should also be used to clarify any contracts or documents that need to be explained or authenticated. When referring to an important document that the witness is being asked to confirm or explain in a deposition, make sure the document is copied and attached as an exhibit. If the witness is going to be used for expert testimony, such as providing technical or professional opinions that support the client's case, the witness should also be asked to briefly explain his or her educational and professional qualifications in the matter before questioning.

Questions in the deposition should proceed in chronological order to make everything clear to the witness. Some witnesses will later try to deny statements made in a deposition, claiming they did not understand a question and, therefore, answered it incorrectly. However, if you state before and after that any question he or she answers is assumed to be understood, the witness cannot use this as an excuse to deny anything while being questioned during a trial. Their answers in the deposition cannot be refuted.

Using emotional incentive is also a valuable technique for getting a confession during an interrogation. Contrary to popular portrayals on television, effective interrogators are more likely to use methods that make the suspect want to reveal information rather than being threatened into a confession. The experience of most investigators working criminal cases is that many criminals possess a superiority complex that can be exploited. Sometimes, the superiority complex is so prevalent that the criminal is subconsciously dying to show how easy it was to fool the authorities. An expert interrogator can bring out these secret desires by playing along. By figuring out what motivates the suspect, you will be able to push the right emotional buttons and get the confession.

The Work Product Rule

Under Exemption 5 of the Freedom of Information Act, work product constitutes any materials or notes attorneys plan to use to support their client's case. Work product may be transcripts from depositions or evidence from the investigator's report. When a case goes to trial, both attorneys are required to present a list of their witnesses to one another. When both attorneys see the witness list, they schedule depositions for each to find out what information the witness has regarding the case. Work product is anything else that the attorney is not required to show the opposing counsel when preparing for litigation. In other words, the materials are not subject to what is known as "discovery." If work product is shared, the attorney sharing the information loses work product privilege, which means it is now in discovery, and the opposing counsel is allowed to use the material in court. For example, if your client's attorney gives the transcript from the deposition or the report from your investigation to the other attorney, the materials are no longer considered work product and become legal possession of opposing counsel as potential evidence that can be used against your client in court. The opposing counsel can then bring in experts to refute the evidence or use your transcript during cross-examination of the witness.

Attorneys covet work product because it allows them to build their case while preventing the materials from being used by opposing counsel to build theirs.

Although the work product rule is not applicable in civil cases, the attorneys you work with in criminal cases will want to protect their materials from discovery. Many attorneys employ in-house investigators, so if you are hired by a client as an outside investigator, you must deal directly with an attorney if it is a criminal case that is going to trial and the attorney wants to retain work product privileges. If the work is coming from an attorney, invoice the attorney's firm rather than the client on all services pertaining to your time in court, even if the subpoena comes from opposing counsel. Invoices should also be sent there regarding the work product materials you collaborate on, such as investigations, depositions, and interrogations.

CASE STUDY: HOW WORK-ING WITH LAW ENFORCEMENT CAN TURN INTO REFERRALS & PROFITS

Rocky Pipkin, President
Pipkin Detective Agency
California License PI16269
2211 W. Whitendale, Suite D, Visalia, California 93277
www.pipkindetectiveagency.com
info@pipkindetectiveagency.com
Phone: (877) 730-3532
Fax: (559) 622-8890

Lawyers and police officers do not generally like dealing with private investigators, so if you can get referrals from lawyers and establish key contacts in the police department, you can carve a great niche for yourself. One of the reasons I decided to specialize in dealing with law firms and law enforcement agencies is because I went to law school and learned about criminal law, procedures, torts, contracts, legal research, writing, and professional responsibility. I also receive annual training from post-certified instructors and attend training classes conducted by private investigation associations, law enforcement officers, and members of the California State Bar. Through these functions, I was lucky enough to meet an attorney who made the mistake of liking me. He has contracted me for all of his criminal investigation cases, which allowed me to network with other lawyers and obtain work from them.

After my first ten years as a private investigator, I came to the realization that criminal investigation was not the most profitable area in the field. We believed that marketing our agency to private businesses and entities would be far more profitable, as the government paid the lowest hourly rate in the industry. Our target niche is to act as a liaison between private businesses and law enforcement agencies. We will usually receive a call from a business indicating that it believes it has a problem with employees either embezzling business assets or products and/or engaging in drug use while at work. We then establish a protocol for capturing evidence of the misconduct and providing it to the business owners. If the owners want the employee prosecuted, we present details of the case to our key law enforcement contacts, and they make an arrest.

CHAPTER 9
Ethical & Legal Issues

When someone does something wrong or against a set of established rules, we call their conduct unethical, or against ethics. Ethics is the cultural or professional philosophy relating to what is considered the difference between right and wrong in human behavior. Ethical rules are created when professionals or members of society have the freedom to make choices. As a form of guidance, those choices need to be defined as right or wrong so the empowered individual or professional understands the gravity of his or her actions as well as how it affects them and others.

While laws are designed to promote ethical behavior, ethics are not always enforced by laws. The act of lying is considered illegal in some cases and simply unethical in others. In other words, although two types of lies may both be unethical, the consequences may vary depending on whether or not the behavior is against written law. For instance, lying to a family member in a culture that promotes honesty may be unethical and may have consequences on your relationship, but there is nothing illegal about it. If you lie to the Supreme Court under oath, it is unethical *and* illegal, and the consequences will be enforced by perjury laws. Maintaining ethical behavior at all times should be one of the highest priorities for a private investigator. The ethics of private investigation are your guidepost. Knowing where the boundaries fall between right and wrong will always determine how to deal with any given situation.

The best way to understand the proper conduct of a private investigator is to understand common examples of how *not* to behave. Unfortunately, unscrupulous practices in this field are not unheard of. Information is power, and in some cases, unethical people will use it to harm others. For example, in 2007, an investigator with the Nevada Department of Taxation was accused of extorting money from business owners after discovering they were in violation of state liquor laws. Extortion is a criminal tactic used by one person to obtain information, property, or money from another person by means of coercion and threats. In the case of the Nevada Department of Taxation, the investigator agreed to quash his report to the Department of Taxation in exchange for monetary payments. Many times, the victim is compelled to cooperate, but occasionally, the extortionist's crime is reported, as was the case in Nevada when the investigator was charged with eight criminal counts of extortion. In this example, the investigator's behavior was illegal and unethical.

An extortionist will often use information to bribe someone. Other times, he or she may take the information and resell it in order to double the earnings. For example, suppose an investigator is asked to compile evidence of parental abuse in a child custody case. He or she gathers evidence, but then promises the target not to report the evidence in exchange for money. That way, the investigator is paid by the target, tells the client no evidence was found, and bills the client for his services.

Worse than the extortionist is the investigator who coerces people into giving information by physical threats or actual battery. Unless you are a bounty hunter and a bondsman has granted you the power to arrest a fugitive, physical coercion is against the law. If someone uses a verbal threat, it may not be illegal, but it is highly unethical. No investigator should behave in a manner that harms or intends harm to another person.

Artificially inflating a bill of service may not be illegal, but it is also highly unethical, and anyone caught doing such a thing risks being reported to the Better Business Bureau (BBB). If you misrepresent your investigative credentials or charge clients for less than your best effort, you are essentially committing the unethical practice of defrauding the client. The BBB has offices in every state, and its purpose is to report information on businesses and alert the public to various frauds and scams that abound. News stations that do troubleshooting segments will often mine the local offices for stories about area businesses that have been investigated by the BBB. The last thing any investigator running a local agency wants is to cement a reputation as a scam artist on television for everyone to see. Many businesses have paid dearly this way — all for a little extra money they thought they could get away with making.

One of the most common unethical practices in the field of private investigation is corporate or industrial espionage. Corporate espionage occurs when one business engages in the practice of acquiring its competitor's trade secrets. Trade secrets are anything that a business designs, formulates, researches, to improve their product or service. Corporate espionage is essentially an attempt to steal intellectual property to gain a competitive advantage. According to Pat Choate, author of *Hot Property: The Stealing of Ideas in the Age of Globalization,* corporate espionage has grown from an American problem to a worldwide issue, especially in Russia, China, and Taiwan. According to Choate, "Among the 3,000 Chinese firms in the United States, a large number of them are engaged in piracy or stealing secrets and sending them back to China."

Computer hackers are trained to break into databases that contain trade secrets. Though it may be tempting for a cop to take impounded drug money, it may be equally as tempting for a computer forensic specialist to steal from companies without any regard for the law. If stealing trade secrets does not sound like a common unethical practice, consider the fact that a legal form of espionage can be achieved by reverse engineering a product. Reverse engineering is the process of discovering how a publicly sold product is made by analyzing its structure, function, and operation. For instance, if a drug company releases a pill for pain relief, another company can use technicians to study the ingredients, create a similar pill, and market it at a cheaper price. Many no-frills products will go as far as to state on the box what brand it resembles.

The greatest responsibility an investigator has is keeping the trust of a client. Ethical investigators not only refrain from practices they know are unethical, they find better ways of conducting their investigations when they sense the boundary between ethical and unethical is about to be crossed. By adhering to the division of licensing rules of privacy covered during training, you protect the client, the profession, and yourself. For investigators, trespassing and wiretapping are two of the major issues. Trespassing occurs when someone enters private property without permission. It is considered an offense against the person who owns the land. There are two types of trespassing offenses enforced by law: civil and criminal. Criminal trespassing is the act of unlawfully entering an enclosed property such as a home or business. Criminal trespassing is enforced by police, sheriffs, and private security. Civil trespassing occurs when property damage has occurred and requires the landowner to file the matter in court and sue for damages that have resulted from the offense.

Trespassing can be difficult to prosecute because some level of intent needs to be proven. In this case, the trespasser must knowingly enter private property without permission. More than likely, if a subject catches someone prowling around his or her home and neighborhood, it may be easier to prove intent over someone caught trespassing on the grounds of an office building or hotel. Most states agree that entering abandoned property does not constitute trespassing. However, there is some varying interpretation between states as to what constitutes abandoned property. For example, some investigators conduct a trash cover search by milling through the contents of a garbage can. Conducting a trash cover search can yield information about the subject's consumption habits or letters that reveal who he or she has been associating with and, in some instances, can provide the investigator necessary information to begin a background search, such as billing statements.

Some states say the property is not considered abandoned until it is picked up by the sanitation department, while other states say anything discarded by the owner is abandoned, even if it still remains in the owner's garbage can. If a client requests a trash cover search, and you think it could be considered trespassing, consult with a lawyer and ask if the state allows this type of action. If the act is legal, call the sanitation department to see what day the trash in that area is picked up. People usually set out their trash the night before pickup. Intercept the subject's trash regularly for a period of two or three weeks and sort through it carefully with a mask, noting all of the items.

Wiretapping is also stringently defined and enforced if privacy laws are violated. In Chapter 5, we explored the difference between a bug and a wiretap. Wiretaps involve the interception of phone lines by a third party. If a client requests a wiretap, it is strongly recommended that you deny the request and not condone it in any way. Wiretapping is illegal conduct for a private investigator without government security clearance. If you do have clearance, expect to abide by what is known as the one or all-party state laws. In other words, a one-party state law allows the recording of an intercepted phone conversation if only one party in the conversation has expressed knowledge and consent of the recording. Other states mandate the all-party state law, which requires the knowledge and consent of both parties in a conversation. Parents who want to record the phone conversations of their children in one-party states are allowed to record conversations in which the parents are not participants because minors forfeit consent to the parent or guardian. This technicality would not be applicable in all-party states. The following states require two-party notification:

- California
- Connecticut
- Delaware
- Florida
- Massachusetts
- Maryland
- Michigan

- Montana
- New Hampshire
- Pennsylvania
- Washington

* All other states require one-party consent

Peeping Tom Law

When working an infidelity case, be aware of the Peeping Tom Law. This law states that anyone who secretly "peeps" through windows for the purpose of seeing undressed women or couples making love can be charged with a Class A1 Misdemeanor. Even if an investigator is assigned to record evidence of infidelity, taking a nude or lewd photograph of two people in a bedroom, restroom, shower, or dressing room without their consent violates their privacy. If the opportunity to record infidelity arises, always try to get pictures of the couple before they fully engage in a sexual act. The best way to record marital infidelity and avoid violating any laws is to keep it G-rated and get amorous actions in public on record. To protect yourself from violating privacy laws, never record graphic sexual activities within private rooms or locations protected under this law. Be aware that if it can be proven that a nude photograph was taken for the purposes of arousing sexual desire, the penalty upgrades to a Class 1 felony.

Drivers Protection Privacy Act

Knowing state and federal laws establishes the line between having access to information and understanding what is considered theft of information. Pulling information from the DMV used to be routine for private investigators, but over the last 20 years the amount of information the DMV will release has grown increasingly smaller due to the Drivers Protection Privacy Act (DPPA). The DPPA was enacted as a result of a stalker by the name of Robert John Bardo who hired a private investigator to retrieve the home address of an actress named Rebecca Schaeffer. The investigator retrieved the information through the DMV and gave it to Bardo, who wound up killing the actress at her residence. How your clients choose to use the information you provide them is their responsibility. You will, however, be held responsible if the information is obtained in ways that clearly violate an established privacy law designed to protect the public. The DPPA lists licensed private investigators as one of its exceptions, but the investigator can only obtain the information for specific reasons, which include:

- Information considered relevant to an ongoing investigation (such as auto accidents or hit-and-run)
- Working in conjunction with government, court, or law enforcement activity
- Conducting employee background checks
- Investigating for civil, criminal, or arbitration cases
- Working insurance cases
- Written consent by the individual

A licensed investigator can send for a request form to the DMV. The form will ask the investigator for personal information (name, address, social security number) as well as the nature of the request. Unlicensed detectives may be tempted to exploit the DPPA by using someone who falls under one of the exceptions — such as a cop, automotive marketer, or licensed detective — but doing so is considered theft of information by both parties. Theft of information depends on the method used to obtain information rather than who is obtaining it. If you plan to retrieve a person's financial information from a credit bureau, you will have to contend with the Gramm-Leach-Bliley Act, which makes it illegal to use pretexts to gain an individual's financial data. The Federal Trade Commission enforces the law by conducting sting operations on detectives who publicly offer services that may involve retrieving information on personal assets or credit information. As discussed in Chapter 5, there can be a difference between what is considered pretexting and what is considered a deceptive practice.

Gramm-Leach Bliley Act

The Gramm-Leach Bliley Act only prohibits the act of using pretexts on financial institutions. A deceptive practice, however, can be used to obtain information directly from a consumer or non-financial institution if you already have a parcel of information pertaining to their financial records, such as a social security number. For example, obtaining a social security number through a pay database and pretexing a hospital as an insurance company representative to verify or obtain a patient's records would not be considered illegal under the GLBA. According to FTC Commissioner Joel Winston, acting in such a manner might be considered a deceptive practice, but is not considered pretexting because you are not contacting a financial institution. However, the FTC may determine the legality of such actions on a case-by-case basis, so make sure the information is not resold or made privy to anyone unconnected to the case. If a client such as a spouse or insurance adjuster requests a background search that involves obtaining financial information, write a clause into the contract acknowledging that he or she has been explained the rules of the GLBA and can be held responsible if proven to be in violation of the law.

Knowing Your State and Local Laws

Because some states vary on licensing requirements, any investigator operating with an out-of-state license can potentially run into some legal trouble with state or local authorities. For example, a private investigator's license from California may grant you the privilege of conducting a surveillance operation in a residential area, but if you try it in Texas, your license — along with the privilege to operate — might not be recognized. Activities covered under federal law — such as pulling information from the DMV — should protect you from getting in the type of trouble that would cost you a license, but you may have a harder time getting information protected by another state. The offense could also wind up being very expensive. In Nevada, for example, first time offenders operating without permission to conduct business out-of-state can be hit with penalties of up to $1,500, even though some investigators consider the act of fining a licensed private investigator to be a restraint of trade. Restraint of trade refers to the act of unlawfully placing restrictions or penalties on an individual who has been legally granted the freedom to conduct business.

Quite simply, states are not inclined to encourage out-of-state investigators from conducting an investigation in their jurisdiction. The concern for most states is that these investigators do not meet their licensing or insurance requirements. If an out-of-state investigator were to be sued for damages by someone, the investigator may not have enough bond or liability insurance to cover the damages, or the investigator may come from a state that allows one-party consent and may break a privacy law by wiretapping an individual from state that requires consent from both parties. In states where gun permits are strictly enforced, the penalty for carrying an unlicensed firearm could mean jail time. Private investigators routinely operate without firearms. Those who carry licensed firearms from another state should report their firearms to the out-of-state division of licensing to avoid getting in trouble with the law.

Despite the legal entanglement involved, some states have recognized the need for cooperation, and have formed *reciprocity agreements*. Reciprocity agreements between states are mutual agreements designed to allow licensed investigators to follow a case across state lines without having to obtain a license in the state they are traveling to. According to the California Department of Consumer Affairs, some states require no agreement and will allow you to operate with your out-of state license. Detectives who anticipate out-of-state leads should check with their own division of licensing office to see what reciprocity agreement, if any, exists with the state in question. For example, the Florida division of licensing office has reciprocity agreements with California, Georgia, Louisiana, North Carolina, Oklahoma, Tennessee, and Virginia. Under a reciprocity agreement, an investigator is privileged to operate, but only in deference to out-of-state laws. If no reciprocity agreement exists and a state license is required, it is better to contract the services of a licensed investigator from that state rather than risk any legal complications.

Reciprocity agreements are also temporary in nature. In other words, detectives allowed across state lines have investigative privileges for the duration of that case only. Never offer services to an individual, attorney, or business located in a state you are not licensed to operate in. If you plan to expand your business to another state, you will have to obtain another state license or expand the payroll to employ investigators licensed in that state.

The ever-changing nature of state laws only demonstrates the importance of consistently maintaining contact with the division of licensing. For example, if a state furthers its restrictions on obtaining records, you will need to know how it affects your relationship with information brokers. Because these brokers are considered research and marketing companies, federal law allows them access to records. Federal provisions list brokers — along with licensed investigators — as exceptions under laws such as the DPPA. Detectives rely on information brokers to retrieve information they may have had trouble finding, such as unpublished numbers or consumer credit card charges. If the information broker retrieves information in ways no longer considered legal, you will also be held responsible in conjunction with violating a privacy law.

When it comes to knowing state and federal laws, no one may know less about privacy laws than clients who request telephone wiretaps on their employees in states that require two-party consent. In fact, not even surveillance operations with a video camera should be accompanied by an audio recording, as Title III of the federal wiretap statute makes it illegal to intercept not only electronic communications but oral communication as well. Investigators who forget to turn off the audio and get caught recording the subject's conversations in public are guilty of violating the statute if the video footage is accompanied by audio and handed to the client or introduced as evidence in court. On the other hand, employers are allowed to use extensions to monitor telephone conversations during the day for business and "quality assurance purposes," but Title III states that the recording must be cut out or omitted from record when conversations venture toward personal subject matter. To learn more about U.S. telephone recording laws, visit the Reporters Committee for Freedom of the Press Web site at **www.rcfp.org/taping**. In 13 states, privacy laws also restrict the use of video surveillance in private areas. Private areas are defined as any place where there is a reasonable expectation of privacy. They include company bathrooms, dressing rooms, private homes, rental apartments, hotel rooms, and bathrooms. If a company wants to install hidden cameras in a private area such as their bathrooms, advise him or her to contact the National Labor Relations Board for approval at **www.nlrb.gov**. Knowing exactly which states protect private areas will make you a more knowledgeable consultant and will keep your client out of trouble with the law. The 13 states that prohibit video surveillance in private areas are:

- Alabama
- Arkansas
- California
- Delaware
- Georgia
- Hawaii
- Kansas
- Maine
- Michigan
- Minnesota
- New Hampshire
- South Dakota
- Utah

If you uncover a crime related to an ongoing private investigation, it is your professional duty to report it. If your client has committed a crime or reporting a crime appears to violate the confidentiality agreement with your client, you have an ethical decision to make. This decision is more ethical than legal because division of licensing laws regarding this matter tend to be somewhat nebulous. You are expected to report a crime, but most division of licensing disciplinary codes do not specifically mention it. For example, under Chapter 11.3 of the California Business and Professions code, otherwise known as the Private Investigator's Act, Article 6 states:

"The director may suspend or revoke a license [if the licensee determines] that any of its officers, directors, partners, or its manager has committed any act… constituting dishonesty or fraud. 'Dishonesty or fraud' as used in this section, includes, in addition to other acts not specifically enumerated herein…"

Some investigators believe specific acts of "dishonesty or fraud" have been left vague by the division of licensing for the purpose of allowing the state review board to enforce the disciplinary laws at their discretion. Either way, it is better to let the client know that confidentiality will be strictly adhered to, though if a crime has been committed, you are ethically obligated to report any wrong-doing. If the client objects, simply refuse to take the case. When reporting a crime, go directly to the state or local police. If you have an evidence report, make a photocopy of the file and get the original documents notarized as originals.

Liability

State liability policies require that investigators carry bond or liability insurance, and the amount differs from state-to-state. On average, investigators will carry between $10,000 to $25,000 in insurance to cover death, property damage, and personal injury. Large corporations are more apt to hire agencies that carry more than $1 million in coverage. Private investigation is considered a risky business. The point of carrying bond or liability insurance is to provide financial protection for you and others should damages or expenses be incurred from legal fees and court costs as a result of errors in judgment, negligence, or wrongdoing committed during an investigation. To find out how much liability insurance is necessary to operate, contact the state division of licensing office or visit its Web site.

Liability can be a costly consequence of negligence, error in judgment, or wrongdoing. In recent years, legislation and court rulings have increased pressure on both private investigators and information brokers, holding them liable for damages caused by selling and obtaining information that resulted in a crime. The death of Amy Lynn Boyer was perhaps one of the most famous cases involving a private investigator whose client used information to commit a crime. In 1999, Liam Youens paid an online private investigation service to obtain information on Boyer, a former classmate he had become obsessed with. By obtaining her social security number, the investigator was able to pinpoint Boyer's employment address, which Youens later used to find and ultimately kill her. The investigator, who used a pretext to obtain employment information from her over the phone, was sued for wrongful death, invasion of privacy, and violation of the Fair Credit Reporting Act. Following the trial, the Supreme Court ruled that any investigator who obtains a person's work address by pretexting and sells information to a client may be liable for damages to the person who has been deceived by the pretext.

It has been argued by professional investigators that wrongful death suits threaten to destroy the business of skip tracing, which has helped thousands of other clients. To support a wrongful death claim, one needs evidence that the investigator showed a breach of duty through illegal action or lack of professional judgment, resulting in a wrongful death. In the case of Amy Lynn Boyer, the investigator was charged with wrongful death because Youen's intentions should have appeared obvious to the investigator based on the purported signs of mental instability exhibited in Youens. Youens committed suicide just shortly after killing Boyer with a gun.

Liability and wrongful death puts professional detectives in an uncomfortable spot because one cannot always know the ultimate intent of each client or be able to judge his or her intent with complete certainty. According to author and 17-year professional investigator L. Scott Harrell, detectives can take measurable precautions against providing information to people with harmful intentions. "We have to act responsibly. This is part of the ethics of skip tracing. The bottom line is when more instances like the Boyer homicide make it to press, and then to legislators, the more our tools are going to be taken away and our jobs will become increasingly difficult and less profitable," Harrell said.

Harrell's solution is to write a Subject's Right of Refusal clause into the contract, which states that a client will not receive personal information about the subject, including their location, unless the subject is notified and has the opportunity to either give consent or refuse to make the information available. The consequence of adding this clause may result in the loss of potential clients who do not wish to make their actions known, but according to Harrell, "…if the client is not willing to follow this protocol, then something is certainly wrong…My gut feeling is that the majority of these potential clients are unsteady; their refusal [to sign the clause] helps me make the final decision not to provide investigative services." Detectives should also think about including an "opt-out" clause, which provides the right to cease investigations if the client has lied about his or her intentions. While a right of refusal clause may not completely avert all the dangers of liability, the practice alone should prove in the court of law that you acted responsibly and should lessen the chance of being held liable in a wrongful death suit.

With legislation constantly being enacted to change, limit, or enhance the way detectives operate, the best way to stay current on new laws affecting the profession is through the Investigative and Security Professionals for Legislative Action (ISPLA). The ISPLA was formed by a group of industry professionals with experience in legislative and regulatory affairs. Their Web site can be found at **www.ispla.org**. The goals of the ISPLA include examination of critical issues in the investigative and security trade, providing educational resources, conducting seminars and workshops, acting as liaison to government bodies regarding bills and regulations affecting investigative security and security professionals, and serving as advocates of legislation that protects the trade. For an annual membership fee of $99, investigators can find a local chapter, which the organization has made available on their Web site, and join other professionals interested in protecting their right to operate professionally and ethically without overarching legal restrictions. The ISPLA also has a legislative tracking system that allows members to track legislation in the pipeline at both the state and federal levels. Through membership, the tracker can be accessed on the Web site and will keep you informed on how the law may affect your investigations in the near future. Knowing what legislators are planning allows you to prepare for the consequences or benefits and may deter the possibility of making an error in judgment because you were not clued in to the new law. *Pursuit Magazine* has made the "bill watch" available for free in its ISPLA archives at **www.pursuitmag.com/author/ispla**; although, without membership, you will not have access to the local chapters.

Types of Insurance

Insurance is not a one-size-fits-all solution. Laws vary by state, so some states will have higher premiums based on a number of factors including the number of claims filed overall. If you are licensed to use a firearm, you may find that your insurance costs for that category of service are higher than for other services you provide.

Many states have minimum business insurance standards. A description of some common types of insurance follows. Insurance companies typically offer private investigators insurance for activities that cover general liability, workers' compensation, bond liability, and others.

General liability insurance may be required in your state. This type of insurance will cover your business against unexpected accidents and injuries. Review the policy for exclusions that might leave you vulnerable to exposure under certain circumstances. Read the fine print — do not ignore it or skim over it. For example, if your policy excludes damage caused by drunken employees, the insurance company may not help you if an inebriated employee loses control of your company vehicle.

Know what coverage you need and what coverage an insurance company is providing. If you employ other investigators, you may need to carry workers' compensation insurance. If your work entails following dangerous subjects who could potentially harm you, carry more general liability insurance. Talk to a number of providers and discuss the aspects of your business. Better yet, ask other business owners for referrals to reputable insurance brokers who deal with a range of insurance companies. He or she will shop around for the coverage you need at the lowest cost. The most important part of this process is obtaining the proper coverage. A lower premium is not worth much if you find yourself without the insurance protection you need.

How much liability coverage is enough? A million sounds like a lot, but in today's world, that amount may not be enough. A good minimum is probably $2 million, but $3 million is even safer. If you can afford it, go higher. You will find that insurance companies price this type of insurance reasonably, assuming you do not have a history of claims and judgments and premiums are not based on a dollar-for-dollar fee schedule. For example, $2 million in coverage is less than twice the cost of $1 million, and so on. An insurance broker who specializes in small business coverage can help you determine what you need. Be honest with him or her and do not mislead the broker, or yourself, about what you will be doing in your business — whether it is talking about your surveillance work or the privacy law restrictions you are obligated to observe. Ask questions, write down the coverage you need and any promises regarding coverage from the provider or the broker, and check these items against the actual insurance policy. General liability typically protects investigators in the event of:

- False arrest
- Errors and omissions
- Care, custody, and control
- Invasion of privacy
- Malicious prosecution
- Libel
- Personal injury
- Incidental malpractice

Bonding

If you already have general liability insurance, do you also need to have company and employees bonded? The answer is — sometimes, yes. Liability insurance covers accidental property damage or injury caused by you to your customer's property or people on the site. A surety bond is an agreement the contractor arranges with a bonding company to pay awards to the consumer if the contractor is judged at fault, by arbitration or legal action, if a job is not completed to the customer's satisfaction. State laws differ, but it is common for states to require investigators to carry surety bonds of a certain level, depending on their license category. Bonding is usually a requirement for jobs with the government or large commercial jobs.

Although it is expensive to carry both liability insurance and a surety bond, it helps attract and keep customers who understand that their property and investment will be protected, no matter what. Plus, you can then charge premium rates for your services, because not every private investigation business carries this coverage. You can find a bond provider who works with businesses in your state at the National Association of Surety Bond Producers Web site (**www.nasbp.org/AM/Template.cfm?Section=Find_a_Producer_in_your_State&Template=/CM/HTMLDisplay.cfm&ContentID=1844**).

Employee bonding is a different matter. Employee dishonesty bonds are surety bonds that guarantee compensation if your employee steals property or is otherwise negligent on the job. You may want this coverage because, frankly, you never know what another person is thinking. Talk to your insurance agent to see if it is necessary.

Product liability insurance

Product liability insurance is a separate category that provides protection from problems arising from the products you sell. For example, if you are a debugging or electronic counter measures specialist, you may be selling surveillance equipment to clients. Be sure your business is covered against this type of risk.

Workers' compensation insurance

Workers' compensation insurance is required in every state. However, the structure of the insurance varies by state. Private insurance companies offer this coverage based on the number of employees on the payroll, the roles each individual performs, and the type of business you are operating. However, some states require that such coverage be obtained from the state government or one of its agencies. This insurance pays medical expenses and lost wages for workers who are injured on the job. There are exclusions for certain categories, such as independent contractors, but, again, check your state's laws. Business owners are generally exempt in most cases. If you have identified an investigator you hire to be a contractor based on the nature of his or her services to you, your state may classify that as an exemption. If you have identified an investigator you hire to be an employee of the agency, you will need workers' compensation in the event that he or she sustains an injury while working on the job.

Home-based business insurance

Home-based insurance is required if you are working out of home office. Homeowners' policies rarely cover business losses. If you are operating from your home or garage, check with your insurance agent to see if anything in your office is covered. The typical homeowner's policy specifically excludes home-based business losses, including equipment, theft, loss of data, and personal injury. Unfortunately, many companies that provide homeowner's insurance do not offer business coverage, so you may need to have two insurance companies covering different areas of your home.

Criminal insurance

Criminal insurance covers you in the event that an employee commits a crime. General liability insurance may not cover theft or other criminal acts by employees. If someone is on your payroll, you may be held responsible for his or her actions while he or she is with customers. Should that person steal something, vandalize customer property, or deliberately harm someone, the customer will expect you to assume responsibility. This type of coverage can also protect you in the event of employee embezzlement. Depending on your general liability coverage, you may want to consider this category of insurance. It is difficult to control the actions of investigators who work alone and hold the privileged information of their clients. If an investigator commits perjury in court, extorts a subject, or violates the civil rights of a runaway teen by forcibly apprehending the subject, you will need criminal insurance to protect the agency from being sued for damages as a result of your employee's actions.

Key man insurance

Lenders who provide capital for businesses may require key man insurance. This coverage applies to the person whose absence from the company would cause it to fail. Most likely, that person would be you or a partner, if you have one. If you have borrowed money to start or operate your business, the lender may require such insurance as a guarantee of payment if anything were to happen to you. Most PI agencies around the country begin as a one- or two-person operation; therefore, key man insurance may be required by the lender because the original PI would be the one solely handling cases. Subcontracting work to another trusted investigator while you are unable to perform your regular duties may be a way to avoid having to pay this type of insurance if you are requested to carry it.

Business interruption insurance

Business interruption insurance covers your expenses if you are shut down by fire, natural disaster, or other catastrophes. Some businesses are not as vulnerable to this as others, so look carefully at your other coverage. Assuming your equipment and vehicles are already covered, you may not want to duplicate coverage. Discuss this with your provider or broker.

Vehicle insurance

Vehicle insurance is the commercial version of the insurance you have on your private vehicle. The same price considerations apply: type of vehicle, history of claims, mileage, location, and drivers. If you have employees who will drive your vehicles, their driving records will be considered in the rate you pay, along with yours. Surveillance vehicles are one of the most important aspects of your business. If employees will be using your vehicles for surveillance operations, check their driving records to make sure they will not increase the rates on your vehicle insurance before hiring them.

Ghostwriting

At the beginning of this book, we said that private investigation is not the glamorous job that Hollywood films portray it to be. Surveillance operations may have hours of tedium before the one important moment arrives to document evidence. Privacy restrictions may hamper background searches. Missing persons cases can sometimes lead to frustrating dead ends. No matter what happens over the course of an investigation, you must never cut corners and take the easy way out by documenting false evidence. The act of creating false reports is known as ghostwriting and carries serious consequences for those who are found guilty. In a worst-case scenario, you lose your license and would most likely face criminal prosecution.

To avoid this, be ethical, and always assume that the evidence in any case you take — even if it involves just a few hours worth of work — could wind up in court. A lazy investigator may be tempted to add hours to a bill by detailing interviews in a report that never happened. While this may seem like a harmless con job, the investigator is in serious trouble if those interviews get used as evidence by an attorney trying to prove a client's case. Suddenly, you are subpoenaed to court and testifying under oath that you conducted these phantom interviews — along with each of the witnesses who all claim they have never seen you before. Behind bars, those extra hours you billed no longer seem worth the lifelong price you just paid.

Not only does the act of ghostwriting aim to deceive the client financially, it may end up deceiving the client into thinking he or she has an airtight case with the evidence you have compiled. Even if most of the evidence in your report is true and accurate, the entire report may as well be fictional if just one part of it is proved to have been ghostwritten. Breaking the oath you have taken as an investigator is an offense to the state that licensed you and to the client who trusted your professional acuity. How the client reacts to your findings are not your concern if it the work has been performed in earnest. You will rest better at night knowing the job has been completed with integrity, professionalism, honesty, and most of all, concern for your own self-preservation.

CASE STUDY: ETHICAL DILEMMAS IN CLIENT CONFIDENTIALITY

Lisa Reed, President
LSR Investigations
PO Box 1006, Flemington, NJ 08822
www.lsrinvestigations.com
lisa@lsrinvestigations.com
Phone: (908) 788-0020
Fax: (908) 788-0054

As a private investigator, the biggest ethical dilemma I encountered came in 2007. I was contacted via e-mail by an individual who said he was looking to locate a friend who had just been released from prison. He also wanted information on the title of a car that belonged to someone else, so I took the case and began working for him. To make sure I was not doing anything illegal, I asked my brother, a car salesman, how to go about obtaining a copy of the title, and he suggested I call the dealership.

When I contacted the dealership, they said they never sold a car to the person in question. My client probably did not anticipate that I would uncover this information, but I was already suspicious, so I ran a back ground check on my client's e-mail address and discovered there was no information that correlated with the name he gave me. After investigating my client, I eventually learned that he was on America's Most Wanted list for having defrauded the Department of Defense for over $8 million. He needed the title because his car had been stolen in Mexico, where he faked his death. As a private investigator, I had an ethical responsibility to keep his case confidential. On the other hand, I knew I had an ethical responsibility to report him to the authorities.

Because he falsified his identity to me and was a criminal at large, I had no ethical or legal responsibility to keep the investigation confidential. I subsequently assisted the Department of Defense by continuing my "relationship" with him. We agreed to meet in Mexico where he was apprehended. The Department of Defense is currently awaiting his extradition to the United States.

CHAPTER 10
Long-term Financial Goals for Your Business

Congratulations! If you have managed to make it this far in your commitment to opening and operating a financially successful private investigation business, it means you have accomplished a lot. You have made a commitment to a career, learned the business, earned a license, worked for an agency, built up your cash requirements, opened an agency, obtained clients, and reached profitability. Now what?

When business becomes business as usual, it is time to start asking certain questions about what your long-term financial goals should be. Are you comfortable staying small and serving local clients? Are you still energized by the challenge of running an agency or tired of the effort it takes? Do you want to expand or sell the business? When do you plan to retire? These are all questions that must be answered at some point in the life of an entrepreneur. So how do you answer them?

When a business reaches the five-year mark, it is a good time to take stock of things. The business plan you created so long ago should have a five-year plan in it. Compare the realities of what you created to the goals you set for the company in the beginning. Are they close to what you projected? How much of your efforts have paid off? Regardless of whether the agency reached these goals or not, you must create a new set of long-term goals to decide exactly what you want for your own future. To accomplish this, start with a checklist of steps:

- **Step 1**: Set another timeframe for the business. If one year is too short, make it five, ten, or 20 years. Then, write down what you want the agency to accomplish over that period and be as specific as possible about how you think these goals can be accomplished.

- **Step 2**: Write down realistic ways these goals can be measured. How can the progress of these goals be tracked? Is it through sales? An increased number of clients? The opening of new offices around the state or country?

- **Step 3**: Make sure you have the resources to attain these goals. If you plan to open more offices, how much cumulative cash flow will it take in relation to what you already have? Can you afford debt funding? Are there additional licensing requirements? If so, how long will it take to acquire them?

- **Step 4**: Define a new set of short-term goals within your new set of long-term goals. For example, if you set a five-year plan to expand regionally and nationally, set a timeframe for how many new offices you can open per year. If you plan to expand in other states, determine how many investigators licensed in that state you will have to hire to form a branch. Time limits should be set for each short-term goal and make sure each short-term goal moves you closer to your long-term goals.

- **Step 5**: Prioritize the list of goals. Arranging goals in a sequence makes the total long-term picture clearer as to how it will be achieved. To determine which goals take precedence, ask yourself which goals can be achieved fastest and which goals depend on the completion of other goals first? Asking these two questions about every goal will help to arrange each one in a sequence that forms the long-term plan.

Before using the checklist, simplify the main objective by summarizing the long-term goal of the business using only one criterion — the most important overall goal you have for the business. Ask, what would the most important overall goal be? To increase profits and client satisfaction? To tap a niche market and offer a specialized service? To take advantage of certain regional or national opportunities? To eliminate a direct competitor? This one criterion should act as the umbrella under which everything else in the long-term plan falls under and ultimately serves.

Increasing profits may not be the overarching goal in the long-term plan, but as exampled by the dangers of rapid growth, you do not want actions from the long-term strategy to compromise future profitability by increasing the risks to dangerous levels. Step 3 should give careful attention to the long-term value of the company and provide ways to monitor whether actions are increasing or decreasing the company's long-term value on a month-by-month basis. If you have to, anticipate costs and make spreadsheets that estimate expenses before and after they are incurred. Total them up on a monthly basis and create annual spreadsheets that form a picture of the agency's long-term value compared to its current value. The difference should answer whether that value may increase or decrease over time.

If you plan to borrow money to increase operations, make sure the borrowed money is earning more than the interest rate being paid. If the profits created from the borrowed money exceed the borrowed money's interest, your return on equity is increasing, which means the long-term value of the company is improving as your strategy proceeds. However, minding the long-term value means making sure you have the sales in place for the actions you plan to take. If sales drop as a result of actions in the long-term plan, accruing interest on loans will begin decreasing the company's long-term financial value and you will have to set a time limit for how long this can be reasonably sustained.

In Chapter 7, we discussed the dangers of rapid growth when growth comes without preparing for it. The same holds true for business owners with ambitions to expand the business beyond their local area.

Expanding Internationally

For some private investigation agencies, the natural progression of success is to expand its offices to service more clients and generate higher revenues. The question is: Where do you expand and how do you identify the right prospects? For some, it makes sense to expand locally, while others look to expand out-of-state or even to other countries. The least disruptive choice for the agency is local expansion. By staying local, you do not have to worry about cross-state licensing issues or trying to form new partnerships with law firms or marketing companies. Local expansion also avails you of doing the kind of extensive research on area demographics that national or international expansion would require. On the other hand, national or international expansion reduces the risk of losing money or going bankrupt if the local economy suffers a dramatic collapse.

If you have conquered the local region and want to expand the company into another state, research potential areas that are similar to the region where the agency has succeeded. Essentially, you want to perform the same research that was used to select the region in which you first opened the business. Go to all the previous Web sites that keep national demographics and look for similarities to the agency's home base. The out-of-state government Web site should also have helpful information on doing business there. Some state Web sites will have pages dedicated to assisting small businesses expand into their state. If the prospective state does not offer assistance, try an online business location service like ZoomProspector (**www.zoomprospector.com**). Through a feature called "Find Communities," ZoomProspector enables business owners to analyze and identify the best location for start-up, expansion, or relocation by inputting information about the current location or by typing the desired characteristics of a region into their database (i.e. community type, number of private investigation agencies, law firms, and so forth). ZoomProspector uses a mapping technology that lists regional matches throughout the country, allowing you to make the best selection based on comparative data.

Most companies have to reach certain milestones before they even think about expanding internationally. Milestones are important dates and goals that help track company performance against the long-term business plan. For example, it is normally a good practice to reach the milestone of becoming a national player in your own country before expanding elsewhere. If the long-term goal is to open an overseas office, set milestones for the types of resources needed to handle expansion, such as building revenues, employees, clients, and supply chains to levels that would allow some parts of the agency and its cost structures to transition into foreign markets.

Expanding the agency internationally can add prestige, create global exposure, and capitalize on economies that are just beginning to boom, but it is by far the largest endeavor, and the unknown quantity that comes with differing economic, social, or political climates may result in greater risk. Cost structures in other countries may be significantly different with regard to supply, labor, and real estate costs. Seasonality may be different elsewhere. Can your domestic supply chain logistics support foreign expansion, or will you need to create a new supply chain inside the foreign country? For example, can you still obtain your needed equipment or hire subcontractors if you expand to another country? How will the new office handle currency conversions? In lieu of these questions, you will need to visit a local consulate office to get international advice on how to go about expanding internationally and what regulations exist. The U.S. Office of Commercial and Business Affairs is a government program that provides critical information to American companies looking to establish their presence overseas. They help educate and assist some of the major international issues facing companies looking to expand internationally, which also include:

- Identifying corrupt activities in overseas markets
- Dealing with export controls on equipment
- Securing business visas for employees, clients, and owners

The U.S. Office of Commercial and Business Affairs can be accessed at **www. state.gov/e/eeb/cba**. You can also get a copy of any country's business regulations from the Doing Business Project at **www.doingbusiness.org/Downloads**. By clicking "economy profiles," you will be able to access the economy of your choice, which covers 183 countries across the world. If you feel more comfortable hiring a consulting expert, the Intrix Corporation and CSSL Group are among the many international companies that customize foreign integration strategies.

Once you have hit domestic milestones and selected an international region that matches the domestic region(s) the agency has been successful in, it will be necessary to think about hiring an international partner or manager to run the overseas office. Hiring a manager takes a great deal of careful consideration and is often one of the main drivers for international success. When looking for an international manager, do not overlook present employees. Hiring from within could be a great recruitment tool for other employees who enjoy working under the person you have chosen. Plus, he or she is a known quantity. The employee has demonstrated outstanding work production and is trusted, and there is a comfort level in his or her ability to oversee the operations.

Seeking a partner or manager from within does carry one major risk: The candidate is less likely to be familiar with the region or have any influence there. If it feels too risky to promote someone without those specific qualifications, you will have to find someone outside the company who has the qualifications you are seeking. Hiring a partner or manager from outside the company will require research into the candidate's background regarding four key indicators: his or her financial status; reputation in his or her business community; understanding and proficiency in the region's culture, economy, and politics; and influence over resources that can help bring business to the agency abroad.

Breaking into an overseas market obviously requires access to capital. If your bank or loan officer cannot assist you in funding the endeavor, the Small Business Administration has created an Export Express loan program that guarantees up to $250,000 of commercial funding. Three other institutions that provide capital for international expansion are:

- The Overseas Private Investment Corporation (OPIC): **www.opic.gov**
- The Private Export Funding Corporation (PEFCO): **www.pefco.com**
- The Export-Import Bank of the United States (EXIM) **www.exim.gov**

Now to the next question: What investigative services are currently booming in foreign markets? The answer to this question alone may guide your decision to expand internationally. Despite a global recession, private investigation agencies are experiencing an uptrend in the need for international background checks and executive security services. Many international agencies — such as Global Investigative Services, Wymoo® International, and Kroll & Owens — are reporting high demand for international background checks in London, the Ukraine, Manila, Ghana, Nigeria, and Moscow due to the rise in Internet fraud and online relationship scams. While Russia's slow economy has reduced demand for pre-employment background checks to an all-time low, corporate fraud cases in Manila have doubled since 2007. Wymoo reports that Australia, Canada, the United Kingdom, and the United States remain the high demand areas for surveillance operations, infidelity cases, and premarital background checks.

Background checks have become an integral part of globalization as companies continue to seek business opportunities overseas. In addition, American companies looking to reduce operational costs have increased outsourcing activities to labor forces in foreign countries. Businesses choosing to outsource and employ foreigners may have to contend with a different set of privacy and labor laws, or they may simply want to protect themselves from unsavory people. Therefore, it takes an investigative company with an understanding of that country's laws, languages, and legal processes to conduct a screening that properly adheres to the different standards of compliance. If you plan to succeed in meeting this demand, your goal is to run an office that specializes in the regional market and minimizes the legal risks of conducting due diligence for corporate clients within that market.

During your training as a private investigator, you may have also obtained a license in bodyguard or private security services and now want to offer those services abroad. Executive protection services are growing all over the world as CEOs more frequently make trips to foreign countries to meet their global partners or inspect industry plants. Terror alerts at major venues like the Olympics and the World Cup have also ratcheted the presence of security firms. Although security firms handle major venues, its officers do not have the power of arrest. Instead, they are trained to assume a defensive posture by providing safe means of escape from trouble rather than confronting it.

If you want to open an international private security firm, be prepared to deal with a foreign country's regulatory agency. If one exists, your staff may need to be licensed. The Security Industry Authority (SIA), for example, regulates private security firms based in England and conducts random compliance checks on licenses. Under the SIA, all security firms are required to join the Approved Contractor Scheme. Security companies that are regulated under SIA are certified as being in compliance with training and licensing regulations, and the regulation serves as a form of quality assurance to consumers. If you have received a state security officer license and plan to operate internationally, check to see whether the overseas region has a regulatory agency and whether your state certified license falls under compliance to work internationally. If not, find out what the requirements are. If the foreign country has no regulatory agency, then private security training, rather than licensing, may be the only requirement. To find out if a regulatory agency exists in a specific country, contact the U.S. State Department's Bureau of Diplomatic Security at **www.state.gov/m/ds**. The Bureau of Diplomatic Security is a U.S. government law enforcement agency with representation in almost every country in the world. Their role it is to provide protection to U.S. foreign affairs and will have critical information on the foreign community.

International training courses are provided by many private security firms around the globe. It might even be a service your own firm can offer at some point. Trojan Securities International, for example, is a private security firm that offers training solutions in celebrity and executive protection, corporate security, risk management, vulnerability assessments, industrial and maritime security, confidential investigations and intelligence, defensive tactics, and NRA certification in tactical firearms. They have offices in Mexico, Nigeria, the U.K., Bangladesh, Kuwait, Trinidad and Tobago, and Italy. When choosing a training course, ask how long the firm has been offering its services. Also, learn about its accreditations, the qualifications of its instructors, what the curriculum covers, and its student success rate.

The Exit Plan

At some point in the future, you will want to leave your business. You will either be ready to retire or you will wish to sell the business and move on. Other choices include going out of business or leaving it to your heirs. When you are ready to sell, you will know why it is important to build a profitable, saleable business. When you start your business, you should be thinking about your exit.

You can build a profitable private investigation business with a loyal customer base and an efficient business structure that will earn you top dollar when you sell. You will want to consider the fact that with an investigation business, if you remain the only investigator, you are the most prized asset. You will not have inventory and equipment as assets, but you will have the loyal customer base and solid business reputation that you have built for your investigation agency.

Now is the time to develop an exit plan. You will not need as much detail for the exit plan as you needed for your business plan, but you want to develop it now and review it each year so that you can make any necessary changes. Your business situation will inevitably change from year to year, and you will want to revise your exit plan. Here are some of the basic items your plan should cover:

- **Your best-case scenario**: Do you know when you want to retire? Decide whether you want to sell the business or leave it for your family to manage.
- **Current value**: If you were to sell your business today, what is it worth?
- **Enhancing business value**: What changes would make your business more appealing for a buyer? Consider these carefully and realize that there might be some changes that you do not necessarily want to make, but that will enhance the value of the business when it is time to sell.
- **Worst-case scenario**: If you had to get out of the business today, what could be done?
- **Preparing for the sale**: What would be the tax implications of the sale?
- **Leaving**: Are you in a partnership or corporation with others? If so, how does this affect how you leave your business?
- **Financial health for your family**: Do you have a will? Is your family trained and prepared to run the business without you?

Meet with your attorney and your CPA for advice about how to create a realistic exit plan. To see some examples of exit plans, go to:

- Principal Financial Group®: **www.principal.com/businessowner/bus_exit.htm**
- Family Business Experts: **www.family-business-experts.com/exit-planning.html**

Leaving Your Business to a Family Member

There are millions of large and small businesses that are operated by families. Some owners pass their business down to family members or heirs. Another option is to pass or sell the business to your business partners or employees.

There are tax implications if you leave the business to a family member. These issues include inheritance tax, trusts, and tax-free gifts. Each of these issues is complicated, and you are advised to consult with your attorney, banker, estate planner, and CPA to make sure they are handled well. More resources include:

- The U.S. Chamber of Commerce: **www.uschamber.com**
- CCH® Business Owner's Toolkit: **www.toolkit.cch.com**

Selling to Your Employees

You might not have family members who are interested in carrying on the business without you, so you might consider selling the business to your employees. They would need to have adequate financing, and you will want to make it a very professional transaction and include your attorney or accountant. Be aware that this can be highly emotional, as the employees buying your business might have different plans and ideas for how to "change" your business. The other issue is that it might feel uncomfortable to negotiate over money issues with friends.

Your employees might want to talk with a professional so that they clearly understand the transaction. For advice see:

- The National Center for Employee Ownership: **www.nceo.org**
- The Beyster Institute for Entrepreneurial Ownership: **www.fed.org**

There are many ways to handle this transaction, including transferring your business to a worker co-op or transferring directly to employees, similar to transferring it to family members, so it is a good idea to get advice and understand the process for everyone's sake.

CASE STUDY: WHY OBSERVING BUSINESS AND SOCIAL CUSTOMS ABROAD CREATES INTERNATIONAL SUCCESS

Paolo Bourelly, President
International Security
Operations Group, Inc.
Office Address: Calle 58-E Obarrio,
Building C.C. Panama, Office 3-1,
Panama, Republic of Panama
Postal Address: PTY 5999, 1607 NW
82nd Ave., Miami, FL 33126, USA
www.isog.org
pbourelly@isog.org
Phone: (507) 390-4268
Fax: (507) 390-4439

Because I specialize in international cases, I deal strictly with big international banks to receive money from clients and pay sources around the globe. Foreign operations can be very dangerous. In some Middle Eastern countries, taking any kind of photo or video in public is illegal. You can be sentenced three to six years in prison, so it must be done in a way that the subject and the authorities do not understand what you are doing. Having faced this kind of danger before, I carry a high definition Japanese 520 lens camera in a small bag with a tiny hole cut out, so no one would suspect anything. You also need to have an understanding of why certain tactical operations work in some countries while others do not. For example, in the Middle East, we employ the same ABC scheme that is commonly used by the FBI. In old European cities, this surveillance tactic would not work because there are many back streets and narrow passageways.

Having worked as a private investigator for more than 20 years with international corporations, I know how to build an international business. It requires having knowledge of the customs and languages that are indigenous to the countries in which you are operating. Knowledge can be acquired through research, a professional consultant, or spending an appreciable amount of time in other countries. To internationalize, you need to show the proper etiquette, even if the foreign values significantly differ from your own. If you are not willing to adapt, it is not possible to expand internationally because no foreign client will trust you with his or her case.

What may seem like the most insignificant gestures to us can have drastic effects on international business relationships. For example, when you exchange business cards with someone in the Arab world, it is considered unprofessional to give or receive the card with your left hand. In Asia, business people use both hands to take the card and remark positively about the appearance of the card. Personal space is also very important to international clients. In the Middle East, men can never make physical contact with a woman. Slapping someone on the back in Mexico is OK, but in China it is considered a personal offense. Some cultures talk loudly, others softly, directly, or indirectly. Knowing the culture you are dealing with helps establish trust, which is the key to building stronger and longer-lasting international business relations.

Conclusion

Our hope in writing this book is that you have come away with a better understanding of what it takes to open and operate a financially successful private investigation business. If you started with the assumption that detective work was the stuff of Hollywood cinema, you are certainly wiser now. A good detective uses many methods to determine the facts of a case. Over the course of your training, you will learn all of them, gain experience, and become licensed to help others find out what they need to know. When information lacks, that is where you come in. You will be a master of desired information, entrusted to help others and use your experience to the best of your ability. The way information is delivered may change over time, but its demand will always create new and exciting opportunities for professionals in the field. Should you choose to pursue it, the road ahead is both challenging and rewarding. We wish you luck.

Before closing this book and heading off to begin your future, examine the questions at the end of this conclusion, as they will help you determine just how ready you are to become a private investigator. If the goal of all men and women is to find the truth in themselves, perhaps yours is in finding the truth for others. As Woodrow Wilson once said, "You are not here merely to make a living. You are here to enable the world to live more amply, with greater vision, and with a finer spirit of hope and achievement. You are here to enrich the world. You impoverish yourself if you forget this errand."

Questions to ask after reading this book:

- Do I want to be a private investigator?
- Do I have the skills and personality for it?
- Is it financially feasible to become a private investigator and open my own business?
- Am I ready for such a large undertaking?
- Is there any information I am unsure about?
- Where can I find information (in this book or elsewhere) that will answer my remaining questions?

Appendix A
Checklists and Forms

Retainer Agreement

Retainer Agreement

Name of Agency:
Name of P.I:
Agency License #:
Address:
Web site:

This Agreement, made this _____, day of _____, 20_____, between ____
_____, (name) of _____, _____
_____, _____, (City, state, zip) hereinafter known as
"Client" and [Agency name], hereinafter known as "Agency."

(1) Client retains Agency for the purpose of:
_____
_____
_____
_____
_____
_____

(2) Client agrees that Agency is empowered to perform said services for and on behalf of Client, and to do all things necessary, appropriate, within the law, or advisable in performing said services.

(3) Agency agrees to conduct this investigation with the due diligence to protect the interests of Clients and agrees that whatever confidential information is obtained while conducting the investigation will only be given to Client unless Client instructs otherwise.

(4) Client herein acknowledges and understands the investigator(s) and their agents are not attorneys or police officers and cannot give legal advice to Clients.

(5) Client agrees to pay a retainer for services of Agency or its Agent(s) in the sum of $ _____. The hourly rate shall be $ _____ per hour, plus $ _____, flat research fee, plus $ _____ per mile, plus actual costs and expenses for each Agent authorized by Client to work on Client's behalf. The hourly rate plus costs and EXPENSES will be deducted from the retainer.

(6) All Services require a retainer to be paid in advance.

(7) It is also agreed upon that in the event investigator(s) appear as a witness in a court of law on the Client's behalf, Client agrees to compensate investigator(s) at the same hourly rate, same mileage fee, and all expenses for said court case on an as needed basis.

(8) Any portion of the retainer not earned by Agency at the termination of the investigation will be promptly refunded to Client.

(9) It is agreed that Agency has made no guarantee to Client as to the results regarding the above stated matter.

(10) Client further agrees that all monies owed to Agency at the competition of this investigation will be paid in full at the time of completion, i.e., before any reports, pictures, video or any evidence is to be turned over to Client.

(11) All reports furnished to Client by Agency are for the express use of Client only. Client agrees to hold Agency harmless from any and all damages, which are occasioned by any disclosure of any part of said reports, photos, videos, or actions while in the commission of the investigation on Client's behalf.

In Witness Whereof, the Parties have hereunto agreed to enter into this contract.
Client: _____
Date: _____
Accepted For Agency By: _____
Date: _____

Itemization Checklist
for Surveillance Operations

- Spare tire
- Leverage pipe
- Car jack
- Lug-nut wrench
- Jumper cables
- Local map
- Audio recorder
- Extra Sets of batteries
- Flashlight
- First aid kit
- Glass cleaner
- Cigarette lighter
- Fire extinguisher
- Notepad & pens
- Camcorder
- 35mm camera
- Memory card
- Laptop
- Tripod
- Electrical tape
- 12-Volt charger
- Curtain rods
- Window tint
- Cell phone & car charger
- Professional license & identification
- Change of clothes
- Ziplocked food
- Thermos
- Change for tolls

Surveillance Log

Date: _____ Day: _____

Time: _____

Target(s): _____

Location: _____

Participating Agents: _____

Time-In Date	Time-Out Date	Agent Initials	Observation

Sample Income Ledger for January 2010

Date	Taxable Sales	Sales Tax	Non Taxable Services	Total
1/26/2010	552.58	38.42	$75.00	**$666.00**
1/27/2010				
1/28/2010	400.00	32.54	$50.00	**$482.54**
1/29/2010	665.50	65.00	$120.00	**$850.50**
1/30/2010				
1/31/2010				
January Totals	$6,947	$193.46	$478.85	**$14,985.98**

Sample Expenditure Ledger for January 2010

Date & Payment Method		Phone Bill	Gas	Video Film	Total
1/5/2010	Visa	$87.20			**$666.00**
15/2010	Cash		$38.42		
1/28/2010	Visa			$30.00	**$482.54**
1/29/2010					**$850.50**
1/30/2010	Debit		42.89		
1/31/2010	Cash			$30.00	
January Totals		$87.20	$193.46	$180.00	**$2,565.45**

IRS   **Cost**

Appendix B
Additional Resources

Online Private Investigation Resources

eInvestigator.com (**www.einvestigator.com**)

PI Magazine (**www.pimagazine.com**)

Pursuit Magazine (**www.pursuitmag.com**)

PIMall (**www.pimall.com**)

Net-Trace Careers (**www.nettrace.com.au/careers**)

Net-Trace Resources (**www.nettrace.com.au/resource/investigation/private.htm**)

Investigator Resources (**http://investigator-resources.com**)

Private-Investigator-Info.org (**www.private-investigator-info.org**)

Worldwide Private Investigator Network (**www.privateinvestigatornetwork.com**)

Networking Organizations & Directory Sites

United State Association of Professional Investigators (**www.usapi.org**)

National Association of Legal Investigators (**www.nalionline.org**)

National Association Of Investigative Specialists (**www.pimall.com/nais/dir.menu.html**)

Infoguys (**www.infoguys.com**)

The Investigator Network (**http://pinetwork.ning.com**)

World Association of Detectives (**www.wad.net/site/pages/home.cgi**)

LawInfo (**www.lawinfo.com/private-investigators.html**)

Books

Requirements to Become a P.I. in the 50 States and Elsewhere: A Reference Manual, by Joseph J. Culligan

Public Records Online, 6th Edition: The Master Guide to Private & Goverment Online Sources of Public Records, by Michael L. Sankey

PI School: How To Become A Private Detective, by Wayne Harrison

Private Investigation in the Computer Age: Using Computers to Revolutionize Your Work and Maximize Your Profits, by Bud Jillett

Process of Investigation, Third Edition: Concepts and Strategies for Investigators in the Private Sector, by Charles A Sennewald and John Tsukayama

Appendix C
Glossary of Terms

Accelerated depreciation method: Method of calculating an assets depreciation by expensing most of the cost at the time of purchase or at the beginning of the assets life expectancy.

Bugging: The act of hiding a microphone in a room to record a conversation.

Business plan: A written document that details the operational and financial objectives of a business.

Chain of custody: The chronological documentation of evidence showing its collection, possession, transference, and analysis between individuals and agencies.

Circumstantial Evidence: Provable evidence that provides only a logical indication that a theory related to it may be true, but does not directly prove it.

Corporate espionage: The act of obtaining confidential corporate information through spy tactics.

Cryptographic hash: A computer function that allows a computer forensic specialist to know when stored electronic data has been accidentally or intentionally altered in some way. Used as an information security application regarding digital signatures and authentication codes for electronic data.

Cumulative cash requirements: The total amount of cash needed to cover a company's start-up costs until the business begins to turn a profit.

Direct evidence: Evidence that supports a theory without question or doubt.

Ethics: The study of morals and moral choices made, established, and adhered to by an individual, group, or society.

Ghostwriting: The act of creating fictional case reports to avoid working or to inflate a client's bill.

Horizontal integration: A business strategy in which an agency seeks to acquire an agency with similar service offerings to increase its market share.

Indirect evidence: Evidence that can only be used in limited ways because it comes directly from hearsay, and does not fully eliminate doubt or questions regarding the validity of a theory.

Information broker: Companies that research and sell all types of information; they also specialize in advanced searches.

Junction box: An enclosed box that contains connected electric circuits.

Letter of credit: A bank note or document that guarantees payment upon an investigator's completion of services.

Liability: A financial obligation, debt, claim, or potential loss.

Lineman's handset: A device that an investigator looks for to determine wiretaps on active calls.

Perceived value: The value the client places on the service versus the actual market value of the service.

Permissible deception: Any act of deception that does not result in the personal harm of the individual being deceived.

Pretext: A fabrication designed to obtain information from or about someone.

Pure retainer: An agreement made between a client and an investigator that retains the investigators services and prevents the investigator from working for the client's direct competitors.

Reciprocity: A mutual collaboration of favors and privileges between two or more states whereby an out-of-state detective may be granted investigative privileges to operate out of his or her legal jurisdiction.

Registered agent: An agent who represents a company or organization and deals directly with a process server in receiving all legal documents pertaining to lawsuits, subpoenas, and tax forms for that company or organization.

Restraint of trade: To create laws that inhibits a professional's ability to perform their duties.

Results billing: The type of billing that is justified in certain cases in which the perceived value of the results achieved by the investigator is higher than the amount of hours the investigator actually worked.

Reverse engineering: A legal form of espionage in which commercial products already made public are taken apart, analyzed, copied, and sold.

Reverse search: Privately published directories that contain lists of names, addresses, and phone numbers. Frequently used to build or verify current information on a subject in order to locate them.

Straight-line method: Method of depreciation in which the assets depreciating value is calculated by spreading the cost evenly over the life expectancy of the asset after purchase.

Subpoena: A government issued document that summons an individual for testimony or orders the production of evidence.

Unearned and expected income: Money noted in a financial ledger that has been paid to the company, but the service for that payment has yet to be completed.

Wiretapping: The act of intercepting telephone wires from outside a residence or office in order to record a conversation.

Work product: Any evidentiary material that, under law, is protected from being discovered by opposing counsel.

Wrongful death: Any negligent act that results in the death of another person or persons.

Bibliography

The A-Z Guide to Federal Employment Laws For the Small Business Owner. Atlantic Publishing Group, Inc. 2010.

Accessreports.com, "Permissible Uses of pulling driver's license information," **http://www.accessreports.com/statutes/DPPA1.htm,** 2009.

Acfe.com, "Becoming a Certified Fraud Examiner," **http://www.acfe.com/ membership/becoming-cfe.asp**, 2009.

Allbusiness.com, "Negotiating an office lease," **http://www.allbusiness. com/operations/facilities-real-estate-office-leasing/593-1.html**, 2009.

Asginvestigations.com, "The History of Private Investigation," **www.asginvestigations.com/history_of_private_investigations.php**, 2009.

Blogspot.com, "SEO Tutorials," **http://searchengineoptimization-tutorials.blogspot.com/**, 2009.

Brown, Bruce C. *Google Income: How ANYONE of Any Age, Location, and/ or Background Can Build a Highly Profitable Online Business with Google.* Atlantic Publishing Group, Inc. 2009.

Brown, Bruce C. *How to Build Your Own Web Site With Little or No Money: The Complete Guide for Business and Personal Use.* Atlantic Publishing Group, Inc. 2009.

Brown, Douglas Robert. *The Restaurant Manager's Handbook: How to Set Up, Operate, and Manage a Financially Successful Food Service Operation 4th Edition — With Companion CD-ROM.* Atlantic Publishing Group, Inc. 2007.

Brown, Steven Kerry, *The Complete Idiot's Guide to Private Investigating, Second Edition.* Alpha Books, 2007.

Bureau of Labor Statistics, **http://www.bls.gov/oco/ocos157.htm,** 2008-2009.

Castle, Janessa. *Your Complete Guide to Making Millions with Your Simple Idea or Invention: Insider Secrets You Need to Know.* Atlantic Publishing Group, Inc. 2010.

Cohen, Sharon L. 199 *Internet-Based Businesses You Can Start with Less than One Thousand Dollars: Secrets, Techniques, and Strategies Ordinary People Use Every Day to Make Millions.* Atlantic Publishing Group, Inc. 2010.

Cohen, Sharon L. *Amazon Income: How ANYONE of Any Age, Location, and/or Background Can Build a Highly Profitable Online Business with Amazon.* Atlantic Publishing Group, Inc. 2009.

Cohen, Sharon L. Yahoo Income: *How ANYONE of Any Age, Location, and/or Background Can Build a Highly Profitable Online Business with Yahoo. Atlantic Publishing Group,* Inc. 2009.

Compasspointpi.com, "Internship programs," **http://www.com-passpointpi.com/pages/private_investigator_internship.htm**, 2009.

CTKinvestigations.com, "Car Accident Injury Stats," http://www.ctkinvesti-gations.com/car_accidents.php, 2009.

Department of Energy Labor and Economic Growth, "Application for Licensure in Michigan," **http://www.dleg.state.mi.us/bcsc/forms/detect/application.pdf**, 2009.

Ehow.com, "Web developers and Web designers," **http://www.ehow.com/how_2097834_choosewebdesigner.html?ref=fuel&utm_source=yahoo&utm_medium=ssp&utm_campaign=yssp_art**, 2009.

Ennislaw.com, "Toyota recall," **http://www.ennislaw.com/toyota-recall-runaway-toyota-lexus-news-11082009.html**, 2009.

Entrepreneur.com, "Tips for naming a business," **http://www.entrepreneur.com/startingabusiness/startupbasics/namingyourbusiness/article21774.html**, 2009.

Expert.law.com, "Business contracts," **http://www.expertlaw.com/library/business/contract_clauses.html#**, 2009.

Federal Trade Commission, "FCRA Rules on pulling Credit Reports," **http://www.ftc.gov/os/statutes/031224fcra.pdf**, 2009.

Florida Department of Agriculture and Community Services, "Classes of Licensure in Florida," **http://licgweb.doacs.state.fl.us/investigations/C_CC_requirements.html**, 2009.

Florida Department of Agriculture and Consumer Services Division of Licensing, "Florida Division of Licensing Handbook," **http://licgweb.doacs.state.fl.us/application_instructions/Investigator_C_ApplicationInstructions.pdf#page = 6**, 2009.

Fontana, PK. *Choosing the Right Legal Form of Business: The Complete Guide to Becoming a Sole Proprietor, Partnership, LLC, or Corporation.* Atlantic Publishing Group, Inc. 2010.

Gater, Laura. *How to Open & Operate a Financially Successful Medical Billing Service: With Companion CD-ROM.* Atlantic Publishing Group, Inc. 2010.

Granite Island Group, "Debugging and TSCM Pricing," **http://www.tscm.com/howtoengage.html,** 2002.

Granite Island Group, "TSCM Training," **http://www.tscm.com/training-gov.html**, 2002.

Homeland Security of Ohio, "Classes of Licensure in Ohio," **http://www.homelandsecurity.ohio.gov/PISG_information/Classes_Licensure.htm**, 2009.

Illinois Department of Commerce and Economic Opportunity, "Illinois Detective Agency License Fee and Registration," **http://spinotew.commerce.state.il.us/dfsim.nsf/ef155608d8fab5c88625657f005bc355/4e7f9488df25a5688625663a0072179a?OpenDocument**, 2009.

Invest-2win.com, "Income tax brackets for 2009," **http://www.invest-2win.com/Brackets.html**, 2009.

Irbsearch.com, "Networking Organizations," **http://www.irbsearch.com/links_resources.shtml**, 2009.

Jacques, Kevin, *Trade Secrets of Private Investigations.* XLibris, 2009.

Leone, Diane. *How to Open & Operate a Financially Successful Interior Design Business.* Atlantic Publishing Group, Inc. 2009.

LifeTips, "Top Criminal Justice Programs," **http://criminaljusticedegree. lifetips.com/cat/65079/criminal-justice-schools/index.html**, 2009.

Lovelady, Larisa. *The Complete Guide to Google AdWords: Secrets, Techniques, and Strategies You Can Learn to Make Millions.* Atlantic Publishing Group, Inc. 2010.

Managementhelp.com, "Sample Articles of Incorporation," **http://www. managementhelp.org/legal/articles.htm**, 2009.

Manresa, Maritza. *How to Open & Operate a Financially Successful Import Export Business: With Companion CD-ROM.* Atlantic Publishing Group, Inc. 2010.

Mitchhowie.com, "Personal injury cases," **http://www.mitchhowie.com/ personalinjury.htm#3**, 2009.

Nebraska Secretary of State, "Nebraska PI Agency License," **http://www. sos.state.ne.us/licensing/private_eye/pdf/title-435.pdf**, 2009.

Netmechanic.com, "SEO Tutorials," **http://www.netmechanic.com/products/SE-Tutorial.shtml#2**, 2009.

Pakroo, Peri H. *The Small Business Startup Kit,* Fifth Edition. Nolo Press, 2008.

Paulson, Edward. *The Complete Idiot's Guide to Starting Your Own Business,* Fifth Edition. Alpha Books, 2007.

PInow.com, "Collection and repossession," **http://www.pinow.com/news/2007/01/09/understanding-the-repossession-process/**, 2009.

Private-investigator-info.org/, "Accident Reconstruction," **http://www.private-investigator-info.org/car-accident-investigation.html,** 2009.

Pursuitmag.com, "Marketing Tips for Investigators," **http://pursuitmag.com/staying-alive-in-tough-times-tips-for-marketing-your-private-investigations-business/**, 2009.

Ratz.com, "Good and bad web design features," **http://www.ratz.com/features.html**, 2009.

Rominger Legal, "Server processing, Marketing and SEO Tips," **http://www.romingerlegal.com/pi_process_marketing/**, 2009.

Rose, Bryan. *How to Open & Operate a Financially Successful Photography Business: With Companion CD-ROM.* Atlantic Publishing Group, Inc. 2010.

Secrets of Top Private Eyes, "How Much Income Can I Expect to Make?" **http://secretsoftopprivateeyes.com/index.html**, 2009.

Smith-Daughety, Desiree. *Using Other People's Money to Get Rich: Secrets, Techniques, and Strategies Investors Use Every Day Using OPM to Make Millions.* Atlantic Publishing Group, Inc. 2010.

Stephens, Sheila, *The Everything Private Investigating Book.* Adams Media, 2008.

Technical Surveillance Countermeasures Services, "Debugging and Technical Surveillance Countermeasures Surveys," **http://www.tscm.co.za/services. html**, 2009.

Texas Department of Public Safety, "PI Agency License in Texas," **http:// www.txdps.state.tx.us/psb/forms/forms/PSB-27-GeneralInstructions- forC-L.pdf**, 2009.

Travers, Joseph A. *Introduction to Private Investigation,* Second Edition. Charles C. Thomas, Publisher, Ltd. Springfield, Illinois, 2005.

Trinitypi.com, "Infidelity stat," **http://www.trinitypi.com/infidelity_ investigations.htm**, 2009.

USLegal, "Retainers," **http://definitions.uslegal.com/r/retainer/**, 2009.

Wikipedia.com, "Alan Pinkerton," **http://en.wikipedia.org/wiki/Allan_Pinkerton**, 2009.

Wikipedia.com, "Bounty Hunting," **http://en.wikipedia.org/wiki/Bounty_hunting**, 2009.

Wikipedia.com, "Communications forensics," **http://en.wikipedia.org/wiki/Computer_forensics**, 2009.

Wikipedia.org, "Death Master File," **http://en.wikipedia.org/wiki/Death_Master_File**, 2009.

Wikipedia.com, "Divorce Laws," **http://en.wikipedia.org/wiki/Divorce_law#Legal_aspects_of_divorce**, 2009.

Wikipedia.com, "Marketing Strategy," **http://en.wikipedia.org/wiki/Marketing_strategies**, 2009.

Wikipedia.com, "Registered agent," **http://en.wikipedia.org/wiki/Registered_agent**, 2009.

Biography

Michael J. Cavallaro was born in New Hyde Park, New York, and was educated at Villanova University. Following his years as a staff writer and publishing editor, he has worked as a freelance commercial writer, and enjoys contributing the occasional article to magazines. This is his second book.

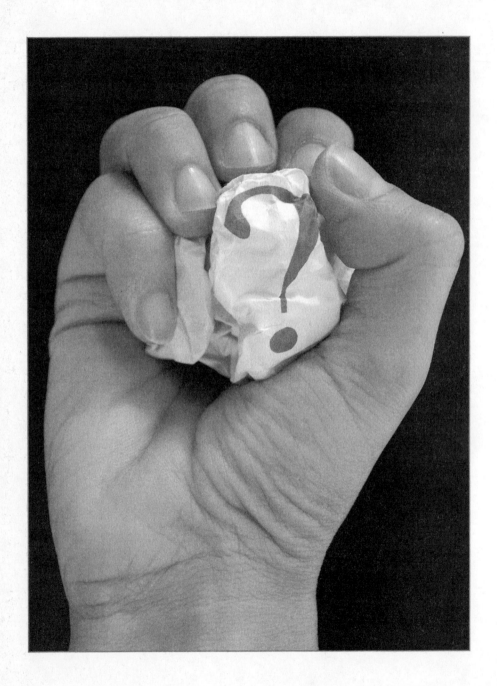

Index